Discovery and Experience

A New Approach to Training, Group Work, and Teaching

Leslie Button

London
Oxford University Press
NEW YORK AND TORONTO
1971

Oxford University Press, Ely House, London W1

GLASGOW NEW YORK TORONTO MELBOURNE WELLINGTON
CAPE TOWN SALISBURY IBADAN NAIROBI DAR ES SALAAM LUSAKA
ADDIS ABABA BOMBAY CALCUTTA MADRAS KARACHI LAHORE DACCA
KUALA LUMPUR SINGAPORE HONG KONG TOKYO

ISBN 0 19 215433 8

Made in Great Britain at the Pitman Press, Bath

Preface

The story I have to tell is about the adventures of a large number of people from several walks of life who involved themselves in experimental situations on trust. To this large band numbering several hundreds I owe a great debt, both for the privilege of having led so bold a team, and for the material that forms the basis of this book. I am most grateful to them all for their willing help, their fortitude and their common sense approach. At all times they kept my feet on the ground. I am particularly indebted to the inner fraternity of about fifty people who have contributed so generously through their personal efforts, encouragement, and criticism.

The work we did together was part of a wider programme of research and experiment, dealing with the influence that small groups of young people have on one another, and the ways in which those who seek to serve groups of young people may best do so. This book therefore owes much to the team of thirty or so field workers who have been helping with this research, and have offered insights that have illuminated our purpose in training and education. I express my gratitude to this team, and to my colleagues who coped with the clerical work and typed the manuscript.

My account of what took place is a personal one, and includes an attempt to crystallize into a coherent rationale the methods of training through discovery and experience that we developed. It is offered as a contribution to the never-ending discussion about methods of training, teaching, and of helping people to cope with life that changes with increasing rapidity.

Contents

1

Introduction

The beginning of appraisal and experiment. Training and courses of study. Building on immediate experience

It is not very often that we can recall the exact time when something new started with us, but I can pinpoint the moment when I was launched into the series of discussions, experiments, and courses that are to be the subject of this book. It all began during a seminar involving a small group of students. I remember that we—mainly they—were discussing a topic that I had covered at some length in a lecture a week or so before. They were making heavy weather of it and raised in me so much doubt about whether I had actually covered the subject that I stole a surreptitious look at my notebook in order to see what I would have said. Yes, there could be no doubt: my notes for the lecture were quite clear.

It was not the first time that one of my lectures had appeared not to have penetrated, so I asked the students if they would look up their notes of this lecture to see what they had managed to get down. I found the response most reassuring: they had in their notebooks a very good summary of what I had said. But this led us, as a group, to question why, in spite of having all this in their notebooks, they did not have it in their heads, or—even more important since we were discussing matters affecting professional conduct—in their hearts. Was it I who was ineffectual as a teacher or was it the methods we were using; and how was it that I had never faced this question before? Could it be that the approach through lecturing carried its own protection against the discovery of one's own ineffectiveness by the absence of feedback?

Examinations showed my students no less successful than most, so presumably the pre-examination swot period made sure that the students dug the material out of their notebooks and managed to retain it at least until the day required. Are we to conclude from this that examinations are a necessary corollary of lectures, because otherwise, there is a very real danger that the material will remain in the unattended storehouse that a notebook can become?

Once disturbed I continued to ruminate. I had been most conscientious in a reappraisal of the material before each cycle of courses, but much less frequently had I considered how the material was to be taught. I was reminded, too, of my disappointment about the lack of success, as practical workers, of some students who seemed to have such an excellent grasp of the principles we were discussing, but failed to apply them; could this be a result of our methods of teaching? As I thought about it and observed people's behaviour with a new curiosity, I became more and more impressed by the way in which we seem to be able to keep one part of our personality and experience separate from another.

It is astonishing the degree to which we can entertain a body of intellectual knowledge, ideas, and precepts without their seeming to penetrate our system of thought and feeling. It is as if we can receive a flow of precept and knowledge into an insulated container, which we carry under one arm whilst we attend to our professional concerns with the other. We may study science without developing a feeling for scientific method; we may study the history of painting without developing any real sensibility to what we are examining; and we may entertain ideas about democracy and self-determination without any awareness that we are directing or using other people, or are behaving in an authoritarian manner as a teacher, youth worker, or as a family man. The human capacity to keep intellectual understanding separate from actions, feelings, and attitudes is very considerable, and many students approach their practical work during and after training in ways suggested by their ingrained attitudes, to the apparent disregard of so many ideas entertained during their training.

At the time, I was receiving invitations to lecture at in-service training courses in various parts of the country, and would attempt to cover in a single lecture what would take considerably longer with full-time students. Having persuaded myself that so much of what I had been doing of this kind was pretty futile, I doggedly refused all invitations, saying that I thought we needed to give more time than we had hitherto given to each topic, and to use a different kind of approach. The colleagues who sent me the invitations seemed to accept my aberrations good humouredly and looked elsewhere for more willing partners. A few became curious, a dialogue with several of them ensued, and interesting things began to happen.

So began a long reappraisal of training methods and a series of experiments, which were informed by psychological insights into selective listening and learning, and recent studies of attitudes and group controls. In a way we were fortunate in being concerned, in large measure, with the theoretical background to everyday life. All students had a lifetime's experience to draw upon, and we were able to break new ground by introspective studies—as long as we could find questions that would help the student delve into this experience in a reasonably logical and analytical way. In dealing with group behaviour, the immediate events within a study group can also be part of the subject of study.

At about the same time, our own research into adolescent behaviour was facing us with new experiences and knowledge that made many of our former dearly held views quite untenable. Thus we found ourselves being changed by our own discoveries and quickly realized that, if only we could provide our students with similar opportunities for discovery, they in turn would be challenged to evolve an approach and philosophy that fitted actual situations. As I shall explain in greater detail later, an important step in our experiments occurred when, having run several courses at which students were asked to search their past experience for relevant material, we next encouraged others to engage in field studies and experiments that produced more immediate and sharper experience upon which theoretical discussions could be based.

So it was that we came to evolve a system of training that has at its core the student's personal discovery and experience. In so doing, we would not claim to have invented a new form of education. Rather we have adapted and applied ancient and well-tried heuristic approaches to education to an area of expertise where they can contribute so much.

The reader will have noticed my use of 'we'. This expresses my consciousness of all the collaborators who have been involved in these experiments. Above all, I have a sense of a running dialogue, and I have reason to be very grateful to the large circle of people who have so generously collaborated with me, often when they could not quite see where it was all leading us, and suspected that I did not know either.

Training through Discovery

The reader might reasonably ask whether a book on training through discovery is not a contradiction in terms: am I not trying to offer a blueprint to the reader, which will short circuit discovery in a way I would be at pains to avoid when face to face with students? I have been very hesitant to set all this down as a definitive statement, especially since the actual courses are as much an experience as an assimilation of knowledge. I can only plead that I know of no other way of reaching a wider circle who may like to engage in the kind of experiences we have been having.

It may be argued that it is just not possible to 'benefit from other people's experience'—that we cannot have experience through somebody else, as it were by proxy. Indeed, the purist may suggest that true learning through discovery can only take place in an unstructured situation where a student may truly make his own discoveries. It is clearly not possible for each generation to fumble its way anew through the development of mankind. Shortage of time dictates that we should present the student with shorter paths to experience and understanding, though it may be important not to leave out any of the earlier steps that are essential to the logical development of the topic. Margery Gascoigne Cooper has made a useful summary of the public dialogue about this.[1]

I find myself taking a pragmatic view about all this: to some degree we are interested in the student's discovery for its own sake, but much of the value of his making discoveries is the effect of so doing on his state of mind, on his attitudes and sensitivity as well as his assimilation of material. It is not my purpose to suggest that the lecture or other forms of didactic teaching have no place in training; the reader will find in these pages plenty of examples where material, that was not discovered by the students, was fed into the discussions. It is only that the students' personal discoveries and experience have formed the core of the training described.

Much of the material for this book has been gathered during the training of group workers. Group work, as the term is being used here, means not only working with groups but also working through groups, making use of the opportunities and influences inherent in group situations in order to encourage the personal development of those concerned, or to support the objectives being pursued. Companionship is a basic human need; but the demands made of the individual by his companions may not always be helpful. It may be the purpose of the group worker from time to time to liberate individual people from the undue pressure of the groups to which they belong.

Anyone who is professionally concerned with the well-being of other people is inevitably caught up in the mesh of the influences that people exert on one another. Be he teacher, parson, probation officer, or family doctor his effectiveness is going to be conditioned by the powerful forces impinging on the pupil, parishioner, client, or patient. To this extent all those whose business is to help others are both subject to

[1] In *The Times Educational Supplement*, 12 January 1968, p. 73.

group forces but also an influence, sometimes a powerful influence, on them. In the case of most of us our part will be unselfconscious, whereas the group worker will be endeavouring to play his part deliberately and with as much knowledge as he can bring to it.

It is strange how slow those who serve other people as their profession have been to appreciate, not only the formative part they play in the situation that surrounds people they serve, but also how that social situation may undo all their efforts. The teacher, for instance, is helping to create a social situation and a social experience for his pupils by his every move, but at the same time the unspoken person-to-person controls may be working against his effectiveness as a teacher, as, for instance, by limiting the effort of the pupil. Inescapably the teacher is both a creator and a victim of social situations, and his effectiveness can be enhanced considerably by the knowledge, skill, and personal resource that will help him to play a more formative part in this social situation. The vital part played by inter-personal relationships is common ground to a wide range of professional work.

The relevance of this approach to learning about other people extends far beyond the bounds of professional training. Modern urban life implies a growing mobility, and the security of relationships within a settled community can no longer be assumed. The increasingly impersonal nature of urban communities has far-reaching consequences. No longer can the individual rely upon his immediate community making a place for him; his social and mental health may depend upon his own capacity to make the running in developing relationships with other people. Similarly, our social obligations are no longer inescapably brought to our attention, and we may need help in developing a concern for others and a sense of social responsibility. It is little wonder that increasing attention is being paid to these topics in school. An approach through discovery and personal experience has much to offer in this area of work.

Training and Courses of Study

Training is sometimes confused with courses of study, courses taught in a didactic manner at that. It is curious how readily we sometimes expect students to assimilate quite complex concepts. If we were teaching a practical skill, a manual skill for instance, we should not expect to accomplish our purpose merely by demonstrating the operation—we should anticipate the need for the student to practise the skill. Yet when dealing with verbal expression, with concepts that may be much more difficult to handle than practical operations, we often assume that it is enough merely to tell the student. Sometimes we offer him no opportunity to practise the handling of the statements and concepts for himself. Our skills in various departments of life may be quite different, and each may need specific training. For instance, it is not uncommon to find students who are able to write ideas but are quite inarticulate when asked to discuss them, and it has been my experience that many students need to clothe an idea in words from their own mouths before it can be absorbed into their intellectual armoury. Storing and regurgitation should not be confused with assimilation and use.

Perhaps we have not, in the past, given sufficient consideration to the nature of the material to be assimilated. If the new information is likely to conflict with the attitudes or the present emotional position of the student, then there are additional and very considerable barriers to be overcome. Training is usually of this kind. Whether it is as a teacher, youth worker, athlete, or medical practitioner, it is in some measure concerned with the way in which the student should conduct himself. He usually has a set of attitudes about this before he starts training. If he is not likely to be called upon to change any of his attitudes there may be a little problem, but if we are hoping that he is going to examine his existing position and achieve a new and perhaps flexible approach, then the resistance to learning may be considerable. This can apply as much to work with children in a class-room, the persuasion of a congregation in church, and the inspiration of adults in extra-mural classes, as it does to courses of professional training. One of the major objectives of our experiment in training has been to surmount these barriers. If this style of learning has any contributions to make to a lessening of prejudice and tension, the principles may also have a wide application to daily life.

Abstractions and theoretical concepts present their own difficulties of assimilation, and our methods in training need to be sddressed to this problem. Through grafting conceptual abstractionᴇ on to the immediate experience of students it is hoped that they will both be seen as relevant and be properly understood. Some of the illustrative material used in this book is drawn from courses for part-time and voluntary workers who included in their ranks a wide range of intellectual ability. It is a good test of training methods if they can engage those who are not accustomed to study and to whom theoretical concepts may not come easily.

Perhaps I should offer some explanation about the treatment of the material in this book. I have attempted to describe, however inadequately, some of the feeling that accompanied the experience. I recorded in some detail a number of the courses as they proceeded and I have illustrated the text from my recording. Very detailed records were kept of an early experimental course. Every person associated with the course, including the administrator, tutors, individual trainees, and even visitors recorded every session. This individual recording was brought together as a report of the course, from which I have taken a number of quotations.

Many of the concepts considered are drawn from the literature dealing with group dynamics; some represent an application of recently published sociological research, and others are drawn from our own current research. There is a growing amount of really exciting material available to the practitioner in the human sciences, although it has not yet been drawn together in the kind of coherent form that would make it easily accessible to him.[1] It is not possible for me fully to describe and develop this material without overloading the text; so I shall have to content myself with stating the concepts without arguing them, and offer references for the student who wishes to give more detailed study to them.

I feel that I must emphasize that because we are dealing with an approach to training that works through a continuous dialogue between all those involved, the content and practice is subject to continual amendment. This book I could not have written several years ago, and I suspect that were I to postpone its writing for several years it would be different in a number of respects. It is not only that everybody connected with the courses is having important new experiences, but we seek quite deliberately to liberate the contribution that students can make from their own experience. There has also been a most intimate interplay between our experience during full-time professional courses, in-service training courses, our own current programme of research, and discussion with fellow trainers from other parts of the country.

This book is therefore addressed to those who share our interest in evolving effective means of helping trainees to discover themselves, their responsibilities, and the potential within them. It is not offered as a blueprint, but it is rather an attempt to expose, for the scrutiny of colleagues, the attempt being made by an interesting fraternity to chart new paths to very old goals.

---

[1] Although there is no single general book that meets this need, a number of useful sources are listed in the selected bibliography.

2

The Trainer's Dilemma

The trainer's purpose and approach. Intuition and analysis. The integration of theory and practice. The development of the courses

The relationship between the trainer and the student is a matter of great importance, because one of the prime influences on the form of leadership the trainee is likely to adopt is the leadership he has experienced himself as a follower. When experience and precept are in conflict, it is usually experience that is most influential. How helpful is it, I wonder, to tell a student by lecture or other didactic means that he should work through the discovery or self-determination of his charges. The ideas being expounded may be well understood, but will the student do as his instructor has said—or as he did?

Authority and Dependence

Didactic methods may induce a dependence of the student on the teacher, which may be quite the reverse of what is intended. Batten[1] suggests that, when training community development officers, he must prepare the officer to be self-reliant, for he is likely to be very much on his own in the field. The officer in turn must, as one of his main objectives, liberate the self-help of the communities he is serving. I have repeatedly found, when faced with a group of students accustomed to didactic methods of training, that they become anxious and sometimes hostile when invited to take an active part in their own education and training. And incidentally, groups of students who have been brought to a point of self-reliance in their contact with tutors, are sometimes hostile to teachers who approach them as recipients of information. The group's expectancies about the role of the teacher are always an important factor, and anyone in a position of leadership who disappoints the expectancies of the group he is leading is likely to cause anxiety and resentment.

Commitment to didactic methods may be very strong in some teachers as is illustrated by the experienced and senior teacher of mathematics:

[1] T. R. Batten, *Training for Community Development*.

Tom said he felt that there were times when he 'must do a chunk of solid teaching—tell them what they must know—and they must get it before they leave the classroom.' Later, when we were discussing our ability to grasp the concepts we were dealing with on this course, he was foremost in saying that until we actually spoke the words for ourselves we did not seem to gain full possession of the material. I think he saw the relevance of his later statement to the position he had taken up about how he should teach maths. in school, because after a pause he added that it was 'difficult to talk with a group of twenty to thirty pupils'.

The difficulty in achieving the active participation of larger groups has been one of the interesting problems to which we have given considerable attention, and I shall be returning to this point.

I find it interesting also that the people who in their daily life are giving instructions are often the most forward in pressing for clear direction and information. Of the first meeting of a group of tutors, I recorded:

John, who described himself as something of a disciplinarian at school, led the groups's demands for a clear lead from me. By lunchtime he was so ill at ease, and I suspect angry, that he moved round to several other members of the group to gain their support.

As our work together proceeded and we became firm friends, he confided in me that he had felt like doing me some physical mischief that day, though he really could not understand why.

There has been considerable reaction against didactic methods of training in recent years, especially amongst trainers who are responsible for in-service training, or who work with mature and experienced people. Attempts have been made to draw upon the experience of such trainees to a much greater degree by providing a setting where they are free to pool their ideas. Through free and open discussion it is intended that they should deepen their understanding of human behaviour, and of what has been taking place in the professional situations with which they have been concerned. It is hoped that the behaviour of these students will be influenced by giving them an opportunity to work through their own attitudes. In cases where this method has been taken to its extreme, groups have been brought together for free-flowing discussion without any guidance at all, and I have even heard it suggested that it is almost unethical to try directly to influence the behaviour of others. Those who hold this kind of view tend to take the same attitudes into, say, their contact with young people, and I feel constrained to ask why, if they are not to influence young people, they are in the business at all. It is not always appreciated that as soon as we accept a position which is thought by others to carry some responsibility, particularly the responsibility of leadership, we are influencing as much by our omissions as by our commissions—indeed, sometimes most of all by our inactivity.

For certain purposes the unstructured group, in discussion without an agenda, may be particularly suitable, but to imagine that a corporate wisdom will always arise from it would be somewhat naïve. In fact group controls may cause the group to draw quite wrong conclusions, and at its worst the discussion may be a process of substituting the opinion of one person for that of another, without any sounder basis for the new position than there was for the one that has been forsaken.

A good tutor can do much to help a group to sift its material, to face awkward issues, and to embark on new lines of thought. The sensitivity of the trainees may be increased by, for instance, role playing[1] and case studies,[2] and their forethought and planning by simulation exercises. Much of the training should be aimed at sharpening the trainee's insight and heightening his intuition. Some forms of training may rely too much upon the worker's intuition, for there is a place for a more analytical approach informed by knowledge and a framework of concepts. An analytical approach is needed in the school, and it is particularly relevant to British youth work. Face-to-face work with small groups might reasonably be conducted at an intuitive level (although I would argue that a conceptual understanding of the social forces at work is a great asset in this kind of situation also), but the British youth worker is usually dealing with quite large numbers, as well as with small groups within it. In his work in the larger and more complex institution, he is particularly dependent upon his understanding of the total situation.

Framework of Theoretical Concepts

We are sometimes very light in our conceptual tools for analysis. For instance, changes are made in the internal organization of individual schools that are based on nothing more than a hunch. It is true that a hunch may hit on a better solution than a carefully thought-out analysis, but the people concerned may so lack a conceptual language that it is

[1] F. W. Milson, *Social Group Method and Christian Education;* Irving, Janis, and King in Jahoda and Warren (eds.), *Attitudes.*
[2] T. R. Batten, *The Non-Directive Approach in Group and Community Work.*

difficult for them to conduct an informed discussion about what is being proposed, and to check the results of the changes made. Until an institutional worker has made a specific study of the social processes involved, he may be completely unaware of the ripple effect of his own actions, and attribute the effects that he himself causes to factors outside his control.

In the past we had no choice, we could only work by intuition; but the understanding of human behaviour, and particularly of group dynamics, has increased so rapidly in recent years that there is a lot of exciting material awaiting the practitioner's exploration and use. The importance of our taking possession of this material is one of the reasons that has made me doubtful about the wisdom of relying upon unstructured group discussion as a basis (rather than as an adjunct) of training. Not only are the students without certain important knowledge: they may not even know that relevant material exists. It is part of my ambition to introduce a trainee to as wide an area of relevant knowledge as he is able to assimilate and use.

I have heard colleagues talk about replacing intuition by science. This seems to me to be an over-enthusiastic assessment of what we are attempting: a better statement of our ambition would be that we should help the student to reach a heightened and better informed intuition. Personal judgement will remain a vital element of the situation, for when the factors have been examined and described as far as we have the ability to do so, a number of alternative choices are likely to remain and a decision will need to be made.

The basic problem is not so much whether information and theoretical concepts should form part of the training programme, but how the material should be fed in. If we are not to rely upon didactic methods, then what is available to us? Kelly[1] describes a series of in-service training courses for teachers in the Education Workshop of Wayne University, U.S.A., where groups of teachers were brought together for free discussion rather after the style of working parties. After a good deal of experience, the business of introducing new information to the groups was one of their 'unsolved problems'. Every positive move on the part of the tutor carries the danger of inviting the dependence of the group upon him, instead of the responsibility remaining firmly with the students. This has been one of our basic problems too: how to enable, indeed almost require the students to grapple with new material without ourselves becoming the fount of knowledge and authority figures.

[1] E. C. Kelly, *The Workshop Way of Learning*.

Whether we managed to overcome this difficulty the reader will be able to judge for himself.

The intellectual difficulty of some of the theoretical material is a further complicating factor. Not all trainees, it may be argued, are capable of analysing their situations, and there was a time when I doubted the wisdom of introducing this kind of material to, for instance, part-time youth workers. But having watched their insights grow in little jumps as they have come to understand the relevance of each new principle, I am no longer in doubt about the value of exposing them to this kind of experience. Of course, 'part-time' is not synonymous with 'less able', since many part-time youth workers are highly intelligent, but there is usually a fairly wide range of ability amongst them. In any case what better way is there of introducing theoretical material to less able students than through practical experience and their own discovery?

Objectives of Training

It is so much easier to lay plans if only one can state objectives clearly, and it may be profitable at this stage to summarize the purpose of training. First, not because it is most important but rather because it is most obvious and concrete, there is a body of knowledge and theoretical concepts upon which practice is based. In the case of work with young people this will concern their physical and emotional growth and condition, and the type and effect of their social background. Most work with young people goes further than working with them just as people, and personal service is usually within a specialist context which provides a further element of content for training. For instance, the teacher is likely to be interested in a subject or subjects, together with methods of presentation; the recreative group worker will be concerned with recreative activities, their discipline and essential background; and the social group worker, and in particular the group therapist, may need a much deeper knowledge of psychology, social psychology, and methods of psychotherapy and social therapy.

Second, there will be a series of skills underlying successful practice, for, as we have already stated, knowing how something should be done is not synonymous with being able to do it. For instance, I have found that the ability to make easy and intimate contact with young people is less general amongst teachers and youth workers than I once imagined to be the case, and I have been interested to see that trainees can acquire confidence and skill in this kind of activity. When we speak of 'born teachers' or 'born youth workers' we are probably referring to people to whom this kind of thing comes more easily and naturally, but I shall later be producing evidence which suggests that people's skill in human contact can be improved very considerably through training.

Third, beneath the surface of personal skill lies the attitudes and outlook of the people seeking to exercise those skills. In practice, the skill and the personal outlook and qualities are difficult to separate, except in so far as people are able to develop a professional style that does not flow into the rest of their lives. There is little doubt that within limits, attitudes can change and may need to be changed as a result of training.

It is not only that practice is conditioned by a framework of attitudes: it is also possible for precept and practice to be kept apart, so that the attitudes that actually inspire our behaviour are camouflaged by a set of ready responses that we keep near the surface. A worker may subscribe to the principle of self-determination for young people, but in practice, hardly give them room for breath. It is as if there were a public model and practising model. It is this kind of inconsistency that can come into the open in group discussions, and it is possible to quote many examples of students recognizing the emotional basis for the arguments they have been using, and acknowledging that the position they have taken up is irrational. I am anxious not to suggest that this happens easily, for attitudes and emotional positions are often deeply rooted and extremely resistant to change.

Fourth, one of the reasons that attitudes can be so resistant to change is that they are rarely held singly but are part of a whole complex of attitudes, which in turn may be embedded in deeper personality factors. Ultimately the trainee's effectiveness will be bound by the kind of person he is, how flexible and inventive, how resilient in the face of discouragement and hostility. Can we have any impact in training on these more basic personality factors, or have we to be content in helping people to be more efficient at their present state of personality development? Certainly in common parlance we continually speak as though it were possible to change people. Phrases such as, 'Can't you get him to be more reasonable?' 'I must try to help her over her shyness,' 'Can you persuade him to put a bit more effort into life?' 'I wish I could ease the chip off his shoulder,' all imply that people's personalities may be altered. But I suggest that we leave personality adjustment and development as our fourth objective, and explore the possibility of whether training can make any contribution in this respect as our story unfolds.

A statement of the objectives of training, set out in this way, should help us to feel towards them. If we determine our approach according to the purpose we have in mind, we may get away from the commitment to any particular approach to training as a point of departure. In theory it would be possible to consider each of the stated objectives in turn and plan for its accomplishment. For instance, real understanding on the part of the student probably requires his being engaged and committed to the interchange between teacher and student. Similarly, proper assimilation means acceptance as well as understanding, for we may understand but disagree, or understand and absorb the material into an intellectual conserve. Real assimilation may mean absorbing new material into our thinking and working framework, sometimes material that is uncomfortable to us because it is in conflict with our existing framework of attitudes and values.

Just how proof we may be to the blandishments of the educational persuader has been brought home to me on a number of occasions. For instance, I attended a meeting of heads and senior staff of secondary schools, which was addressed by a visiting professor who had a particular message to convey. I thought his material was well ordered and his presentation convincing, and by the time he had finished his talk my reservations about the effectiveness of the lecture were greatly lessened. But when the meeting was thrown open for contributions from the audience I wondered whether some of those who spoke had been listening to him at all. It was as if they had come with prepared speeches, which they were going to make no matter what the speaker had to say. If anything, they reinforced one another in the belief that their own previous practices were the right ones. The public statements of several, whose situation I knew personally, seemed to me at considerable variance with what actually obtained. We seem reluctant to change a position bound up with previous attitudes even if there is little at stake, as if the effort of making a change is in itself enough deterrent.

Methods to Suit Objectives

We need to consider the suitability of our methods of training to the attainment of these objectives. I have sometimes invited trainers to place various methods of presentation on a scale of influence or persuasion. Where, for instance, do we place the lecture to a large audience, and how would this compare with a small seminar? How do we evaluate the way in which the seminar is conducted; would it make a difference, for instance, whether the occasion is dominated by the tutor or the initiative is in the hands of the students? What is the impact of a demonstration or explanation followed by practice, and how should we rate the students' reading and private study? And is there a special quality attaching to the student's own inquiry and discovery? In reality, it is quite impossible to rate any of these methods of presentation away from the more intimate details of situation and personalities. For instance, the effectiveness of a lecture will be dependent upon the status, efficiency, and persuasiveness of the lecturer, though the view may reasonably be advanced, that the more accomplished the lecturer, the more dangerous he may be in suspending the judgement of the students by his competence and authority.

A matter of outstanding importance would seem the degree to which students are committed to, and engaged in the learning. I have watched my own behaviour in this respect, and this is how I recorded the impact of a lecture on me when I was first questioning methods of training. The occasion was a lecture by a visiting speaker about counselling.

I was full of admiration for the way he ordered his material and his excellent presentation, and I found myself taking his points one by one with an inward affirmation. I had just said to myself: 'B, you're wrong about the lecture old man', when he said something I disagreed with. Almost out loud I said 'no, no!' but by this time he was on to the next point and then the next. As I came away from the lecture I recognized that he might be right and I wrong, but that he was not likely to move me unless he engaged me in a dialogue. Is this a general pre-condition of people moving their position?

A conversation between several students that I recorded will also illustrate the importance of engaging the commitment of the student to his studies.

Jane: 'How do you like the transfer to your new course Bob?'
Bob: 'Oh, its all right. It's funny, I was thinking only this morning that back in the other department we were so wrapped up in our discussions in seminar that terrific arguments used to continue over lunch or coffee. But here, once the lecture is finished, we all just go out of the room and that's it.'
Prue: 'That's true of our place in the main—except our Tuesday class. We were so shocked at being made to talk, that we talked about being made to talk, and now the discussions always continue outside.'
Jane: 'You know what we are like—we're all discussion. I can't remember the coffee time when we didn't talk shop.'

Is the attention of our students sufficiently caught that they want to share their thoughts with their colleagues? Do the studies stir them enough as individuals to cause the material to be absorbed into their way of thought ? We began these experiments recognizing that we would have to engage the students' participation if they were fully to grasp the material, but we were unprepared for the amount of reiteration and consolidation that would be required before we could be satisfied that it had really got home.

Even if we do succeed in winning the student's commitment, and he fully grasps the theoretical concepts we are discussing, it does not follow that he will apply theory to practice. Anyone who has been concerned with the training of teachers is likely to have met students who were able to present an excellent rationale of the approach they wished to adopt, but their actual performance in the class-room in no way resembled their theorizing. Effective work is much more than understanding or even accepting: to put ideas into practice may need a daring that will only be reached after gradual exposure and acclimatization to new experience, and may need considerable tutorial support.

The First Steps

I do not wish to suggest that the series of experiments I have to describe were inspired by the kind of analysis outlined above. It is true that we were working with a hazy rationale, but the approach was pragmatic. Many of the lines of thought suggested above only became clear on the journey—which is, I suppose, in itself a demonstration of these theories in operation. I spent some months in the wilderness as a result of my declining invitations to single or short series of lectures, until a good friend responded to the plea that we should spend more time in relaxed contact with a group of students, dealing with a topic sufficiently limited to make some impression on it in the time available. He brought together a group of part-time youth workers to whom we were to attempt to introduce some theoretical material under the title of 'The study of groups—why bother ?'

I had been very much impressed by the relevance to youth work of some recent group studies, and wanted to share my excitement about them with a group of practitioners in order to see whether they agreed with me about their value. My notes of the occasion remind me that I suggested to them that the youth worker could be on the verge of a major break-through; and that whilst other social services had taken advantage of the insights provided by the social sciences, the youth service had been slow to do so. Was it that the academic had not taken the trouble to address himself to the practitioner, or was the youth worker resistant to a theoretical approach? Today we would examine some of these questions. It would be an exploratory journey and we should need to develop a technical language together; but we should try not to move forward unless everyone were clear about the terms we were using.

Although this happened over five years ago, as I turn the pages of my notes it is all very fresh to me, and I am forced to smile at the scramble we had that day in getting through the programme I had planned almost to the minute. The plan stood in sorry contrast to the ambition of a relaxed discussion with a group of practitioners. My introduction took less than ten minutes, but already by then my audience had settled down with beguiling receptiveness, some with legs crossed, others stretched out as comfortably as the seats would allow; and they sat up with quite a jolt when I suggested that we should share the load more evenly than usual, and were they ready for work with pencil and paper?

In developing methods of presentation I have been helped very considerably by the nature of my special interest in human behaviour, particularly behaviour in groups. Most of the members of this course were mature people of long experience in teaching and youth work, and the material I had prepared was not only relevant to life in general, but also to their work with young people. Really, they already knew what I might have been tempted to tell them except that their knowledge was not ordered, or illuminated by general concepts of behaviour. It was my purpose to help them to make explicit what they already knew intuitively.

My plan of action on this occasion was to cause the members of the course to draw upon their experience by asking them a series of questions, and so enable them to base a theoretical framework on their actual experience. My problem was so to frame the questions that we would be able to elicit the material in some kind of logical and usable order, and so that each new question did not constitute too big a jump from the position that they had just reached. At this stage it was a proper understanding of the material that was my ambition. I was, as yet, not much troubled by the need to practise the newly learned concepts, or the restatement and reiteration I have since found necessary, or the support that they would need if the new understanding was likely to challenge old positions.

The group I was facing numbered about forty, and I knew from past experience that individual statements in so large a body would come very slowly and that a few people would do all the talking. I had had experience of working through very small groups and I wondered whether we could achieve what I was seeking by addressing questions to groups of three or four, who would explore their ideas for a few minutes and then come forward with their findings for the benefit of the group as a whole. This procedure should not be confused with discussion groups that sometimes follow a statement by a specialist speaker: there are several important differences. Our groups were to produce the raw material and not to consider material presented to them; and they would be considering a strictly limited question, not ranging over a wider, more diffused agenda. The size of the groups would be limited to three or four so that they could all participate spontaneously without having to organize themselves. They were not intended to prepare a report of their findings or even to talk the question out, but rather to produce a number of spontaneous ideas that could be fed into the corporate discussion of the question by the group as a whole.

So we sorted ourselves out into groups of threes and fours, 'encouraged' by my studied, rather jocular prodding. There was a brief hiatus when I asked whether we could organize ourselves in this way and I wondered for a moment whether they were going to play at all—but the hesitation was quite momentary and was probably only whilst everyone was finding his new bearings. I was very nervous about it at the time and the pause seemed to me an age, but I do not think I had anything to be anxious about, judging by what we have lived through since then. Now, I would regard any unwillingness of a group to co-operate as a valid starting point for a discussion that could touch on many vital issues. There was some tittering and we were all a little sheepish at first, but this phase soon passed as the groups eased their way into their discussions. But as the members of the course began to realize that progress would depend upon their own contributions, I thought I sensed some anxiety and even a little hostility.

The small group discussions got under way quickly and intently, and there was, for me, a surprising readiness by individuals to contribute to the open corporate discussions. The contributions were ragged but alive and spontaneous, and a real dialogue developed rapidly, which seemed to involve everybody either through their spoken contribution, or by gesture, or active assent or disagreement. I challenged statements fairly freely and my contributions were received with respect but not without question. I had planned to crystallize the findings at the end of each step and then move forward to the next question. By the end of the day, the animated way in which the company was tackling quite subtle material convinced me that there was something here well worth further exploration.

Before long I was invited to lead groups for longer periods, and I had the opportunity to experiment with two-day residential meetings. On each occasion we tackled a different programme, and I began to learn how much time was needed to deal adequately with specific topics, how better to frame the questions, and how far I could go in challenging the audience about, for instance, the clarity of their meaning or the clichés they were using. Step by step we found new ways of reaching a point of understanding, and introduced new features to the courses. For instance, at one week-end course we did a sociometric test of the whole group, and I stayed up half of the night with several of the students to draw the sociogram so that we could examine our own sociometric profile when we reassembled the next morning. It provoked an immediate and intense interest and seemed to bring to life a number of points that we had been seeing in a somewhat confused way the day before. I realized that some kind of sociometric exercise should find its place in subsequent courses, and I was very encouraged also by the ready way in which a small group of students had actually prepared the sociogram with relatively little guidance from me. We included a similar study in several subsequent overnight courses.

Introduction of Field Studies and Experiments

We began to realize that we were meeting recurring difficulties, but also that there were even greater prizes round the corner. First, the time was still too short to enable us to take a sizeable chunk of material to a sufficiently sophisticated level, to help trainees gain insights and tools that would be usable in their work. There was a danger of unsettling the trainees' present intuitive approach without enabling them to resettle at a new level. At the time I likened it to the danger of asking the centipede which leg he moved first. Second, if the training could be spaced over intervals of time it could be more relaxed, and we could also introduce an element of supervised field study and practice. Third, we had so far been dragging the material out of their remembered experience, but their levels of experience, of life as well as of youth work, were very uneven. How much better would it be, we thought, if only we could structure new, relevant, and sharp experience as part of the course, and at the time it was required for the study.

This kind of thinking was stimulated by other relevant experience we were having at the time. We were conducting an experiment in systematic recording in which we had found the going hard, mainly because our collaborators had great difficulty in analysing their own situations to the point that made recording helpful. They had difficulty with the theoretical insights required, and had even more difficulty in illuminating the work of their colleagues so that they, in turn, could record their work. From the point of view of encouraging the growth of systematic recording amongst youth workers the experiment cannot be said to have been much of a success, but we had learnt a great deal from it, particularly that recording can only proceed hand-in-hand with a growth of understanding, insight, and sensitivity. But we had also learnt that recording could itself constitute an excellent vehicle for training, not only in the hands of those running courses but even more spectacularly when used by the worker in charge of a centre who wished to encourage and supervise the recording of his assistant staff.

A second timely development was the rapid extension of our own research which was bringing to us new discoveries that were confounding our old ideas. We were finding it quite impossible to hold on to time-honoured theoretical positions, and we were having to construct new theoretical bases for our approach to field work. Seen in the context of the training courses we were developing, we were impressed by the way our discoveries were influencing us, and the obvious question presented itself—could we in any way help the student to similar experiences ?

At about this time I happened to be making some visits in connection with our research, when I came across one of the youth workers who had attended an overnight course at which we had used a sociometric test. He showed me proudly that he had continued from there and had undertaken some sociometric studies on his own account. The tests and sociograms were impressive, but he startled me by some of the conclusions he was drawing, which were without proper foundation and could have been quite seriously misleading. I immediately saw both the dangers and the potentials of the situation. If only we could so plan the course of training that students were enabled to carry out field studies and exercises under supervision, we would surely have the spring-board for the leap forward I had talked about so many times. It was at this most opportune moment that a colleague raised with me the possibility of conducting an extended course of in-service training in his area, which could include periods of field work, and the seeds of a pilot course were sown.

I worked out the actual form of the course with the group of people who were to serve as tutors, and it is worth pausing to consider the kind of situation we faced at our first meeting. Some progressive and very sharp experiences had led me to see possible approaches to training that were probably outside the experience of my colleagues, and yet I was anxious to benefit from anything I could encourage them to suggest. Also, I did not want to present them with an already finalized plan, since I felt that their mere acquiescence was not the kind of partnership as a tutorial team that we should be encouraging. At the same time, however much I protested that we should take joint decisions, I would have been disappointed if they had wished to stick to methods that I had discarded; and my assurance arising out of recent experience, together with the inevitable deference accorded to me as the visiting specialist made it anything but an even encounter. What does one do when faced with a situation of this kind?

First, I did my own home-work thoroughly. It had already been indicated that we might be able to devote three residential week-ends to this venture, spaced at about monthly intervals, so I did a feasibility exercise to see just how much could be tackled in the time available. I assumed adequate opportunities for field studies and experiments before each week-end, and the possibility of additional intervening tutorial meetings. I prepared what seemed to me a viable plan.

It was not my intention to present this plan to the meeting as a *fait accompli*, and I approached the occasion by inviting my colleagues to conduct the meeting in the same manner as we might a training session, both to consider the acceptability of the approach, and to examine the kind of material that should be included as the content of the course. The meeting provided me with a number of new insights, but we finished by settling on a plan which represented only minor adjustments of the plan I had prepared. I asked myself, as I travelled home, whether my approach was genuine or had the whole operation been something of a confidence trick in order to gain the acceptance of my pre-arranged plan. I have had it suggested to me several times that the approach I adopt is no less inductive than traditional methods; it is only that I endeavour to use more subtle but equally persuasive methods.

The line between genuine joint study and consultation, and subtle persuasion must at times be very fine. The specialist who meets a group of people who consider themselves much less experienced than he is, finds himself in a strong position if he wishes to persuade, and a weak position if he wants to draw suggestions from his colleagues. Our conduct in this kind of situation will be conditioned by our whole attitude to training. We shall be beset by questions: we may wish to liberate the contribution of the other participants, but are the discussions to be informed only by their present level of knowledge and experience? Have we a duty to bring new insights to them? If we take a formative role, how do we avoid our colleagues expressing a dependence upon us? I am still learning to walk this tightrope. I suspect that the touchstone of our genuineness is whether we are open to change ourselves, accepting, indeed seeking knowledge and insights that our colleagues can bring to us. This is a dilemma that will be faced continually by the trainer, or, for that matter, by all teachers who wish to engage their students or pupils as full partners in their own education.

In designing this pilot extended course we were anxious to ensure that there would be effective transference from practical experience into theoretical concepts, and of theoretical concepts into practice. We endeavoured to design a series of field studies that would inform our theoretical discussion, and we hoped to apply each principle as it was established, in some kind of field work. This decision involved us in, what was for us, a new concept of field work.

Interconnection between Theory, Practice, and Tutorials

Most of our previous experience had been of training divided fairly clearly into theoretical work, field work, and a bit in between called tutorial supervision. When a trainee was allocated to a centre for this field work, it was often quite by chance that any of the theoretical part of the course became relevant to his immediate situation. He usually understudied the work or followed the direction of the person responsible for the practice centre, and the kind of experience he had would be dependent upon the course of events and the particular interests and insights of the worker-in-charge. In tutorial sessions, we would help the trainee to look more deeply into how people were behaving and what the centre or agency was setting out to do, and to discuss critically his own contribution to it. Often it was not possible to point the direct relevance of the theory considered on the course. The trainee would be trying to cope with an extremely complex situation in a single step, and the social phenomena which he should be noting and coping with did not stand out singly or sharply enough for him to recognize them. Yet in training him to recognize social phenomena in tutorial sessions we were mainly dependent for our material upon his eyes and reports. In most teacher training, the interconnection between theory, practice, and tutorial supervision has been even more tenuous than that I have outlined.

We had tried to improve the trainee's skills through encouraging him to record his work and to discuss his recording with his colleagues in his tutorial group; but we gradually realized that this method tended to limit our discussion to what the trainee had attempted, and this could represent a very narrow range of action. Often we felt at the end of a course, that the student was just beginning to see that there were alternative ways of working. We also realized that now that the support of the training situation was ending, the trainee was much less likely to venture into new realms of experience. Would it not be possible to face the trainee more sharply with a series of graded problems and exercises as part of the field work?

We asked ourselves whether we could get away from the situation where the trainee was dependent upon the chance of what happened to turn up in the practice centre. In planning the field work for the pilot course we tried to pin-point one social phenomenon at a time, so that it could be recognized, discussed, and possibly influenced by the trainee. All this has naturally involved us in the need for close consultation with those in charge of the centres in which the students have been doing their field work.

The practice is sometimes followed, even when conducting in-service courses, of insisting that the trainees should undertake field work in an establishment other than their own. We have come to see the value, on the contrary, of trainees doing their field work in their own place of work. There is much to be gained from the trainee's examination of his own situation with new eyes, and from the practical exercises that may feed, for instance, into his regular contact with young people, which he may take to a much deeper level. In this way, in-service training does not steal the worker's time, but rather feeds in to his normal work at a more sophisticated level. We saw this only dimly when we were planning the pilot course; it is part of what we have learnt as our experiments have proceeded.

In portraying the development of this work, I will briefly describe the subject-matter in the kind of order in which it has been dealt with. Whilst the several fields of learning are inseparable—for any one piece of work may serve several purposes—an attempt will be made to draw out some of the main lines of development in order to reveal our intention and the actual experience. I will also attempt to describe some of the more subtle experience involved, much of which first came to us as a

by-product of the programme of work. I shall illustrate from the recording I made at the time, including the report of the pilot extended course
already mentioned, which was based on detailed recording of everybody
concerned.

3
The Approach

Preparatory field work. The central position of the tutorial group. Feeling for theoretical concepts. Interviewing. Processing the material collected

In this chapter I will begin a description of the kind of material that might be included in a course about human behaviour. The relevance of this kind of study in the training of those in social work and education is generally accepted, but it is not always appreciated how vital these topics are to, say, the nurse, the architect, the industrial manager, or to anyone else who intends to serve or direct other people. Indeed, it is the kind of knowledge and insight that illuminates everyman's normal relationships with his fellows, and much of it may profitably find its place in, for instance, the social education programme at school.

Before outlining the content, I will refer briefly to some of the main approaches to learning that have been developed in the courses. At this stage I shall do no more than outline the methods used, leaving a more detailed analysis of method until Chapter 9. I should like to emphasize that, when studying human behaviour, the method of learning and the experience arising out of it—in so far as this is made explicit—is also an important part of the content.

A Course as a Group of People

The anxiety level at the beginning of the course of training may be very high. It seems to stem partly from a feeling of inadequacy. One student's comment, 'I feel as if I were five' reflects the considerable uneasiness felt by many mature recruits to training as a result of their returning to the role of the student.

I usually try to begin with something that puts the student in a strong position by using his material as the basis of discussion. When he is describing something that he and he alone knows about, he tends not to worry so much about some mythical depths of knowledge unknown to him. If this can also be something practical he will feel even less under strain. On many of the courses students have begun by describing the youngsters they have met in inquiries about their social backgrounds. Generally, confidence grows fairly quickly. In fact, there is often a honeymoon period when people are so excited by what is going on that they forget to be anxious.

Considerable care must be given to the volume of material prepared for a course—some of our earlier courses were seriously overloaded—and the placing of the sessions also needs to be carefully considered. Although logical order sets limits, there needs to be a balance between the kinds of activity—e.g., theoretical, practical, discussion—that follow one another. On residential week-end courses, the two special spots of after dinner on Saturday evening and after a solid lunch on Sunday have their own problems. It took me some time to appreciate that the difficulties, including hostility, I was facing on Sunday afternoon were not necessarily a result of the kind of material we were handling or my own mismanagement. I learnt to provide for the treatment of a piece of the students' own work for this period, particularly something concrete that was likely to provoke a lively discussion. The difference to the atmosphere led me to surmise that they took more kindly to rousing themselves to do battle on their own account, than to my personally provoking them out of their Sunday afternoon lethargy.

The heading 'A course as a group of people' reminds us that each individual will have his unique experience within the total group situation, which will be conditioned very much by the kind of person he is. Any disturbing experience calls up our defences, and this seems particularly prevalent in the early stages of training. But as the general spirit of the course becomes one of free and frank discussion, mutual probing and more confident self-examination grows. 'Harry was obscure during the earlier discussion, and now seems very disturbed by the suggestion that he was "smoke screening". I wonder why it is troubling him so much.' And once this kind of conversation has begun it is likely to be a continuing feature of the interchange. 'About Harry—he is unable to engage in a dialogue; he expects to make definitive unchallenged statements. What prevents his entertaining other people's ideas?'

Preparatory Field Work

We have come to see field studies and experiments as a major source of material—indeed it would not be going too far to say as the basis of training. As a logical corollary of this, the student should have accomplished some field studies before the actual theoretical sessions begin. Preparatory field studies are important, not only for providing the material upon which theoretical discussions may be based, but also because they affect the student-tutor relationship quite fundamentally. For the trainee's position becomes that of a person who has something to contribute about which he is the specialist.

How this is organized will depend upon whether the course of training is to be held as, say, regular meetings on a weekly or some other continuous basis, or as regular but more widely spaced meetings, such as, for instance, residential week-ends. When planning courses as a series of residential week-ends, we have felt bound to initiate some preparatory field work even before the first meeting, which has involved us in the problem of briefing the trainees about what they were being invited to undertake. If they were all within easy reach of a single centre —as in the case of a medium sized town—it has been easy enough to bring them together at a central point for a briefing meeting, but many of the courses have been drawn from wide geographical areas which has made a single briefing meeting impossible.

We have gradually come to realize just how difficult it is to inspire a clear response through a written briefing without a supporting tutorial meeting. The difficulty seems to be less a lack of clarity and more a matter of strangeness, needing confidence, courage, and flexibility on the part of the trainee. Our practice on a number of courses has been to devote time at the end of each meeting to briefing for the next assignment of field work—much of which, let it not be forgotten, will have arisen naturally out of the present work—and after the briefing the trainees will have had an opportunity of a few minutes' tutorial discussion to make sure that the message has been received clearly. This has been followed within, say, a week or ten days by a written confirmation of what has been agreed, and tutorial meetings will have been timed to follow this fairly closely. We have learnt not to be disappointed or disconcerted when, after all this, several trainees arrive at the next session with reports of field work which show that they have failed to understand what it was all about. Some examples of confirmatory written briefs, as they may have been sent to students, are included in Appendix 2.

The actual field work would vary according to the stage of training. It might be to make certain contacts with a number of people for a specific purpose; or to gather information, usually by interview or conversation; or to involve young people in discussion about a specified topic, so that they might inform us about their views and feelings. Trainees might follow up a theoretical discussion by trying to discern in practice the social process that had been identified, or attempt to influence some element of group behaviour that had been studied. They might be invited to practise a certain skill that had been tentatively established; and above all to study their own behaviour whilst enmeshed in and influencing all this. The reports of the field work would usually be presented, in the first instance, to a meeting of the tutorial group.

In the more advanced courses students have shouldered a very significant load of field work during the later stages of training. The following is an example of a fairly crowded four weeks of field work undertaken by some institutional group workers following an in-service training course:

(a) a continuing piece of informal group work with a small group, which they recorded regularly;
(b) having introduced a colleague to informal group work with a small group, guide and encourage him in this work, and record progress;
(c) a deliberate and closely reported exercise in delegating leadership;
(d) a study of their own style of leadership on the basis of criteria they had established;
(e) having previously studied some of the norms of certain groups in their own centre, an attempt to influence certain of these norms if this would be helpful to the people concerned;
(f) a personality test of themselves, which would be processed and interpreted at the next week-end.

Of course, this would have been quite impossible if it were all *in addition* to their regular service to young people: by this stage in the training the actual methods that we were using had become an integral part of the way in which the trainees were doing their jobs. This is one of the important saving graces of training through field work. The assignments build into the trainee's normal work and do not detract from it, but they do so by bringing him to quite a new level of practice. The training and practice are one. I do not wish to suggest that everybody always does all the home-work. There is room for a certain amount of vicarious learning, which may arise when the field work is fed into tutorial discussions.

In merely listing bits of field work, I may make the plan of action seem more haphazard than it is. A logical sequence is essential for several reasons. Training that is encouraging trainees to venture into new experiences needs some orderly steps, so that each experience can build on those that precede it. Similarly, in the thread of conceptual learning that runs through the courses, there must be a sequence if one principle is to be based upon another. Exploratory field studies need to be geared to the principles to be considered, and in theory it should be possible to design a field study that will throw up just that kind of material necessary to lead to the next principle. Perhaps now I am making it sound too tidy, but I fear that this kind of training can lose its way unless it is carefully, though flexibly planned.

Tutorial Sessions

In the earlier courses we regarded the division of a course into smaller groups as an organizational device to make discussions more manageable. We were only dimly conscious of the subtle personal support and development inherent in the tutorial situation. It has become our practice to channel nearly all the reports of field work into tutorial sessions so that colleagues can look over one another's shoulders. The central position occupied by tutorial discussion is illustrated by Figure 1.

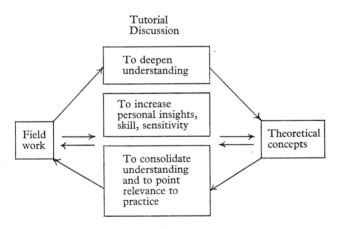

Fig. 1   The central position of tutorial discussion in the courses

The tutorial group has several functions. First, its members must be helped to get through a programme of work and to examine fact and opinion. Second, it should afford its members opportunities to work through unhelpful, conflicting, or irrational attitudes. Third, it may enable individuals to experience the emotional support of the group, and to take advantage of any personal therapy that it can afford. Some refinement of these separate functions will be found later.

It is possible for these several elements to be in conflict with one another, and this occurred in the earlier stages of the experiments without our appreciating what was happening. I had failed to see the competition that could exist between the tutorial group as a working group, dealing with a programme of concrete and factual business, and its function as a supportive and therapeutic group, which may need a complete relaxation of all urgency. The attempt to combine these roles has its own difficulties, and its special potentialities. I shall return later to the need for the tutor to learn when and how to switch off the business, so that personal exploration and resolution can take place.

It follows from this that the experience offered by the tutorial group to its members depends to a great extent on the skill of the tutor. Good tutoring has often been seen as helping the group to discuss its business efficiently; our experience has caused us to realize that the ability to discern the emotional undertone of what is being said, and to lead from the business to a discussion of the feelings of the people concerned, may at times be a vital part of tutoring. How to prepare for an informal and therefore unpredictable discussion is a recurrent problem in tutor preparation. Whilst tutors may see how to agenda a discussion of the business, they may find it very much more difficult to conceive of an agenda to guide them in a discussion that may roam over very subtle matters of personal feelings. I shall be returning to this topic particularly in Chapters 10 and 11.

Open Sessions

Although training offered by these courses can be conducted completely through the tutorial group, a course often consists of a larger number of people who both work as a single unit and break into tutorial groups. However the course may be conducted, there is the third element of training beyond the field work and tutorial exploration—the formation of a theoretical framework. If this is done through the tutorial groups, it will need to be approached consciously as a different kind of operation. In the larger courses, that meet together regularly, we have usually accomplished this part of the work through corporate sessions. Note how the corporate sessions are placed in the order of learning. First comes the field work, second, the tutorial discussion of the experiences, and third, the conclusions and principles that may be drawn from the material.

They also serve to develop the corporate feeling of the courses. Whoever is leading the course will find in the corporate sessions one of his main opportunities to contribute both to the development of the study and to the tone of the course. The corporate sessions have usually occupied a quarter to a third of the total number of sessions. We have also usually begun each tutorial session by coming together as a whole group for a short briefing, with some questions, explanations, sometimes some brief discussion and, of course, some good natured cross-talk.

We have had difficulty in deciding what to call the corporate sessions. We began by calling them 'information sessions', until people repeatedly and sometimes rather pointedly brought to our attention the fact that we offered little information during these sessions. Somehow we were never quite happy with 'corporate sessions', because although the term expressed the fact that everybody came together, it certainly made no comment on what went on and how. 'Plenary' we found conjured up a picture of formality quite out of keeping with the occasion, and for a time we seemed to hover between 'study sessions' and 'open sessions'. Study sessions could have described the whole course, and particularly the tutorial sessions, and we seemed finally to gravitate to 'open sessions', which does express at least something of the spirit that pervades them. This is the term that I shall use.

Making Contact with People

I should like to illustrate the use of these three vehicles for work by focusing on some areas of study and experience that might find their place in the earlier stages of in-service training. Workers whose business it is to offer help to people will need to know as much as possible about the kind of people they are, their background, and their personal needs. They should also be capable of easy and flexible contact with them. Both these attributes are a matter of pride, for instance, with many teachers and youth workers. When it is suggested to them that they should take steps to come to know their young people better, it is fairly predictable that someone will respond by saying that any finding out about them will merely be repeating what they already know.

On one occasion I was discussing this with a group of about thirty youth workers, many of whom insisted that they had a very full knowledge of their youngsters. I invited them to put this to the test. We began by working out the personal details they felt a youth worker should know about his members if he were to serve them intelligently. They then put this to the test by dividing into groups of three, one of whom would name four of his members and proceed to inform his colleagues about these people on the basis of the check list that they had prepared. Many of them were very shaken to find how much of this 'minimum' information they could not provide. They were even more disturbed by the fact that the people they had named were either the particularly helpful or the difficult members, with whom they most came into contact, and they began to ask about all those people in the anonymous middle.

Many youth workers and teachers believe that any direct questions to young people would be resisted by them, would jeopardize their relationships with them, and in the case of youth workers, even cause them to leave the organization. I held this view for many years, until I found it at variance with our experience in research, for our inquiries and interviews with young people were well received and could lead to continuing relationships between the researcher and certain of the youngsters involved. At first I put this down to our privileged position as a university research team. When we launched an experiment in systematic recording, I accepted our collaborators' view that it would be dangerous to let the youngsters know that records were being kept. But as soon as the workers began direct questioning they found themselves at the centre of friendly and animated conversation with young people who, sensing the new personal interest in them, were keen to reveal more about themselves than the youth workers had dared to think of asking.

Workers may resist a direct approach to young people on ethical grounds: have we any right to inquire into a youngster's personal affairs? This is difficult to answer except by the suggestion that we should not take the decision on the youngster's behalf, but let them choose whether they accept or reject our interest in them. We always impress on trainees the importance of maintaining the confidentiality of any exchange, and of genuinely making it easy for the youngster to avoid our advances without loss of face.

Often the trainees' own fears of rejection are the most stubborn and general barrier to their making a direct approach to young people about personal matters, and what has surprised me most about this has been the great anxiety shown by many long experienced workers. I should not have been surprised, because I can remember quite clearly my own anxieties when I first conducted interviews dealing with fairly intimate matters.

The point I am making is well illustrated by the recording I made of a venture several years ago. I was with a panel of very experienced full-time professional youth workers and we were trying out techniques on ourselves in order to asses their value in training.

As we climbed into the mini-bus I was struck by a growing tension and anxiety amongst the group. I noticed that Averil seemed pale and particularly tense, and Fred's hand was shaking slightly as he held his papers. The atmosphere seemed contagious and I found myself becoming steadily more anxious, particularly as we walked up the path to the club and caught sight of a tough looking bunch of youngsters inside. Well, there was nothing for it but to get on with our plan, so I moved over to a boy leaning on the handrail of the stairs and engaged him in conversation. Yes, he was quite willing to be interviewed he said. He was an interesting boy who had been in lots of trouble. The interview took a long time, and I became somewhat anxious about the welfare of my colleagues who were out of sight. I need not have worried, as I realised when Fred approached me for an additional form: there was a little girl who seemed to be longing 'to be done'.

As we left the club we were all very excited about the whole experience.

I find teachers and youth workers fairly generally resistant to and incredulous about the possibility of making this kind of approach. I do not spend a lot of effort trying to convince them about it, because I have found that they are proof against any of my blandishments. On the other hand if they try it for themselves it is they who are pressing the message on the doubters. The excitement and enthusiasm reported above has now been repeated many times, as one group of people after another have tried the interviews for themselves.

An example of the kind of interview form that might be used is included as Appendix 2(a). The questions that trainees fear most—as, for instance, about how youngsters fared at school and their family background—are more often than not the most productive. It often seems that these are the aspects of life which touch the youngsters most deeply, and many of them welcome the opportunity of talking about them.

Trainees have been surprised at the generosity of young people in conversation with them, and have asked themselves why they had not done this before. Many have uncovered situations that show that young people were in urgent need of their support. For instance, a middle-aged married woman who was a part-time youth worker discovered that, by the very act of conducting an interview, she had become the only adult in intimate contact with the boy she was in conversation with. He was at odds with his family, in trouble at work, and had

indifferent friendships. The boy seemed deeply grateful for the opportunity of discussing himself, his troubles, and his anxieties with her.
Tutorial discussions tend to centre around the dramatic cases and it is
often necessary to focus attention on the so-called ordinary youngsters.
Trainees can then see what a wealth of interest there is in them also.

We have learnt to spend more time in helping the trainee to consider
his approach to interviewing:

Cedric confessed that he had some difficulty in making this kind of
contact with youngsters, and as we were slow to understand his difficulty,
we suggested to him that he should role play an interview. He startled us
with his inward looking anxiety and the abruptness of his approach. We
suggested to him that he should project his concentration on to the person
he was meeting and thus forget his own anxiety. When we tried it again
the interviewee seemed to occupy his whole attention and his anxiety and
awkwardness largely fell away.

We first introduced interviews into training as a means of gathering
information and acquiring skill, but we gradually came to realize that
perhaps its greatest contribution was in the emotional experience it
brought to so many of the trainees. We found that when discussing
what they had discovered with their colleagues in the tutorial groups,
many of them were deeply moved. They had been faced by needs that
called not only upon their compassion but also for their help. Much of
the tutorial discussion ranged around what they could do to help the
youngsters concerned.

Group Observation

Sensitivity to inter-personal behaviour is very important to anyone who
seeks to serve others. We all express much of our personality through
our behaviour to others, and it is largely through our relationships with
them that we satisfy our own emotional needs. For the group worker,
who seeks to help people mainly through the groups to which they
belong, sensitivity to people's behaviour in groups is vital. He should
be able to penetrate the subtleties of the situation.

To become skilled in this is a long journey, and it is important that it
should begin early and at quite a basic level. It is to this end that trainees
have been invited to undertake careful and detailed observation of
group situations. Fortunately our laboratory for this is all around us,
for small groups are to be seen in school, club, at the street corner, in
the pub and cafe, at the bus queue, and in public transport. We have
encouraged trainees, as their first exercise in the observation of groups,

to choose a simple situation involving only a few people, and to observe them for only a few minutes, but to do so in great detail. An example of a brief report of a few minutes' observation is included as Appendix 2(b).

There is more to this than most of them at first imagine. When they bring the reports of their observation to their tutorial groups for discussion, they realize what they have missed and the obvious questions that they are unable to answer. They are encouraged to describe the setting, the participants in terms of age, sex, general appearance, dress and, if they are near enough, speech. They learn that 'the events' may be as trifling as a flick of the finger, and they are soon asking one another about the personal characteristics shown by each person observed, as suggested by gesture and facial response. The flow of events is important—who initiates and what response each of the others makes, and any outward expression of feelings for one another. They often discover that to do nothing is to be doing a great deal. There is a tendency to consider that behaviour is not worth observing if it is not in some way dramatic, and one of the values of this exercise is to bring home to the trainee how much is going on in the most mundane or languid exchanges. When trainees describe their examples to their tutorial group, omissions may have to be brought to their notice as obvious as whether a young woman is wearing an engagement or wedding ring.

Many trainees have reported that noticing groups has soon become a habit with them, and small groups keep popping up wherever they go. In particular they begin to see their own establishment with new eyes; less as an agglomeration of people, and more as people in varying relationships with one another. We find that this part of the training can profitably be extended by encouraging the trainee to observe a small group that may come repeatedly to his attention, in order to build a cumulative awareness of what is taking place, and to follow this by the detailed observation of situations in which he is one of the participants.

Feeling for Principles

Unless professional work is securely based on a theoretical framework, the approach adopted by individual workers tends to be subject to opinion and prejudice. There is a danger that the worker may first strike a posture, and then look selectively for the kind of theoretical material that supports his position. In this training the procedure is quite the reverse. The student is first invited to examine what needs to be done, and he looks for this in real life situations in contact with young people whom he comes to know fairly intimately. As the social processes become clearer, theoretical principles may be evolved which help the worker to establish objectives and to develop methods based on sound rationale.

When the preliminary field work has been submitted to examination in the tutorial groups, the next step is to draw out some general principles, if this is possible. Where the courses are conducted through weekly tutorial meetings this will occur as part of the normal tutorial sessions, but when tutorial groups can be brought together for corporate occasions, we have usually drawn out the principles in Socratic small group discussions in open sessions. This is the way the course administrator recorded an open session in the pilot course, dealing with basic emotional needs. He timed the actual events by the minute.

9.50: General session. L.B. explains that the purpose of the session is to build on the studies already made in order to draw out some general principles. He asks whether this can be done in small groups, and the whole group breaks into threes and fours.

9.58: General session. L.B. asks question, 'What is the purpose of our work as youth leaders?'

9.59: Small groups. Half a minute's hesitation and sorting out, then immediate and animated discussion.

10.02: General session. L.B. draws out the many groups to say what is in front of their minds. Quick response. Ready repartee between L.B. and students, and sometimes disagreement amongst students. L.B. challenges and probes. L.B. underlines the general emphasis that our work is to help young people—the activities and programmes serving this main purpose. L.B.: 'So if we are to help young people what needs do we serve—what are the basic emotional needs of young people? Each group name two basic needs.'

10.09: Small groups. Immediate and animated discussion. L.B. moves around and engages in conversation.

10.15: General session. Very quick response. Number of members queuing up to say their piece. L.B. has to act as chairman so that only one person speaks at once. He challenges a number of suggestions that are abandoned as too superficial. L.B. summarises the suggestions that have stood up to criticism, e.g. love and companionship, significance, security in the lives of other people, adventure and new experience, and infers from these the vital part played by group membership.

L.B.: 'Examine this for yourselves. Get one of your group to describe the case history of someone he knows well, and consider the influence in the life of that person of some of the groups to which he has belonged.'

10.38: Small groups. Animated social climate and quick, free exchanges. Students have forgotten the strangeness of this mode of learning and are thoroughly enjoying their work. *Everybody is working all the time.*

10.42: L.B.: 'Have you made any progress?' Several advance pieces of information they have discussed and others indicate 'message received'.

10.47: L.B. refers to students' recording, encouraging them to increase their personal probing.

10.48: Recording and coffee break. Some record individually, others discuss the matter with another member of their small groups.

This method of operating through small working commissions should not be confused with the use of small groups sometimes called 'buzz groups' or 'huddles'. The purpose of the latter is often for the discussion and digestion of material that has been given to them, whereas we were using small groups as a vehicle for actually producing the raw material upon which the general principles might be based. It must be apparent from the above recording that the person leading this kind of session is in a very formative position. The small groups are used to tease out a wide and sometimes confusing range of ideas, which are then freely, often eagerly fed into a general and open discussion, to which a large proportion of the total group may contribute. The person presiding is more than a chairman: he challenges statements in his own right. Although his main contribution will be to obtain a clarity, a logical order of ideas, and a crystallization of the discussion by causing one contribution to be considered in the light of another, he may also be making his own contribution to the discussion, particularly by way of feeding in supplementary material that would not be known to the students. Although it may seem and be claimed that the small group discussions are the basis of progress and learning, it is in the open interchange that follows the small group discussions that order and synthesis are established.

The account given above of a discussion about basic human emotional needs is only one of the studies that might be sparked off by inviting trainees to interview a small number of young people. The personal experience they gain through the interviews is probably even more important than the information they gather. For instance, it can serve as the basis for discussion about the setting up of two-way communication between the worker and the client. We could proceed by asking what is meant by a two-way communication, and try to make explicit the experience of the trainees, that it was not until they, as seniors in the relationship, caused communication to flow, that intimate matters were discussed between the youngsters and themselves. It is impressive that many youngsters seem anxious to continue the conversation beyond the confines of the inquiry, and once the channels have been opened, they may take the initiative in keeping it alive on subsequent occasions. It is not very difficult to point the relevance of this to the amount of conversation on intimate matters that takes place or does not take place between parents and children. It is as if an area of communication must be made legitimate by the action of the senior partner.

We have come to realize that though these insights seem clear on the occasion, they will rapidly become blurred unless the trainee puts them to some use. So it is customary for any new principles that have been arrived at to be fed back immediately into tutorial discussion, in order to consider their relevance to the practical situation. They may then be practised as some actual work in the field, either as an *ad hoc* exercise, or as a new thread in some on-going piece of work. In the case of the discussions already considered—of basic emotional needs and easy communication—the students could be asked to build these into their diagnostic skills, by making them a major point of emphasis in their next period of recording.

4
People and Their Relationships

Sociometric studies. Relationships and the function of interaction. Personal styles of relationships. The trainee emotionally involved in his studies

Having launched the trainee into a study of both the individual—his background and his needs—and of group behaviour, we are ready to deepen the penetration into both these areas, and in particular into the inter-relationships between them. Already the trainee will have seen that a statement of personal emotional needs is in large measure an expression of the way in which the individual realizes himself in the lives of other people. At the early stage the trainee's understanding is diffuse and generalized. His appreciation of the needs of individual people must be sharp, and some deliberate attention is likely to be required before he can discern the uniqueness of each person's position. We have found that sociometric studies are one of the most valuable means available to us to sharpen all this.

Sociometric Study

The really vital experience comes from actually using sociometry and not merely hearing about it. From the moment we first introduced sociometry into training it had an immediate impact.

Each trainee had been asked to interview the members of a small group with the aid of a questionnaire we had provided, and they were now to draw a sociogram depicting the relationships diagrammatically.

The trainee who recorded himself as 'amazed at the new ways of looking at groups, and what was revealed', was fairly typical, and several admitted to having 'preconceptions shattered'.

It is important that sociometric testing should be seen in its broader context and not as an end in itself. It may be necessary, in order to familiarize trainees with the techniques, to enable them to conduct their first test more or less as an exercise. But it would be far better if, from the very first moves, sociometry could be used as one of the diagnostic tools available to the field worker, so that it can form part of some ongoing contact with a group of people. In practice this is not always possible, not least because it is the actual experience of sociometric testing that may be the first real entry to an understanding of group structures by the trainee.

We have used friendship as the criteria upon which most of the sociometric studies have been based, making use of definitions that we have borrowed from our research into friendship amongst young people. Most of the trainees have reported that young people have been frank and earnest in their statements, though the reliability of the material is obviously dependent upon the quality of the interview. For this reason a sociometric study, conducted in this way, is a two-edged experience, the contact and discussion with the young people being as important as the experience of sociometric techniques. Questions about friendships seem so often to touch vital chords in young people, and they may lead very rapidly into a conversation about hopes and joys, fears, and failures. Trainees often choose as their subjects of study, young people whom they have known for some time. Many report that they have made more intimate contact with these young people through an inquiry about their friendships than through all their previous conversations.

We have found that using friendship as our criterion for a sociometric study has features of particular value. Most sociometric studies are concerned only with choices of people within the group being examined, but a study of friendship produces a picture of a youngster's choices both inside and outside the group. Thus the worker can see more clearly the part that the group is playing in the total life of its members. For instance, youth workers are quite often surprised to find that, whereas they believed a certain youngster had several inseparable friends in the club, a friendship study reveals that these are no more than associates, and that the more important relationships are with friends met in other walks of life. Even more important is the discovery, made not infrequently, that a certain youngster, whom the teacher or youth worker sees as co-operative and socially able, is at odds with his peers, is lacking firm friendships, and is possibly leaning on the adult as a result.

The definitions of friendship being used were made clear to us over a period of time by youngsters describing their own feelings and experience. We differentiate close and intimate friends from other friends with whom the youngster does not share intimacies, and differentiate also friends from associates and acquaintances. The friendship studies seem very often to lead the trainees into a fairly significant introspective experience.

The actual arrangement of the diagram is a fairly mechanical exercise and is only a preliminary for the real work that must follow in order to induce a reasonably rigorous attitude to interpretation. Of the pilot course I reported:

The first example, presented to the course as a whole, was an activity group. The worker had thought it to be a fairly close friendship group but the actual study revealed that very little friendship existed within the group. Members of the course were not slow to notice the similarity of the structure of this group to a number of other cases they were considering. After the person responsible for the project had given a brief description there was a pause, which seemed to indicate that either the assembled company were assuming that the topic had been fully ventilated, or alternatively they did not know what to do with it, and I found myself for the first few minutes leading the questioning. The idea soon caught on and questions quickly moved over to a discussion; at times everybody seemed to want to speak at once and I found it necessary to restrain several members who wanted to hold the floor at the same time.

The interesting thing that came out of the next example was the distinction, which we have met not infrequently, between a sexual relationship and a friendship. Here were couples who, there was reason to believe, had travelled a long way along the path of sexual experiment, and yet the sexual partner was said not to be a 'friend' as we were defining it.

The third illustration was most effectively introduced by the student responsible, and the question and discussion followed rapidly. There was a general tendency to read too much into the evidence before us and even to draw conclusions that were quite unjustified. So I took the opportunity of feeding in several other sociograms that I had with me, which were of a kind that inevitably brought a note of caution to the discussion.

The kind of material that has been produced by part-time students on courses of this kind is illustrated by Figures 2 and 3. Figure 2 is a simple study of the friendships existing within a group of boys who spend most of their leisure time together. The worker became particularly interested in Ginger, who seemed to move around with the group as if on equal terms with the others, yet the study showed a very different situation. This was really the beginning of the worker's more sensitive work with this group.

The sociogram included as Figure 3 is an interesting example of the worker's thinking about her problem. The group depicted included a number of somewhat unsteady youngsters. They formed the inner circle

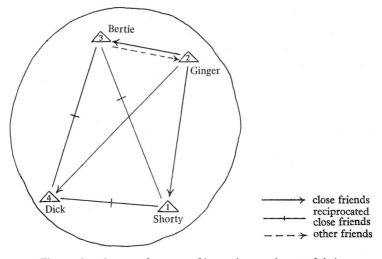

Fig. 2   A sociogram of a group of boys who spend most of their
leisure time together

of a wider group centred around informal drama, but the inner circle included much more in their activities together, including a good deal of undirected and introspective discussion. It will be seen that the worker has indicated whether the choices were within the group, within the club, or outside the club; and has identified the relationships that were operative exclusively within the context of the group activity.

A worker who has made a study of a group in this kind of detail will have gained a completely new view of the situation. It should not be forgotten that what has been set down in the sociogram is only part of the experience: the youngsters will have offered the worker a lot of enlightenment about themselves during the conversations about their friendships. One of the important discoveries we have made in developing these courses, is that studies of this kind are within the capacity of, for instance, very modest part-time youth workers, as long as they are offered suitable tutorial support.

Whilst sociometric studies may deepen the trainee's insight into group structures, care has to be taken lest he becomes obsessed with the function of the group as a whole, to the neglect of the personal qualities of the people within it. The direction of the discussion can be changed by drawing circles around the individuals included in the sociogram in order to reveal what may be called the social atom of the persons

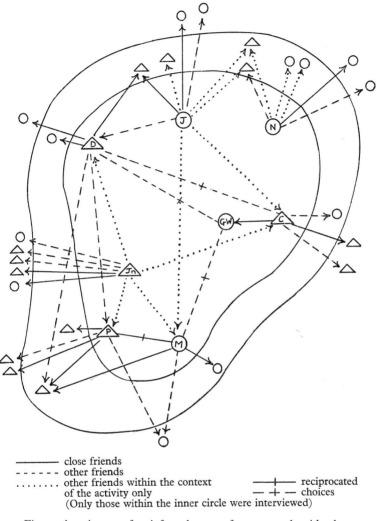

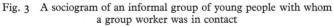

——— close friends
- - - - - other friends
. . . . other friends within the context   ——+—— reciprocated
of the activity only   — + — choices
(Only those within the inner circle were interviewed)

Fig. 3   A sociogram of an informal group of young people with whom
a group worker was in contact

concerned. The briefest examination usually reveals sharp differences
between individuals that might reasonably be linked to their personalities, and to the circumstances in which each finds himself. Before
long trainees will be searching for the roots of these differences. Figure
4 illustrates the very sharp differences that may exist between two

people who are rubbing shoulders with one another in the same group. There is reason to believe that the differences shown by this diagram indicate fairly long-term tendencies on the part of the people concerned.

Girl of 15

Girl of 16

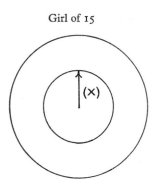

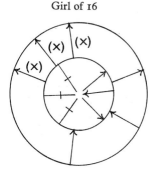

One choice of close friend
outside the group

All choices of close friends
within the group
Three of the choices of other
friends outside the group

Inner circle—close friends
Outer circle—other friends
(Choices marked (x) were to
people outside the group and
it was therefore not possible
to check whether they were
reciprocated.)

⟶ choice of friend
⊢ reciprocated choice

Fig. 4   The social atoms of two girls who were members of the same
scout-guide group

The Function of Interaction

It is possible for several separate paths of study to converge in a consideration of relationships. The inquiries into personal backgrounds, the study of basic emotional needs, the link of both these with our need for a place in other people's lives, the observation of groups in action, the group worker's recording and sociometric tests—all these studies converge at an inquiry into relationships. By this time the trainee will have gathered for himself a very considerable amount of material, and for good measure we usually invite him to engage in discussion with small groups of people, to explore with them how it was that certain of their own relationships came to be started and developed. It should be only necessary, therefore, to ask the question, 'What is it that sparks off a relationship?' in order to begin to capitalize on the trainee's intuitive grasp of the topic.

The first round of answers to the question are almost certain to include factors like a common interest, mutual attraction, and personal compatibility. It will be necessary to consider situations in which none of these may be present and yet a relationship grows, and to remind ourselves that we are seeking any ingredient common and essential to every situation. It is characteristic of this discussion that people will tend to have a pleasant or friendly relationship in mind and it may be necessary also to focus attention on the range of relationships possible, including hostility. In ensuing dialogue someone will edge towards the fact that there must be some kind of actual contact before any relationship can grow, and the group will begin to see that most of the other factors they have suggested will remain potential forces unless actual contact does take place.

If it is intended to use the term interaction in order to describe the contact that must take place, it is possible to feed it in at this stage; but we need always to be conscious that any technical term will remain strange and distant to the student until he becomes accustomed to using it himself. It is profitable to spend a little time in considering the various forms that interaction may take, and it is not very difficult to demonstrate this to one another by eye contact, touch, and gesture, as well as speech.

Several people have suggested that I am just being tiresome in causing students to go through the process of sorting this out for themselves, when I am only waiting for them to come to the 'right' conclusion, that is, the conclusion I want. One reply to this is that, though a ready acceptance of a solution may be gained by didactic teaching, this is a long way short of real understanding which seems only to come when the student has made some of the journey himself. The effort is worth while for another reason. The really important realization that may come out of this discussion is that, not only is interaction a prerequisite before a relationship can begin to grow even if it is desired, but that enforced interaction may of itself necessitate some kind of relationship.

This far it is not a very difficult intellectual exercise, though I have found that most students' grasp of the concepts is vague and precarious. Before it can become a usable tool there must be a considerable consolidation. We have a choice at this stage either of concentrating on the various facets of interaction, or of postponing this whilst we see the part played by interaction in the general flow of human behaviour. It is essential that we should give students an opportunity of converting their abstract understanding of interaction into a concrete recognition of it. But I should also want to reach the realization that, just as interaction is an essential pre-condition for a relationship to begin, so must there be a fulcrum, some kind of activity that serves as a focus of interaction between two people.

This again is of considerable importance to the group worker because, although he has no control over people's *chosen* interaction, he may be able to structure into a situation all kinds of events, and bits of business, minor as well as major, around which people may gather. In this way the spiral of human behaviour may begin, with some focus of activity serving to promote interaction, which in turn heightens the feeling between the people involved. The relationship that grows between them may lead them to do other things together and so the spiral may continue. The reader will find this argued in rather different terms in Homans's *The Human Group*.[1]

In the context of the school or club, although the teacher or group worker may have no direct influence on the contacts the youngster chooses to make, he may have considerable influence on the interaction that the youngster is forced to accept as part of his schooling or of the routine of existing in the establishment. The impact of this *essential* interaction may extend far beyond the confines of the original situation, which can easily be illustrated from the actual events during training. Many of the trainees will have interviewed people whose close friend was the first person they sat with in class, or the boy who lived in the same street, or the person who occupied the room next door in the hostel.

In bringing all this home to trainees, I have sometimes illustrated from case studies that we have made of a teacher in a class-room or a leader in a club. The situations are often very real to the people concerned, so much so that on occasions some hostility has been aroused because the examples are rather too near home.

We considered a case study of a teacher whose approach to teaching seemed to focus nearly all the interaction on himself and to keep the interaction between the members of the class at a minimum. Tom jumped to the defence of what he called 'the traditional approach to teaching', in which he had some support from Ron. Later when we were discussing

---

[1] G. C. Homans in *The Human Group* refers to the external and internal social systems of groups. See chapters iv–vi.

the case of a shy girl who had come through school with very few contacts and had badly needed help in her relationships with other people, Ron was deeply affected and seemed to be arguing both ways at once. It was he who was pressing upon us the importance to this girl of the pattern of interaction in the classroom.

When I first worked through a programme of this kind I left the discussion at an abstract understanding of the principles, and I was very satisfied at having reached so far. The first time that I felt forward to a concrete application of that abstract understanding I was shaken to find how big a step it was. Many trainees failed completely in their attempt to apply it to real situations. I realized how inadequate my previous programmes must have been and how little help I must have given the trainees to convert our theoretical discussion into usable methods of work. In its practical application we have the very real advantage of being able to illustrate interaction from the immediate behaviour of the training group, and I have often asked students to discuss in small groups the interaction that has taken place during, say, the last fifteen minutes and is taking place at the present. Some groups find this surprisingly difficult. They seem to want to deal in wide sweeps—'we discussed'—and are unable to see the blow for blow (perhaps even better expressed in pinpricks) that is really the nature of interaction. They do not see who initiates, who responds, the gestures, the eye contact, and the pattern which arises, putting some people in a strong position and others out in the cold.

It can be a useful experience to ask tellers, say two at a time, to look in and report on the interaction taking place whilst the groups are at their discussions, which they then describe to the whole party. For the people who act as tellers this can be an entry into a new stage of under-standing. But appointing tellers can have the effect of putting the groups into a goldfish bowl and the way it is done needs care.

We moved straight into an examination of interaction by asking small groups to analyse the interaction that had been taking place amongst ourselves in the last few minutes. At the same time we appointed tellers. Some of the groups found themselves almost completely without conversation, because, they said, they had not been given anything to discuss. From my point of view the brief was crystal clear, and yet their inadequacy was so great that the matter was raised a number of times subsequently, as if to penetrate my stubbornness with the realization that I had given them an impossible task. Sam defended the situation by showing that he and his small group had seen the task quite clearly, but I think there was some weight in the criticism. The task was probably too complex. I had combined a first attempt to observe and discuss interaction with making themselves the subject of the observation. I had also complicated the issue by putting the tellers in at the same time.

The time spent on the study of interaction seems to me to be fully justified, for as a concept it is fairly central to the understanding of group behaviour. For instance, it is possible to turn students' attention to their own clubs or class-rooms.

The part of the afternoon's study that seemed to have bitten hardest was the question, 'Name the points of interaction structured into a limited part of your club or class-room situation.' After this had been chewed over in small groups for a few minutes I asked them to raise their heads and amended the brief to, 'the points of *inescapable* interaction structured into the situation'. The small groups I visited found this a severe exercise. It was not just that they lacked the skill to discern the points of interaction that existed, but the opportunities, and even more the necessities for interaction were few. In many of their situations it would be possible for a single youngster or a small group to spend some time there without any wider contacts coming their way. Above all, the students were shaken by the fact that they had never before realized that there was something here to be examined and thought about and, if they deemed it advisable, to change.

This is probably as much as many students can absorb in one step and a period of assimilation would be appropriate. 'Assimilation' is usually not left without something to help it on, and we have, on a number of occasions, asked the trainees to make a study of the interaction occurring in one corner or element of their establishment, and to report to the next meeting. This exercise has usually been attempted but with little distinction, and often it is not until they return to discuss the inadequacy of their understanding that enlightenment begins to dawn.

In order to consolidate this study we have sometimes followed with the suggestion that the trainees might capitalize on their study by causing a slight change at a recurring point of interaction, or alternatively stimulating a new area of interaction that they consider would be helpful.

Many members of the course had not realized that if they disturbed the equilibrium at one point they must be ready for repercussions at some other point, which may be quite remote from the first. Some of the changes attempted were a little short of dramatic, and contrasted sharply with the brief—to make a small change in one particular—and as a result some of the reactions produced were quite strong. At least at a negative level most people had learnt to approach making changes with considerable caution.

The kind of chain reaction that could be set off was illustrated by the youth worker who moved four chairs from their usual place to the other side of the room. The normal occupants, now unseated, moved around until the butt-end of a billiard cue triggered off a brief fight. The combatants were reconciled and one of the unseated boys joined the small party with whom he had so recently tangled.

Gradually we have seen the need to refine the concept of interaction partly as a result of the success and difficulties of trainees, but also because our own understanding has been extended by our research and other experiments. For instance, we have found it necessary to focus attention on the context of the interaction, as the study of friendships has suggested to us that the impact of interaction will vary in accordance with the level of the intimacy of the communication.[1]

There has usually been considerable interest on these courses in the number and kind of relationships formed by the people being studied. Students begin to ask themselves whether the differences have arisen by chance or whether there are sound reasons for them. The work done by a number of sociometrists,[2] and our own studies, give some grounds for the belief that the social atoms revealed by sociometric tests may reflect a fairly long-term tendency for people to relate in the kind of way indicated. It is not that we are looking for 'good' or 'bad' styles of relationships, but when young people confess to a worker that they have difficulties in making friends, and have a sense of inadequacy about making contact with other people, then clearly this is a matter of some importance.

The Trainee Caught up Personally in his Studies

Training programmes based on the trainees' own efforts and discoveries tend to involve them so personally in what they are doing that the challenge to their equilibrium may be quite severe. They may at times need considerable support. Stress, it would seem, may arise from a number of causes, and may be sharper at one time than another.

Almost at any stage of the course the trainee may be involved in introspective contemplation that is usually interesting and stimulating, but it can at times be quite painful. In the early stages, the background and friendship studies can stimulate introspection, and it is interesting that many of those who are moved to help young people, at this time confess that they feel inadequate in their own social skills. The reluctance of some people to make intimate contact with young people seems

---

[1] Button, *Some Experiments in Informal Group Work*.
[2] See, for instance, Helen Jennings, *Leadership and Isolation*.

to stem partly from the fear that they have of doing so. Similarly, the actual training situation, particularly at the early stages, often involves people in new kinds of relationships—notably with authority figures—that they find difficult to cope with.

At one stage, when the tutors were discussing coping with authority, Frances drew the attention of the whole group to herself. It seemed that she was uneasy in her relationships with her tutorial group. When I later happened to meet her between sessions she edged the conversation back to the tutors' meeting. In a confused way she linked her anxiety in coping with her tutorial group with her relationship with her immediate superior, and I asked her gently whether she had 'a thing about authority'. She answered without heat, that she didn't think so, but I learned later that she had been very seriously disturbed by my question.

That was in the early stages of our work together, and the person concerned later became very open with her colleagues in discussing her difficulties. She also became much easier both in her own leadership and in her relationships with senior colleagues.

The actual confession of difficulty can often of itself change the situation.

Donald launched into an almost vicious attack upon Roly for no apparent reason. Almost immediately after the session ended I came across Donald, whose anger seemed to have vanished completely. He looked back to his recent outburst with some amusement and said that he didn't know what it was all about, but he felt a lot better for having got it off his chest. For some unaccountable reason it all seemed different now. We had a few words with Roly who did not seem too shaken by the encounter.

Later we saw changes in Donald which, as he confirmed himself, seemed to date from that outburst.

When we started our experiments I think we saw the function of the tutorial group, in so far as we rationalized its function, as a means of gaining clarity and understanding of the intellectual material. But as our experience has progressed we have come to regard the emotional support of its members as the primary object of the tutorial group. The membership of the corporate training group also carries elements of support, of course, but it lacks the close identification with one another that can arise from a small group of people working together intimately over a period of time. It will be noticed that the emphasis is being placed on the support of the tutorial group as a whole rather than of the tutor.

The term support may seem an imprecise term, and it is difficult to define closely. The tutorial group enables its members to share an emotional experience, to listen, and to have other people listen to them. It offers the therapy of bringing anxieties and cares out into the open so that the person concerned may discuss them, in company with other people, slightly outside himself. In order that this may happen the atmosphere must be generous and open.

It is interesting how certain emotional tones are echoed at various stages of the work. When a group worker encourages young people to involve themselves in new experiences, the young people in turn, may become anxious, stirred, or excited. They too may need support in their venturing, and we have to consider how they may receive this support not merely from us but also through a group of peers. And just as the trainee's need for support may grow as the experiences he is exposed to become sharper, so the group worker's consciousness of his supportive and therapeutic role must keep pace with his involving young people in new experience.

5
Theory into Practice

Building upon experience. Visits of observation; field studies, exercises, and experiments. Exploratory discussions. Practical work attempted in stages. Informal group work. Recording and job analysis

In this chapter I shall attempt to isolate some of the elements common to the field work. It is inserted at this stage because enough theoretical material has already been dealt with to highlight some of the problems involved. It will also avoid the need for further explanations as additional theoretical concepts are discussed. The idea of planning field work as a series of graded steps, that could be provided for and structured into the framework of training, occurred to us only gradually. We saw in it a possible alternative to the placing of students in situations in which they were dependent on what happened to turn up. We had found that some of the most important experience might not come the students' way at all. From the description of the training that has already been given, it will have become apparent that the field work takes a number of forms, each to serve its particular purpose.

Capitalizing on Existing Practice and Experience

Inherent in this approach to training is an attempt to turn the student inward in order to examine the situation in which he is working. It is evolution and not revolution that we seek. The student will weigh existing practice in the light of new concepts and ideas, absorbing the new or adapting the old as he feels appropriate. His new position will, in itself, be only an interim position to be checked against the next series of principles and experiences to be absorbed and practised. The existing situation is always to some degree the point of departure. It is important that we should not devalue the sometimes very considerable accumulated experience and the good sense of the serving practitioner, especially when offering in-service training to experienced workers.

At the same time it would be quite unrealistic not to recognize that, whilst present practice is a source of material, it can also represent a serious impediment. We tend to be committed to our customary way of doing things, partly out of sheer inertia and the effort of making change, but also because our methods are enmeshed in our framework of attitudes, and for this reason alone we may be resistant to change. All this may be reinforced by the fact we are not alone in this situation. We may be a member or the leader of a team, and any change we make may be dependent upon our taking others with us. They too have their fixed positions.

We have had painful experience of the way that a trainee, who is a subordinate in his practice centre, may suffer the denigration of everything he is learning and trying, by those responsible for the establishment in which he is working. And quite apart from our immediate colleagues, we all subsist in a wider climate of opinion. Other people, who may be critical of any changes we may wish to make, are looking in on our work. Is it that those around us dislike our stepping out of line because our difference is an implied criticism of them and their methods? In the school situation the teacher has to cope with the head of the school and even more sharply the staff room, the educational hierarchy, the pupils who can be great levellers, the parents, and the other local members of the profession. In the case of youth workers, the surrounding climate may involve management committees, inspecting officers, colleagues in the adjoining area, the young people, and immediate colleagues.

It is for this kind of reason that we have found it necessary to give very considerable attention to the environment surrounding the trainee. Occasionally, the efforts of trainers and trainees have been sabotaged by the sometimes almost unconscious opposition of the person in charge of an establishment being used for field work. It needs only an inflection of the voice on the part of the worker in charge of a centre for the youngsters to feel shy or antagonistic to the trainee who would like the opportunity of engaging them in conversation. Part of the tutor's ground work as courses are about to begin is to warm up the situation where his students will be doing their field work. It is difficult to convey to someone, who has not had the kind of experience involved in this training, what it is all about. Sometimes the person responsible for the centre will be willing to take an interest in what the student is doing, and to support him by encouragement and discussion. It is significant that a number of workers who have received trainees have later asked whether they may be included on training of this kind.

Certain minimum facilities are required by the trainee. He must have the opportunity of access to a group of youngsters whom he can meet without his relationship with them being prejudiced by the other people in the establishment. He needs the freedom to move from one exercise to another, and the tolerance, if not the support, of the establishment in his on-going contact with a small group of youngsters. He can survive during training in an atmosphere of scepticism, as long as there is no direct sabotage, first, by keeping his own counsel, and second, through the support of his colleagues in the training group. But if he is to remain working in the same establishment after his course has finished, a similar atmosphere of scepticism could undo all the training. The trainee, of course, is himself an agent of change, but we should be very optimistic to hope that the situation would resolve itself on this score— in some cases it would be very much the tail wagging the dog.

Visits of Observation

Visits of observation to a variety of establishments is a valuable way of taking advantage of what already exists, and is an exercise that is particularly suited to weekly tutorial meetings. Somehow it is easier to make a balanced observation of what other people are doing, and it may take time for us to realize that features we find wanting in other places are reflected also in our own practice. Often it is arranged for a tutorial group to operate as two or more sub-groups, each making a different visit, so that there is a considerable accumulation of experience in the group. The common experience built up during the period of visits serves as a frame of reference during so many of the subsequent discussions.

It is important to get clear the purpose of the visits of observation. The more obvious purpose, which trainees seem readily to seize upon, is to be able to gather ideas from what other people do. This is, of course, always present, but it could easily be overstated. The more subtle insights will include seeing the interplay between the personality and objectives of the person in charge and the style of the establishment as a whole, including the experience for the young people inherent in their membership. Visits to several places, and the comparison with the student's own experience will focus attention on the variety of answers, or at least approaches to the same problem, and if visits of observation are well conducted they can be a great loosening up exercise. It will be seen that the emphasis here is less in terms of ready-made answers, and more in the preparation for exploration. Readiness for exploration is as much a question of a state of mind as of tools and equipment.

Success in the operation depends very much on good preparation.

There is limited time available for visits of observation as there is for all the other elements of training, and although there may be some value to be drawn from fumbling along at times, much more will be derived from a visit when the eyes of the trainees have been sharpened in advance. It is very tempting on the other hand to tell a group what to look for, but we have found that most groups of trainees can produce a brief for themselves quite quickly, which results in their almost having begun looking long before they actually make the first visit. If time for preparation is limited, we use working commissions as we do in open sessions, by dividing even a tutorial group into several smaller groups. The small groups first draw up a list of main headings, and then each group can work on one or two headings to bring out the finer points within them. A typical series of headings that might be included in a brief for visits of observation will be found in Appendix 2(d).

Much of the value of the visits arises from the tutorial dicussion that follows, when a good deal will depend upon the preparation, and leadership of the tutor. If there are to be several occasions, as is normally the case, the first tutorial discussion may be a fairly straightforward account of what has been seen, with some questioning to bring out the half-hidden elements. For subsequent occasions it may be possible to arrange for some specialization, either by allocating different parts of the brief to particular members of the group, or by the whole group concentrating on certain aspects of the inquiry. If the trainees are beginning to feel sufficiently secure they might visit one another's centres, and submit them to a similar scrutiny and discussion. An interesting additional use of visits of observation has been brought to our notice by several trainees who have involved young people in similar exercises, and have brought glowing accounts of the effects of the experience on the young people concerned. However, there are limits to the profitability of visits of observation, and the time soon arrives when other work becomes more productive.

Field Studies

It is a little difficult to deal with the trainee's field studies and exercises away from the specific material for which they are a vehicle; but there are certain generalizations that can be made about their use as techniques. It is through field studies that so much of the information is fed into the course, and even more important, they provide a strong sense of relevance to the material being considered. It is interesting that this feeling of relevance does not seem to be restricted to the material actually furnished by the students. Their own studies seem to illuminate similar material, and to make them more capable of assessing and assimilating information that can be fed in from established sources. The fact that they do search out an important part of the material infuses their whole approach with a discipline of criticism, analysis, and acceptance which they apply to material presented to them from other sources.

We have developed our own approach through the pragmatic experience of offering students different ways of reaching valid material, and we have found that the speed of penetration has usually reflected the sharpness of the instrument that we have been able to offer them. This has been brought forcibly to our notice. In several of the more advanced courses there was a slowing of progress, which in certain aspects of the course, reflected the inadequacy of the instruments available to the students. We have been very fortunate in the interplay that there has been between our research programme and the experiments in training, for many of the instruments for student discovery have been suggested by the forms of inquiry used in research.

Interview forms and prompt lists offer short cuts for student discovery and learning, and focus attention on a limited area of interest, avoiding irrelevant details as far as possible. If some information is required on which to base decisions or concepts, theoretically it should be possible to design a form of inquiry that will throw up just the material needed. It is a lack of skill in designing such instruments of inquiry that sets limits to the amount and speed of progress we can make. The form of inquiry guarantees that some information about a certain topic will be turned up, but it is vital that the form should not predetermine the conclusions to be drawn, for herein lies the autonomy of the student.

I have been very hesitant about offering examples of the inquiry forms and briefs that we have been using, for I am anxious that it should not be thought that I am offering a blueprint. This study of training methods is surely only a beginning and the present forms of inquiry will, and should, be rapidly overtaken. They are included in Appendix 2 only in order to give concrete examples in preference to vague descriptions, and to illustrate the principles being discussed. It is hoped that the reader will look at them critically against the kind of purpose they were designed to serve, and set about designing his own framework of inquiry to meet his specific needs.

The trainer who adopts field studies as part of his methods should not underestimate the amount of guidance and support the students require.

I am including in Appendix 2 some examples of the briefs circulated to students in order to encourage them to initiate the exercises. We have not been using them exactly in this form, but usually in the more personal vein of a letter. But perhaps I should reiterate that whilst we have found the written statement helpful in crystallizing previous discussion, it has been quite inadequate in getting the student launched on the actual exercises. For this, some kind of personal conversation has proved necessary.

Exploratory Discussions

We have gradually increased the use of informal exploratory discussions between the trainee and young people as an integral part of his preparation for theoretical discussions. I have already mentioned examples of this in, for instance, the discussions about the basic emotional needs of young people, and about how they have come to establish some of their relationships. It is a happily inexact way of gathering information, and tends to surround the topic with a whole range of considerations that might easily be left out in the discussions. In some ways it is an antidote to the danger of the student's sights being limited by the nature of the more stereotyped inquiries he may be conducting.

The by-products of these discussions are often particularly valuable. First, the student may come to the realization that the youngsters have been there all this time ready and willing to discuss these quite vital subjects; and second, the youngsters may lead the worker on to allied topics about which they wish to express their concern. We have used informal discussion a good deal when we have wanted to research into an area of study new to us, and the gems of insight offered to us by the young people we have consulted have at times been most impressive.

Exercises and Experiments

We have found that when a principle or theoretical concept has been established it is important to use it in some way as soon as possible; otherwise it may become vaguely remembered and quite quickly lost as a working principle. The practice of a principle or concept might be, for instance, by observation, as was the case with interaction already reported, or by consolidation through use, as in inviting students to seek new forms of communication with youngsters.

The report of the practice carried out by the trainee very often provides the material for the next meeting. In this way the understanding of the theoretical principle may be consolidated; or, as with field studies, the next theoretical step may be based on the actual reports of the practice. For instance, through the student's observation of interaction as a practice exercise, a much better informed discussion about interaction may ensue, leading to the identification of the context of the interaction, and its place on the personal-task axis, as mentioned in Chapter 4.

Theoretical concepts are tools to assist both in analysis and action. In analysis, they serve to help the worker examine his own situation, as, for example, by studying patterns of interaction; in action they make it easier for the worker to influence the situation, by enabling him to see more clearly the factors upon which to concentrate his attention. For instance, he may be concerned about certain relationships existing within a small group, and in thinking about the part that he might play he is aware of the influence of the pattern of interaction, and of the context of the communication between the people in whom he is interested.

Of course, the practitioner has always been doing this kind of thing as part of his normal work, usually unknowingly, intuitively, and sometimes extremely well; but if the principles of what he is trying to do, and the social processes that he must deal with are visible to him, is it not possible for him to work with greater judgement and subtlety of influence? Often the trainee is presented with the complete and complex situation in a single step, and has to cope with a whole set of interlocking influences all at once. Would it not be possible, we asked, to isolate individual steps and processes, to focus on each one in turn, and make self-conscious attempts to adapt our behaviour, as workers, to suit the situation we have discovered?

As a result of these kinds of questions we have tried to establish two streams of work: first, a series of *ad hoc* exercises and experiments; and second, experience of on-going work with the same group of young people, which I will describe in the next section. We hoped, in this way, to pinpoint one form of action after another, which, once understood and practised, could be fed into the on-going work of the trainee. For instance, the trainee's *ad hoc* experiment in influencing patterns of interaction throws into clear relief both the problem that he is facing and what he might do about it. He is then able to identify the same factors in action in his on-going work, and his reaction to them should be better informed.

The route to the practice we have developed has not been as direct as my account might suggest. In fact we have fumbled along and at times only realized what we had done after the event. And the development has not gone unchallenged, either from within the fraternity or from friends looking in from outside. We have met phrases like, 'playing God', and 'monkeying about with people's lives', which question the ethics of our deliberate influence on situations that affect the behaviour of those in them. We and our students have all lived through periods of disquiet, when we have appreciated what powerful means of influencing people there must be, still awaiting discovery. But can the group worker escape this responsibility? For instance, a number of objective studies of youth work have shown the strong influence of the worker's long-term policy and practice on the behaviour of the young people in membership, and on the social control operating within their small groups. In his case he is unselfconscious about what he is doing, but he can hardly escape the responsibility for his actions and for the effect he is having upon other people. Does it make it unethical if he studies his effect and tries to make his influence as helpful as possible? What we are seeing is that group work is neutral; it is the policy of the group worker that colours his influence.

Working with Small Groups

The techniques we have described above—field studies, practice, and experiment—have all been concerned with *ad hoc* exercises, isolating and concentrating on single factors. Before these can make their contribution to the actual day-to-day work with young people, ways must be found of absorbing them into normal practice. We have attempted, in doing this, to evolve working models, supported by a rationale, and illuminated by the insights gained in the study and experiments. The expression 'working models' could easily give a false impression. We are dealing with real people, each with his individuality, idiosyncrasies, and a certain unpredictability, so that any approach will need special nuances to suit each situation.

The development of principles is impeded by the very nature of the operation being considered. We are introducing trainees to, say, 'teaching' or 'youth work', or to 'probation service', but included in any one of these single ideas is a whole complex of operations, which can very well baffle the trainee who must struggle with them all at once. This is similar to the problem we face when planning a course of practical study: how can we break down the operation so that the student needs to cope with only one factor at a time? Would it be possible, in some continuing field work, to follow the same practice of isolating single operations, to study the nature and effect of each, and to practise methods of approach to a limited problem.

This is what we have attempted to do, for instance, in training the group worker, by focusing on various facets of practical work in turn. There is a major distinction between group work with small groups and institutional group work, although work with small groups may take place within an institution. Institutional group work will be dealt with in Chapter 8. There are also many separate points of emphasis within each of these two major divisions. For instance, the purpose of work with small groups may have specific objectives such as social remedial work, personality development, recreative activity, and even the support of objectives which members of a group may subscribe to, such as community service or social betterment. Any particular project may overlap several of the areas listed above; only too often it may be spread widely or vacillate from one area to another for the want of a clear statement of purpose.

Group workers may find themselves at different times called upon to undertake work of all these kinds, and in the informal situations in which they operate, the switch from one to another may be very rapid. Are there, we have been asking ourselves, common ingredients and skills that can be distilled into a single line of practical work and approached step by step? In order to meet this demand we have experimented with what we have called informal group work, which centres around personality development and overlaps the areas of social remedial and recreative group work. Central to the purpose is the personal development of young people; and any occupation, task, or activity is seen as supportive to this objective.

Having delimited the area of work, the operations involved are still very wide and complex. The next purpose has been to sort out a number of steps that can be thought about and attempted in turn, not of course isolated from the remaining flow of behaviour, but each being the subject of emphasis individually. We have attempted so to time points of emphasis in the informal group work as to absorb into it the practical application of theoretical discussions as they occur. In some instances, the programme of theoretical studies has been retimed so that new insights may occur in time for the next logical step in the field. For instance, locating groups who might benefit from the attention of the worker is clearly associated with the early stages of informal group work. The methods of making contact, of influencing the level of communication, and of considering the ramifications of the group and the relationships within it are the parallel stages of the theoretical discussions.[1]

It has been found that a similar project has particular value in the training of teachers. It is not difficult to convey to teachers, through the kind of theoretical programme we have been following, that inherent in every class-room situation there is a social experience, which may at times be even more important than the transmission of knowledge. But it is one thing to see this as a theoretical proposition, but quite another to see it in operation through the thicket of the task and the school routine. I find that teachers, particularly those in secondary schools, often have great difficulty in delving behind the fronts presented by working pupils, in reaching the informal flow of behaviour, feelings, and controls present in the class-room, and even seem to fear doing so. In fact, it is probably asking too much of them that they should cope with a programme of work as their prime objective and at the same time get to grips with new understanding of the undertone of emotion and covert expression.

If, on the other hand, we can filter out from the situation some of its more informal elements as a separate experience, we may help the teacher to become much more aware of the factors involved and what response is open to him. We have found that the experience of informal group work can do this. And having seen more of what is taking place, and what his role might be in response, the teacher can feed back the experience into normal teaching situations.

For quite a number of teachers, the experience can be painful. For many primary school teachers it may represent only a rather more self-conscious extension of their present practice, but for many secondary school teachers it may challenge quite fundamentally their whole approach to young people, and, for that matter, the total organization of the school. For many it has brought new life to a flagging experience. Some teachers, who have maintained a distant task relationship with pupils, have found themselves caught up, to their great joy but not without stress, in the pupils' private thoughts, ambitions, fears, and guilts. They have found themselves winning the confidence of pupils who were so recently distant, and even sullen and uncooperative.

---

[1] A brief description of some experiments may be found in Button, *Some Experiments in Informal Group Work*. For a more general treatment, see Konopka, *Social Group Work*.

Recording

In a previous experiment in the systematic recording of youth work we found that many of our collaborators had great difficulty in recording their work with any sensitivity. It was not until we used recording as a medium for training that we really began to understand why.

We began by offering trainees a brief which we believed would stimulate their thought—similar to that used by our collaborators in the experiment—but we soon discovered that by offering a finished brief we were attempting to anticipate a sophistication that could only come from considerable experience. Either the brief became lost and unused, or it could make the whole operation seem so outside the competence of the trainee as to cause him to see recording as quite hopeless. As a result of experience and of this realization we next avoided using a brief of this kind, and instead offered for the first attempts at recording a simple form with a few headings.[1]

As our plans developed we decided to encourage the trainee, as part of the work of the tutorial groups, to evolve his own brief for recording, at first inspired only by what was obvious to him and by the early theoretical sessions, and later to be revised step by step as the theoretical insights grew. The tidiness of the plan has rarely been realized in practice; the basis for recording has sometimes become very ragged and has never really kept pace with the theoretical insights. The trainer is always likely to face a dilemma. Too much can be demanded of the tutorial groups by vesting in them the total responsibility for bringing the recording brief up-to-date: some occasion for the pooling of ideas enables help to be given centrally in moving this forward. At the same time, recording done because we require it and on a basis provided by the establishment, may lack bite and short circuits the personal understanding that arises out of planning the thing for oneself.

I have been impressed in recent years by the enthusiasm of students for recording, which never seemed to be present when I *required* the recording of them. Indeed, I have been charged by full-time students with not offering enough help with recording, and I cannot put this down to dependence on their part because in other ways they have been remarkably self-reliant. The brief for recording in Appendix 3 (b) includes some areas for special attention that may be added step by step by a group of trainees.

The discussion of the trainees' recording is very personal and revealing, giving as it does some almost intimate glimpses into his outlook

---

[1] Appendix 3 (a).

and approach. It is therefore not surprising that many groups of trainees often seem to be *talking about* recording rather than actually discussing somebody's recording. Recording can itself seem threatening. I have noticed this particularly with groups of teachers, some of whom have become quite hostile when it was suggested that they might attempt to record the flow of human behaviour taking place within the teaching situation.

There may be a need for a change in direction in recording as a course proceeds. For instance, a course for youth workers may begin by accepting the recording of general organization as appropriate. The recording at this stage would have the purpose of taking the trainee beneath the surface of his organizing to the more subtle events below. As the course develops the concentration may be switched to the help needed by individual youngsters, and the recording for this purpose would need to be quite different. If the worker is responsible for a fairly large and complex organization, the form of recording will ultimately need to reflect the complexity of his situation.

Job Analysis

Allied to recording, and perhaps to be regarded as an *ad hoc* exercise, job analysis can play a useful part in focusing attention on the details of the job as it is really being done, and by comparing this with what the job is said to be. The account of what the worker actually does should be as sharp as possible. Headings may be offered to ensure that there will be an analysis of the functions undertaken, and a schedule or time scale will pinpoint the use of his time. A job analysis would include a chain of responsibility, showing the persons to whom the worker is responsible and also those for whose work he bears responsibility, together with some idea of the relationships with colleagues and equals.

A careful examination of a statement of this kind quickly reveals inconsistencies, lack of clarity, or conflicting roles, and shows how the worker is using his time. It can also be a salutary experience for all concerned if the person in charge carries through the same exercise with his assistant staff. Much of the value of a job analysis is that it can direct discussion to the heart of what the job is supposed to be all about. The kind of brief that may be formulated is illustrated in Appendix 2 (e).

When trainees lay out this material before their colleagues there is usually a very incisive discussion, especially if the tutorial group as a whole have prepared the brief or have been partners in its preparation.

Once again the tutor will have to decide how much help he is going to give the group in formulating the brief, and it is often possible for his help to be given quite unobtrusively. The tutor will start or encourage useful avenues of thought, as he may warn against unpromising lines of inquiry. The purists may argue that the group should do their own preparation without interference, but it is significant that although we had job analysis in our programme of training from the early stages of our experiments, it was very slow to get off the ground, and did not really contribute to the courses until the teams of tutors, somewhat belatedly, cleared their own minds about the form that the brief might take.

6

As a Social Architect

The inevitability of being a social architect. Cohesiveness in groups. Group goals. Consultation. Group norms and roles. Changes in attitudes in action

The inevitability of his role as a social architect is something that the trainee gradually comes to see in the early stages of training. By the time that he has studied the patterns of interaction occurring in his own place of work and under his own influence, he is usually very well aware of his formative role. And when trainees, as part of the field work, consciously exert an influence on, for instance, some aspect of interaction, and observe the very considerable impact that they can have on the course of events, they may no longer escape the realization even if they would. The exercise presents them with a choice either to change or to leave things alone. This is a choice that they have been making intuitively all the time. They can now see that whichever way they decide, they will be influencing the people in the situation. Perhaps it is more comfortable not to know that our continual influence as a leader is quite inescapable.

Cohesiveness in Groups

It is usually enough to ask a question like, 'What makes a group attractive?' to initiate a lively exploration by the students of their own experience.[1] Often we prepare for this study by suggesting to the students that they should inquire of some of the young people in their establishment about why they belong to the organization (which, of course, doesn't work in a school) or what they mean by a 'sense of belonging'. We find that young people usually take the second question very seriously and begin to explore why they like to have other people around them.

The suggestions offered most frequently in answer to the question about what makes a group attractive, may be summed up as:

[1] There is a useful section on cohesiveness in Cartwright and Zander (Eds.), *Group Dynamics*, and, with reference to schools, in Bany and Johnson, *Classroom Group Behaviour*.

(a) attachment to at least some of the people in the group;

(b) a commitment to the purpose of the group;

(c) some kind of personal investment—this suggestion is usually produced after a little more searching;

(d) the level of personal need, recognizing both that there may be different levels of dependence upon groups from one person to another, and that many people have outlets alternative to the group in question;

(e) the presence of an outside threat;

(f) the climate of interaction, including factors like competition and co-operation.

The attachment to people may be dispatched by a recall of the discussion about interaction. It is when doing this kind of thing that we so often find that either the previous discussion has been forgotten or the students are not able unaided to make the transfer of one piece of learning to a related field. It can be very disconcerting to the trainer who is hoping that trainees will use concepts for an analytical approach to their work, to find that they do not even apply one theoretical idea to the next theoretical discussion.

Group Goals

When turning to the commitment to the purpose of the group as a cohesive factor, we need to consider what terms we wish to use. I find that the accepted technical language—group goals—is seen as strange at first, but students rapidly get used to it. I have learnt that an abstract definition of the term as an initial step is sometimes difficult to reach. It is probably better to work through real images by, for instance, asking, 'What are the goals of your own group?'—that is, the people in the establishment in which they are working.[1]

When this question is made the subject of discussion by small working commissions, some immediate answers usually come readily enough. Most people at first interpret this question in terms of the aims and objects of the agency or the leader's worthy purpose: 'the all-round development of young people', 'mind, body, and spirit', 'to improve their minds', 'Christian witness and experience'. When challenged about whether these are really goals to which the ordinary members subscribe, those who have contributed the statements at first

[1] N. B. Henry, *The Dynamics of Instructional Groups*, chapter x; Cartwright and Zander, *Group Dynamics*.

falter, and may then become confused. An untidy exploratory discussion in full session is usually followed by the small groups' resuming their search very thoughtfully for group goals shared by the members, the leaders, and the sponsors of the organization.

When they searched into their own organizations many were completely unable to state any real goals entertained by their groups (as distinct from the ambitions of the leader). Others, who had thought that there were clear goals in their organization, discovered on looking deeper that it was quite possible that their members did not subscribe to these goals, and in any case they had not been asked.

The difficulty that trainees may have in isolating group goals in their own situation changes from a matter of interest to one of concern as they turn to the impact that the commitment to the objectives of the group may have on the cohesion and strength of the group. They can readily see that a number of institutions, such as, for instance, political or religious bodies, may be held together much more by the cement of ideals commonly held than by personal attachment to the other people. In fact, loyalty may be evoked by a commitment to objectives, with the attachment to the other people following rather than preceding it. If, as they have indicated, the trainees wish to develop an attachment, in some cases a loyalty to their organization, then they are surely neglecting a potentially very powerful factor in not ensuring that group goals are clear and people are committed to them.

Many trainees have been very shaken by the realization that they cannot put their finger on goals that are held by the group as a whole, and even more by the fact that they have not previously seen it as something to be considered. Most do themselves less than justice in their too willing acceptance that group goals are completely absent from their own organizations: their failure to name them sometimes arises from their inability to discern the unspoken, unconsciously held, group objectives. But this does not lessen the seriousness of their not having given any thought to the matter.

It is always a very salutary and practical exercise to apply a new principle to the course itself. For instance, of an advanced course I recorded:

Everybody agreed that it would be a good idea to apply a similar examination to ourselves. A few minutes' discussion produced general agreement that as a group we had, as one of our goals, the mutual support of members of the course, but considerable probing could produce no support for my own fondly held hope that we should see ourselves as a pioneer group, evolving new steps in training. I realized that I had not taken the trouble to discuss this ambition with them. But curiously enough, the very action of bringing this into the open seemed to bring to us a new level of mutual understanding and common purpose.

It is obviously insufficient to leave the concept of group goals as broad as it has been stated above. Students may be encouraged to distinguish between long-term and short-term goals, between commonly held or corporate goals and sub-group goals, and between supportive and conflicting goals. They are usually on happier ground in being able to recognize a number of short-term goals; their main difficulty is to see these coalescing into long-term goals held by the group as a whole. In fact, they quickly see that the unspoken goals of many of the sub-groups and cliques in their organization may be in conflict with the goals of other sub-groups, or be directly counter to their own ambitions. The discussion often sheds new light on recent trouble brewing with the football, drama, or some other sub-section of their organization.

It is useful either to precede or to follow the discussion about group goals by an inquiry by trainees amongst the members of their groups about what they see to be the purpose of the organization. Trainees sometimes return rather cheered by this experience and confess that they have found more consensus of feeling than they expected or felt they deserved: but more often the trainees find only confirmation of their own recognition that no generally accepted goals are expressed in the organization as a whole.

Leaders of uniformed organizations and others with a given framework sometimes find this hard to accept, and they recognize also that they could get into difficulties if their members, when consulted, express an unwillingness to accept the stated objectives of the organization. But it is usually the workers in open youth clubs who are in greater difficulty at this juncture. Their dilemma is very real: they stand between an era when 'loyalty to the club' was accepted as good in itself, and a new philosophy which questions whether any demands at all should be made on young people. Most of them want to have some influence on young people and recognize that this will come in part through the prevailing climate of the place, but for the climate to have any real impact a sense of attachment would be required. Their difficulty seems to be increased by the fact that their organization has been set up to serve a wide range of young people and of interests, and to take personal needs of young people as the point of departure rather than to sell a predetermined line of interest and activity. How, they very reasonably ask, can an organization so conceived possibly have any goals common to the membership as a whole? A reasonable response to their question is to ask, 'Have you consulted your members about this?'

The discussion of group goals has been of particular interest to some of the teachers on these courses, especially those who have been concerned with the overall organization of the school. How far do pupils and staff share common objectives? Do all accept the lessons in the same spirit, or does it vary from clear joint action with the staff, to a dumb compliance during lesson time as a pause in the real business of life? Would it be found, in some cases, that the aims of the staff and pupils are in conflict?

Consultation

There are usually many references to consultation during discussions about group goals, and in particular when considering how goal setting can be approached. Involving people in consultation is one of the basic skills of the group worker. At first we assumed that it would be second nature to practising group workers, but we gradually discovered that this most certainly was not so. We were even more surprised to find how difficult it was to obtain agreement about what was meant by consultation.

Quite a number of people see consultation merely as a more subtle way of persuading people to do their bidding, avoiding the necessity of giving them direct instructions. It sometimes takes time for them to see that consultation can hardly have been said to have taken place unless the person initiating it is himself open to change. The leader who goes into consultation having already decided what he is going to do, will usually quite rapidly be seen as a sham.

Successful consultation must surely be fairly central to a lot of people's jobs—any team leader, headmaster, industrialist, institutional manager—especially since the spirit of the age seems to be growing steadily more resistant to authoritarian direction and pronouncement. If we want other people to be identified with what is afoot we shall do well to involve them in the planning and decisions: do we turn readily to consultation as one of the ways of influencing our situation, and how skilled are we at it? When trainees are invited to initiate consultation as a deliberate exercise they very soon discover that the skill of consultation is more than merely asking people what they think about something. The issues must be clear and well understood by all concerned; the sometimes wide range of influences bearing on the topic must be taken into account, and the alternative solutions brought out into the open. Above all the scope for manoeuvre must be clear to all concerned.

An experiment in consultation has been a regular part of the more recent courses; the kind of exercise will depend upon the level of training and the capacity and circumstances of the trainees. Some of them undertake fairly straightforward discussions with young people about how certain events might be staged, but the consultation undertaken by sensitive trainees working at a more advanced level may take them into areas of anxiety, concern, and helping other people. Trainees sometimes return to their tutorial groups, after this exercise, deeply moved by their experience, as a result of youngsters revealing, through their personal discussions, raw places and unsuspected yearnings.

The commitment that arises as a result of consultation may be very considerable. If we are consulted, especially if we are party to a decision, there is a little bit of us invested in the action that takes place. But consultation is only one of the ways of gaining the identification with what is going on. In fact, almost anything that gives somebody a share or a stake in a venture, or draws any effort from him may help to increase his commitment. An example of this is the identification of some of our students with the course of training that we suffer together, which is usually grudgingly conceded and with some amusement. The effort is certainly there, they say.

During several of these discussions, youth workers have asked whether it is possible to make the access to an organization and its facilities too easy, and some have described an increase in the sense of attachment that arose from their having to limit the membership of their organization and to establish a waiting list. It has been possible to feed in, at this point, an account of clinical experiments which seem to suggest that a more severe initiation may increase the value set on a venture by the people who suffer it.[1]

Group Norms
We began the discussion about cohesive factors in group situations by asking ourselves what made a group attractive, but in the course of discussion there are usually a number of hints that the benefits of group life are accompanied in most situations by some cost. It is usually a simple matter to move the discussion quite naturally into the consideration of group norms, by asking whether a group makes any demands

[1] Aronson and Mills in Cartwright and Zander, *Group Dynamics*.

upon its members as part of the price of the benefits gained through group membership. It will not be long before attention centres around a certain loss of freedom, the fact that we shall be expected to conform to certain kinds of behaviour, which we may identify as conforming to group norms. The term may be strange to most students, but I do not find that they have much difficulty with it and they quickly come to use it with a deceptive confidence.

Students seem to follow fairly readily that group norms are a framework of expectancies, sensed rather than spoken or consciously understood, which guide our behaviour in certain group situations and sometimes outside the group.[1] In particular, the group may express its expectancies over a limited area of behaviour which is of concern to the group, sometimes wide but sometimes very narrow. For instance, a football group may have something to say about how we should play, about turning up for training, and something about loyalty: it could extend to what we do after the match on Saturday afternoon but it could equally be limited to the mechanics of the game. The family, on the other hand, might have much to say to us about many personal things in life—our outlook, our religion, the way we behave sexually, how and what we eat. A group of close friends may have a similar wide area of normative influence.

A difficulty in the study of group norms is that they are so often unspoken and it is possible not to know certain norms exist until we offend them. It is not surprising therefore that the step from an intellectual grasp of the concept to the recognition of group norms in real life situations is not made easily. Once again the on-going events of a course offer an immediate opportunity for the tentative practice of the concept under fairly close supervision. 'Have we developed any norms as a group since we have been together?' sets minds working, and, usually with some difficulty, students begin to discern ways in which they feel they are expected to behave. Some of this, it is recognized, they brought in with them as part of the custom amongst a wider circle, but several aspects of expected behaviour, they will maintain, are peculiar to us as a working group.

The search can be extended by inviting students to project themselves into situations with which they are familiar, and to recount to other members of small working commissions some norms of groups that

---

[1] G. C. Homans, *The Human Group*, for a general statement; J. Klein, *The Study of Groups*, for the evolution of norms; D. H. Hargreaves, *Social Relations in a Secondary School*, for the operation of norms in a specific setting.

they know well. Their response to this tends to be to quote rather more obvious cases, but it is all valuable experience in fixing the concept as something they can recognize in action around them. All this is but a preparation for a field study in their own centre, in which they will examine some aspects of the norms of a group within the centre, or identify certain norms that have a fairly wide currency in the centre as a whole.

Trainees often become emotionally involved during this discussion:

The session about group norms was fairly hard going. We had the almost predictable outburst from Tom, who was claiming the right to be an individual and not to conform, but in all kinds of little ways showed his position to be quite untenable, which he grudgingly acknowledged. He seemed to cheer up considerably at the thought that group work might be about releasing people from the tyranny of group controls as much as using group controls to maintain a reasonable level of behaviour.

The expression 'releasing people from the tyranny of group controls' is well understood by trainees in terms of tough gangs, but it takes time for some of them to see that very strong normative controls can be operating in groups of much more sociable youngsters also. Students on these courses and our research workers have demonstrated that a group may limit the expression of interest by its members to very narrow confines indeed. It comes as something of a shock to a worker to discover that he has allowed situations to develop that severely limit the development of certain youngsters in his establishment.

Another very important realization for the teacher or the group worker is that group norms may be working directly counter to what he is trying to achieve.

Both Ken and John were very struck by the realization that a class, or groups within the class, could be exercising controls that might run counter to the efforts of the teacher. John, in particular, was interested in the thought that one did not merely withdraw one's own authority without seeing that it was replaced by the controls of the class itself. He then expressed anxiety lest the control of the group was more tyrannical than the control of the teacher, but this seemed a bit of a rearguard action. By this time he was quite stirred, and at one point said, 'This may be the turning point with me.'

A field study of group norms is found by many trainees to be quite a difficult exercise. Although they may have been satisfied that they understood what they were looking for, many of them find the actual search for group norms difficult, especially on familiar territory. This is similar to the difficulty experienced in discerning norms that have grown up amongst the members of the course: the situation is close, familiar, and personal and this seems to complicate the issue. Teachers often have difficulty in discerning group norms during their normal work, because of their concentration on the subject material. They have little spare time and energy to look further, and in any case the communication in the class-room is often not sufficiently free-flowing and personal to reveal what is going on under the surface. As soon as teachers appreciate the very considerable influence the group norms may be having, not only on the general behaviour of the pupils but also on their willingness to learn, they often become anxious to achieve a new level of communication and an opportunity to reach the informal influences at work in the class-room.

The study of group norms is usually carried out successfully by enough trainees to give rise to very lively tutorial discussions, and as a result to a real step forward in understanding.

Averil described the norms of a group of girls she had studied in her club. They *must* be friends (not just were friends); they must do everything together or not at all; they will be inactive in the club and none of them may take part in any activity; they must share everything possible to share—for instance, they will all smoke a single cigarette; they must defend one another to the end.

Nolan reported having met a member of a motor cycle group who surprised him by expressing an interest in painting and literature. At one stage the boy stopped the flow of conversation in order to make sure that Nolan would not tell any of his gang about his interest in books. He confided in Nolan that when he went to the public library he had to go by a roundabout way in order to be sure not to meet any of his pals.

An experiment in influencing group norms has been an important exercise in the more advanced courses. Often when the trainees concerned have first planned their action they have still been unclear about the processes involved, but most of them are very much more sophisticated about it after they have discussed their reports with their colleagues in the tutorial groups.

Finding that a fifth form G.C.E. group that he was teaching were unwilling to make much effort and were clearly going to fall below their potential in the examinations, Bob decided to consult them about how the work should be tackled, in the hope that he could change the norms that were limiting their efforts. There was not much room for manoeuvre because of the demands of the examination, but he outlined to them the area of choice open and asked for their suggestions. When he had managed to convince them that he really meant what he said, they made some fairly pointed but sensible suggestions about how he might improve his teaching. The change in the situation was quite dramatic, and the group are learning so much faster that Bob says he is now dissatisfied with the work he is doing with the other forms.

A firm understanding of the way social controls operate, an ability to discern some of the main influences in the immediate situation, and an, in part conscious, and in part intuitive ability to influence normative controls can take a group worker to quite a new level of competence. It marks an important step in the development of deliberate work.

Roles

We usually find that we have been using the term 'roles' quite a lot without having looked carefully at its meaning, and the discussion of group norms raises the matter fairly sharply.[1] Trainees often suggest that the best way of changing the norms of a group is to get hold of the leader, but after some exploration of the position of the leader it is usual for them to see that in some ways it is the leader who is most strongly tied to the norms of the group. The indigenous leader of a group of youngsters may have his position jeopardized by the attention and persuasions of the worker.

Yet we also know that in some ways the leader may depart from some of the behaviour to which other members of the group are expected to conform, and a resolution of this paradox is seen in the way that a framework of norms is attached to a particular role. It is as if the norms are bent to suit the roles accorded to various members of the group. For instance, the clown of a group may be applauded for doing something that would not be tolerated from another member of the group. I have used the word 'accorded' advisedly: the evolution of a role results from the interplay of the individual offering himself in certain ways and the group responding with the role they are prepared to accord him.

All this has pressed itself to our attention during these training courses because of the roles that individual youngsters have assumed in small groups with which we have been concerned, and in particular the not infrequent role fixations that have prevented change and growth in individual youngsters and sometimes also in the group as a whole. We have met cases where there is a gyration of repetitive behaviour

---

[1] M. Banton, *Roles*; K. Heap, *The Scapegoat Role in Youth Groups*, Case Conference, vol. 12, no. 7, January 1966. G. C. Homans, *The Human Group*, pp. 147 and 169–70.

that is really cloaking a deep malaise, which the group avoids facing. There can also be some serious miscalculation about the roles that youngsters think they are expected to fill. Some may play a role according to the rules they think they see reflected in other people's eyes, but the others confess to the worker that far from demanding this kind of behaviour they are reluctantly going along with it. Thus a stereotyped routine of behaviour is maintained by a miscalculation of what each would really ask of the other, if only free to express his wishes.

Clearly a group worker who wishes to help individual young people caught up in situations of this kind, needs a fairly clear understanding of what is taking place. Often it is easier to gain this clarity when a worker is looking into a situation as a field study, than it is if he is coping with the situation as a group worker. Having gained the necessary insights there is some hope that he will be able to feed it into the regular work he undertakes.

Attitudes

Throughout the discussion about group norms there are usually a number of references to attitudes, and, although the term is used loosely, most of the time I have always hesitated to break the flow of discussion in order to define it more exactly. As trainees become more at ease with the use of the term group norms, they often begin to use 'norms' and 'attitudes' as interchangeable with one another, and at this point it may be advisable to clarify what we mean by attitudes.

Group norms and attitudes are obviously related. Group norms are the expectancy of the people around us about how we should behave; attitudes are the pointers within us that represent a predisposition to react in a certain way.[1] We may conform to norms that are not a part of our framework of attitudes; indeed we may do so at times even when we are in disagreement with the course of action we know we are expected to take.

When faced by the expectancies of other people we may react in several ways. We may merely comply and keep our own counsel; we may accept what is required of us as reasonable and just; or we may become so accustomed to the demands or in sympathy with them that we internalize the kind of response that the expectancies have nurtured in us and this response may then become part of our make-up. We can conform without accepting, but we are unlikely to internalize a line of thought or action unless we identify ourselves with what is being

[1] Jahoda and Warren (eds.), *Attitudes*, especially part I.

demanded, and possibly with the people who are demanding it. The attitudes thus formed can be quite a powerful determinant of behaviour; we move with a set of attitudes from one situation to another, and the attitudes we have already assimilated may set limits to how we will behave in a new situation.

Attitudes can be very persistent, and resistant to change. They are part of us, and are usually held in an interlocking system which may be a part of our personality. Our attitudes are often supported by the groups to which we belong and are reinforced by their expectancies. Herein lies one of the hard core problems faced by anyone working with young people who may arrive into the situation we are concerned with, having absorbed anti-social attitudes from the environment of their home or neighbourhood, and come to us not alone but surrounded by a small group of like-minded people who will support and reinforce them in their general attitude to life. When faced with a problem of this magnitude the group worker may reasonably feel somewhat daunted, but at least he will recognize realistically the factors involved and will hesitate to limit his treatment to the individual as if he were an island. Clearly some of our worst problems with young people will only be reached if, in the approach to the youngster, his immediate environment is included, possibly even with the youngster serving as an agent of change in his own environment.

The picture of a young person merely absorbing and conveying the attitudes prevalent in his immediate environment is, of course, too simple by far. The situation is complicated by the personality of the individual concerned, and the interplay of his personality with the environment; for his personality will both be influenced by his experience, and will also have an impact upon it. Any one person will therefore hold a set of attitudes in his own unique way; the worker's approach to him will need to be a combination of direct personal help, plus any influence that can be exerted on the environment.

This could all be made to seem quite hopeless, but an approach through the trainee's own experience during the training course may be an excellent entry to the topic. Since attitudes are largely an emotional position they may be resistant to cold reason, especially since we seem to have very effective defences against allowing inconvenient information to reach our feeling self. The relevance of this to training was discussed in Chapter 2. By the time the subject of attitudes is reached on a course of training, the trainees have not only experienced a number of changes in their own attitudes, but they have become conscious of having done so. It is possible at this stage to initiate an exploration of how and why this has occurred, which brings out into the open the whole ethos and approach of the training. The trainee may thus become aware, for instance, of the impact of new experience and discovery, or of the way in which his being faced with other people's need has called up his compassion. These insights may be fed into the informal group work with young people.

The behaviour of Brinley and Roger in June's tutorial group has shown progressive and interesting changes. They both began as somewhat antagonistic to the course, and for some time they supported one another in their opposition.

At one stage Roger became hostile and rather morose, and finally expressed his hostility in a way that did not seem to be rational. I suspected that this was something of a cartharsis with him. When Brinley next turned to Roger for his support, Roger confessed to feeling a little different about things. However, it was not until Brinley mounted a public attack on the establishment in general, and on me in particular, that he began to be able to identify with what was going on. It was very interesting to see that from that moment he began to make haste in order to catch up with the field work that he had missed.

7
Learning about Leadership

Reducing the mystique of leadership. The leader's behaviour as a response to his emotional position. The spread of leadership; delegation. Authoritarian leadership. Permissiveness and autonomy. Personal styles of leadership

We have endeavoured throughout these courses to reduce the element of mystique that seems so often to permeate the discussion of leadership. Well worn clichés abound: people speak of 'born leaders', they search for leadership types and refer to historical figures and models; and attention may become fixed on a kind of amalgam of qualities that a leader should possess. Leadership is expressed in action however subtle it may be, and it should be possible ultimately to describe and analyse the action as it takes place. Confusion arises out of seeing leadership as qualities attaching to the person rather than as a series of actions taken and prompted by him. In any case leadership, in most situations, rarely resides in a single person.[1]

The whole of the training programme described here is really about leadership, although as a specific topic it is treated fairly late in the training. What could be more central to leadership than the worker's role as a social architect, or his influence on people's experience, feelings, and relationships? All the studies and experiments have represented an attempt to break down leadership into a series of recognizable steps that can be identified, studied, and practised.

However, having abstracted the elements of leadership and social architecture that are embedded in the situation, there remains a number of factors that are more intimately bound up with the face-to-face contact between the leader and the led. Not least of these is the emotional position of the leader himself. His outlook, ambitions, and sometimes his blind emotional need, will colour all his actions, and any attempt to help him pick his way through this morass of attitude and emotion

---

[1] For some useful references to leadership see: Cartwright and Zander, *Group Dynamics*; G. C. Homans, *The Human Group*; H. Jennings, *Leadership and Isolation*. Some supplementary material for the group worker will be found in the Leader-training Workbooks published by Association Press, New York.

is likely to lead to introspection, and may be disturbing and painful at times.

It is not always appreciated that teachers are also leaders.[1] The pattern of interaction that they structure in the class-room, the influence they exert on the norms of their groups, the personal face-to-face exchanges they have with individuals and small groups—all these are expressions of their leadership.

It is important in a study of leadership, to distinguish between indigenous leadership, which arises naturally out of the functioning of the group, and appointed leadership, which is to some degree imposed upon the group. Most trainees are appointed leaders. Although they draw much of their authority from the group which they lead, they have a certain residual power vested in them by an appointing body. It is not usually possible for the group to overthrow their leadership, and it will be impossible for them to abdicate completely. Group workers whose approach is to offer themselves as a support to small groups in their autonomous activity stand in an uneasy position between these two extremes.

Spread of Leadership

In introducing a discussion of leadership into training it is possible to build upon a number of previous studies. The examination of the structures of small groups, of social controls, and individual roles will have led to a—possibly unspoken—realization that leadership, far from being concentrated in the hands of one person, is often structured throughout an institution. A discussion prompted by a few sharp questions will usually crystallize the student's grasp of this fact. Further delving will demonstrate that this varies from one situation to another, and that the variations may have arisen from the policy and behaviour of the appointed leader. Thus the spread of leadership would be a convenient stepping-stone to the next series of discussions.

Allied to this is the 'distance' that exists between the leader and the led. The recall of the trainee's experience when deliberately planning consultation would focus attention on this, for many trainees will have found that the distance between them and some of their members was shortened by the consultation. The young people concerned may have readily demonstrated this by their easy approach to the worker

---

[1] For a treatment of leadership in the class-room, see Bany and Johnson, *Classroom Group Behaviour*; K. M. Evans, *Sociometry and Education*; Saunders, Phillips, and Johnson, *A Theory of Educational Leadership*.

following the experiment. Other relevant experience may be drawn upon, such as the transition from fifth to sixth form in school, for those who suddenly found themselves treated by their teachers much more as equals.

The appointed leader plays a very important part in the way acts of leadership are spread through the personnel of the institution. It is possible, for instance, for the leader to maintain a considerable, and perhaps fairly even distance between himself and his members, or he may invite his members, by various means, to shorten the distance.

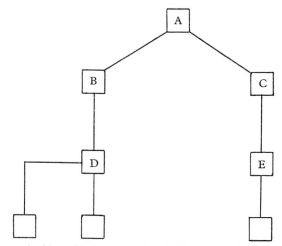

Fig. 5   An hierarchical group with subsidiary leadership at various points in the group

Another element in the pattern of leadership is the kind of hierarchy that exists. If there is a strongly hierarchical structure, the pattern may be of the style illustrated by Figure 5. Even in this situation there is a certain distribution of leadership at various points in the group. For instance, however strongly A in Figure 5 holds the reins, a certain amount of leadership will remain with B, C, D, and even E. Some patterns of leadership are strongly hierarchical like this, but a much greater evenness and interdependence will be found frequently amongst friendship and associate groups, and leadership may be assumed by different members of the group from one moment to the next, or in different circumstances. Figure 6 shows the lines of influence that may occur as the leadership passes, often quite rapidly, from one member of the group to another.

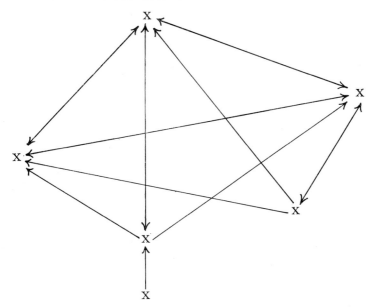

Fig. 6   The lines of influence that may exist in an interdependent
group structure with an even distribution of leadership

Delegation

A discussion of all this can usually be set going by inviting trainees, as
a field study, to distinguish the acts of leadership that take place in their
own establishments. Some find this quite a difficult exercise, partly
because they are being asked to see an old routine in a new way, but
also because they have difficulty in actually recognizing acts of leadership. They tend to expect to see broad sweeps, and miss the passing
jabs of initiative. Often nearly all the initiative is being exercised by
themselves and other adult staff, which leaves little scope for subsidiary
leadership. Many of them do not like what they have to report, for it is
often strongly at odds with their own self-image as a leader.

By this time trainees are usually ready to experiment further, and
we have found that, as a fairly logical follow-up to the study, they are
well placed to attempt a deliberate piece of delegation. It is usually
unnecessary for them to look further for something that they may
delegate, for the previous study has made them painfully aware of a
number of missed opportunities. It would appear that it is part of our
general climate that delegation is a good thing for its own sake, and

most trainees leave very cheerfully and confidently to undertake this exercise. But some of their reports would suggest that their optimism is too often misplaced and the ability to delegate is something that must be as hard won as most other skills. Some trainees seem unable to visualize any intermediate position between doing the whole thing themselves or standing aside completely, even when the person who is taking over is likely to make quite serious mistakes. Sometimes their approach seems so blatantly perverse that I find myself wondering whether they are really wanting to prove their own superiority. They may only gradually come to appreciate the element of support that is inherent in delegation, and support is a topic that recurs with increasing frequency in the later stages of training.

Leadership as an Emotional Position

By making these exercises fairly factual and objective it is possible for trainees to examine their situations without becoming very introspective. However, having uncovered their own situations, it is possible to sharpen the experience by asking why we behave as leaders in the particular way suggested by the studies. It could be that the trainees have adopted their form of leadership as a result of a rational approach (such as we are trying to evolve in this training), but most students freely confess that they have never really thought of analysing their behaviour in this kind of way.

Most have been guided by their intuition, prompted by their attitudes and emotions. The emotional position of the leader will include how he feels about himself, how he likes to be regarded by other people, the deference he feels is owed to him, his need for importance, and probably the pleasure derived from the part he plays in other people's lives. Intuitively he may feel for a certain kind of relationship with his followers, with the inevitable impact on their dependence or maturity, their growing experience or limited horizons. The leader will affect not only their feelings towards him, but also their feelings towards themselves.

In order to be able to discuss with one another how we behave as leaders, we need to develop a common language, and to isolate and identify any separate components that can be distinguished. In my innocence, I used to imagine that the words commonly in use for describing leadership would provide the necessary instruments for this kind of exchange, and having briefly defined what each word meant to me, proceeded to use them. Since I have been working with students through a dialogue, I have realized just how hopelessly inadequate my previous practice was. It is not only that people do not attach the same meaning to the words that they are using, but they often seem also not to want to accept other people's way of using terms. This is true of many words in common use, but the meaning of words used to describe our behaviour as leaders is so heavily bound up with our self-assessment that there is an extra obstacle to overcome. It has certainly been my experience that the discussion of the terms to describe leadership has been accompanied by a good deal of tension and heat. I have therefore learnt to take time in moving from one term to another, not so much clearing the definition as marshalling the sense and feeling behind the word, so that it can be seen in terms of human experience.

Authoritarian Leadership

One of the terms usually used frequently by trainees during discussion is 'authoritarian', and it is even used by one trainee to another as a term of friendly abuse. It is clearly an emotive term, and authoritarian behaviour has been widely condemned even in newspaper articles, radio broadcasts, and other organs of mass-media. Many teachers and group workers seem to feel threatened and under pressure by the mere discussion of authoritarian leadership, which is hardly conducive to an objective examination of the topic. It is important, if possible, to take the discussion into a dispassionate consideration of what constitutes authoritarian leadership, and to give trainees time to acclimatize themselves to new positions as the discussion proceeds.

The straightforward question, 'What do we mean by authoritarian leadership?' can lead immediately into a series of small group discussions of great intensity and considerable heat. Some see authoritarian leadership as simple dictatorship and as highly undesirable, and this has the effect of letting them off the hook, because clearly they are not dictatorial. Others gradually lead the conversation round to include in the definition the giving of instructions that the leader expects others to obey, or telling people what they should believe. It takes time for trainees to grasp the more subtle ways in which we may be authoritarian, and I suspect often that their slowness in coming to terms with this is as much for their personal protection as on account of any intrinsic difficulty about the ideas being discussed. There may be all kinds of diversions, smoke screening, and counter offensives whilst the discussions are taking place. The discussion tends to be in black and white terms, and it is often necessary to lead into a consideration of degrees of directiveness.

When there have been teachers in the group I have usually continued the discussion to consider what we mean by authoritarian teaching. Again the immediate picture is of a dictatorial, almost an unkind person, but this will have been mellowed by the preceding discussion to include someone who directs people's behaviour. I find that the initial discussion about this rarely deals with the way we impart knowledge, and it may take a little time before trainees come to see that a teacher's expectancy that the pupils should accept his knowledge and ideas is also an expression of authoritarian behaviour. One can sympathize with the teacher who resented being called an 'academic authoritarian' for doing a kindly and conscientious job in the way that his whole experience and training had led him to expect that it should be done; but it would be a pity if his indignation were to prevent his examining the suggestion. Do the same things apply to the effects of authoritarian teaching; does it limit the experience of the student and maintain his dependence upon the teacher; can it even mitigate against the student's growth in maturity or, for that matter, his increasing sophistication in study?

Many trainees rightly point out that they are not entirely free agents in the kind of leadership they offer. Any teacher who has wanted to depart from a formal approach within an otherwise formal establishment will be keenly aware of the pressures that may exist to bring him back into line. It is not only his colleagues who will point the errors of his ways; the pupils or students also may become confused, anxious, and hostile. Let us not assume that the groups for which we are responsible are necessarily wanting to be liberated to a personal autonomy and responsibility. The fact that we complain about a régime does not mean that we would relish the responsibilities that a change would bring. Habit has its own inertia.

In this context I find it interesting to observe that it is often the people who are most directive in their approach who themselves demand direction and wish to express dependence on a leader.

The whole group seemed to be waiting for my visit and turned to me for confirmation that the things that they thought might be right were in fact right. Jock, who had led several previous demands of this kind, seemed very disturbed by my unwillingness to take over the reins, and led the conversation, somewhat irrelevantly, to his feelings as a trainee teacher when his tutor arrived to watch him teach. This caused me to ask whether he was particularly concerned about authority, which he considered carefully without responding very firmly one way or another. He did say that he was a disciplinarian himself. . . .

Discipline and the taking of responsibility are recurring themes in this kind of programme.

I asked him what he meant by discipline, and when we managed to sort it all out it was that he insisted on obedience. He was challenged by one of his colleagues, who suggested that discipline involved an effort and a contribution from the person taking the action rather than mere obedience. At this point he retired from the conversation—rather thoughtfully, it seemed to me.

The inter-relationship between direction, discipline, and responsibility usually comes to be understood only slowly by many trainees, and the discussion often falls back on clichés like 'giving people responsibility'—by which it is frequently meant giving people certain things to do, and telling them exactly how to do them.

Cynthia had conducted her experiment in school. She had wanted to reorganize her room for some time, she said, and this spurred her to do it. The girls had previously been working two to a table, and there was always a possibility of one dodging the clearing and washing of equipment by blaming the other. She rearranged the room, she said, in order to ensure that each could not avoid taking responsibility for washing and clearing her own equipment.

It was suggested to Cynthia that for 'could not avoid taking responsibility for', she should substitute, 'could not avoid', since the girls had been relieved of any element of personal responsibility by her new arrangement. But her colleagues did not seem to be able to get through to her on this point.

In fact, it was not until nearly the end of the next week-end of this course, some five weeks later, that she suddenly saw the point.

Permissive Leadership and Autonomy

The natural preoccupation of the trainees has often taken us next to consider permissive leadership, as if authoritarian and permissive leadership were two ends of the same continuum. It is important that this idea should be challenged before it crystallizes. Of all the terms used to describe leadership, 'permissive' is the one about which there seems least consistency. The whole topic seems to be emotionally charged, with some regarding permissive leadership as good and others as bad; and the general talk about the 'permissive society' seems to complicate the issue.

Raymond (a mature and well organized headmaster of a junior school) said that he was permissive in his teaching, and went on to describe my own leadership as permissive. This was greeted by hearty guffaws. It was suggested to him that if he was going to call my leadership permissive, then he would run out of words when he came to describe leadership that was far less directive than mine.

Several students challenged the idea that there could ever be permissive leadership, and I suddenly found myself at the centre of confused hostility. I had proceeded only by question—and not by loaded question at that—and I wondered what could be moving them so strongly.

One of the points of greatest structural sifting in a discussion of leadership, is to distinguish between permissiveness and the encouragement of autonomy. Many trainees will come to the discussion seeing these two things as one, but after addressing themselves to a few sharp questions they may begin to acknowledge a difference between them. For instance, the question, 'Where does the leadership reside if the leader is encouraging autonomy in the group?' may be followed by, 'Where does the leadership reside if the leader is being permissive?' Quite crucial, though subtle, differences emerge in the way leadership is exercised in these two situations. There will need to be some concentration on how real or illusory is the apparent freedom arising from permissive leadership: the individual may be free to please himself—or will he be, after what we have learnt about group controls? And as for the group as a whole, how free are the members to take charge of the situation over the passive head of the appointed leader? The situation is quite different from engaging the members, with the leader's active support and encouragement, in taking as much responsibility as they are able to carry.

When we were describing the course to the head of his department, Sandy surprised me a little by suggesting to his boss that he was perhaps a little too permissive. Sandy greatly appreciated his friendliness, he said, but it may not be enough to say, 'Well chaps, I'll leave it to you', because this did not really involve them in the planning and policy decisions by which their actions were circumscribed. Besides there were all kinds of obstacles, sometimes with colleagues, which they were powerless to overcome by themselves. His manager seemed as nonplussed as Sandy was when we first discussed permissive leadership.

As the discussion proceeds students sometimes advance the view that there is really something rather authoritarian about permissive leadership. This is an intriguing paradox, and arises from questioning where the leadership resides in permissive situations. Although the leader is not active himself, he does not invite other people to take up the leadership but rather tends to sit on the leadership so that nobody else may assume it. It often becomes quite clear during the discussion that this describes precisely the position of some of the trainees, who thought that they were generously setting other people free merely by not exercising active leadership. They can be heard complaining about the lack of initiative on the part of young people; they do not realize that they may have been creating situations that made it extremely difficult for the youngsters to take any initiative.

Gradually trainees come to see that the authoritarian-permissive continuum is a false concept, and that it would be more valid to see it as an authoritarian-autonomy continuum. Permissiveness seems to belong to some other continuum, and it might be reasonably asked whether 'permissive' is the right word to use at all. 'Laissez-faire' might better express the extreme of what we have been talking about, or would it be better to think in terms of a continuum of active-inactive leadership?

At various stages in the discussion the expression 'democratic' will be used, if only because of its currency in some of the American literature. I find it easier to cope with this idea after some of the other concepts have been discussed, and it is fairly straightforward to challenge statements people make about being democratic. Not all of them want to be democratic, but the crunch comes when they consider whether they are really in the position to be democratic. Most of them are appointed leaders and cannot abdicate ultimate responsibility. In any case their members, pupils, or work people cannot dismiss them, and they quickly see that if they might at any time need to apply a veto, they can hardly be called democratic. It is probably much clearer to use the expression 'shared responsibility' for this kind of discussion, since it immediately raises the question of just how much responsibility is being shared and with whom.

Another important element that might be brought into the open at this stage is the effect of the protectiveness of the leader. This is bound up with the essential concern that the trainee will feel for his clients, but this may sometimes amount to over-concern. One sees the very protective mother who always prevents the fall, and we might find it necessary to make a plea for the freedom to make mistakes. Some teachers and youth workers know of no half-way house in this: they either nurse youngsters completely or stand aside and allow the most disastrous mistakes to occur. It is surely a matter of continuous judgement, encouraging young people to stretch out as far as they are ready to go.

Personal Style of Leadership

There is a danger of all the discussions centring on extremes. Each of these elements will enter the behaviour of any leader at different points of intensity. The style of leadership adopted by a trainee will be conditioned by his experience, attitudes, temperament, and personality. The important question is whether his style is a stereotype that remains inflexible before every situation, or whether the worker has a wide repertoire of responses to meet a wide range of situations. To help the trainees check this for themselves, and to practise the elements of leadership we have been studying, we usually invite them to watch themselves over a period of time and perhaps to consult a colleague or two, in an effort to describe their own style of leadership.

I found the group quietly helping Sister Mary through a difficult patch. She had been disturbed by the response she had received when she had asked one of her colleagues whether she was at all dominant; he had said mildly that she usually got done what she intended people should do. This had been reinforced by the fact that she had been shown as assertive in the personality test. Although neither of these things seemed serious in themselves, they apparently conflicted strongly with her own self-image, and particularly with her sense of humility as a religious sister.

From the study of his own leadership it is possible to move on to a deliberate approach in his own leadership, when the trainee will consider rationally what kind of action would best fit the situation with which he is faced. In more advanced courses it is possible to invite trainees to make a study of leadership by using a brief and schedule.

It may be advisable at this stage to add a word of caution. This whole programme of discussion may become deceptive on account of the enthusiasm and obvious effort of the students. The sessions may have their introspective and cathartic moments, and be both painful and enjoyable. But there is always a danger that the advance may remain at an intellectual level; the actual application of the new insights needs personal courage and effort, and often a good deal of support. It is therefore vital that the theoretical concepts should, quite inescapably, be brought into practical work by field exercises, recording, and continuing in-service supervision. Let the last words rest with the student who wrote:

Leaders should have a meeting, not for ordinary youth work, but for self-examination related to the points gained from this session. Question and discussion should take place continually, not just finish with this course.

8

The Institutional Worker

Institutional group work as an element of many people's jobs.
A basis for advanced training. Helping through group work;
diagnostic practices and treatment; counselling. The dynamics
of more complex groups. Guiding the work of colleagues;
supervision. Administration and government

There are important distinctions between the small group worker and
the institutional group worker. The latter bears responsibility for an
establishment as a whole, having within it a series of natural and contrived small groups, which may be separate from one another or be
linked by a complex network of relationships. The total establishment
will be greatly affected by the welfare of the sub-groups within it, and
the parts will, in turn, be similarly affected by the state of the whole.
The institutional worker is himself enmeshed in the very framework
of relationships and controls that he is trying to influence. The worker's
task in influencing this more complex situation involves him in a
greater element of architecture than may be the case in work with a
small group, and because the worker's influence is likely to be more
remote, a greater clarity of analysis may be required of him if he is to
have the effect he desires. Above all, there is a bigger element of team
leadership, whether this be in terms of adult colleagues or in supporting
the actions of leaders emerging from the ranks of the members.[1]

Although it is not always recognized as such, there is an important
element of institutional group work in many people's jobs. It is fairly
obvious in the case of the worker responsible for a recreative centre for
young people, but often not fully appreciated in the adult educational
centre. The outstanding example is the headmaster, and the subsidiary
posts in school. The personal growth of the pupil is the *raison d'être*
of the school, but all kinds of hierarchical relationships and limiting
group influences often get in the way of this major purpose of the school.
Workers in many institutional social work settings—often trained as
case workers—are primarily or equally concerned with group work;
and examples can be added ranging from industrial management to

---

[1] G. Konopka, *Group Work in the Institution.*

hospital administration. It could be argued that the expression 'group workers' should be reserved for those who use their influence self-consciously, and it must be granted that in many of the instances cited the worker may be the victim of social forces rather than the architect.

It is one thing to be able to do the work ourselves and quite another to be articulate enough to guide other people: the institutional worker should be capable of both. In order to prepare himself for this it is desirable that he should be familiar, as a result of his own experience, with what is involved, and this is one of the reasons that work with small groups has taken a fairly central position in the early stages of training. The skill of enabling other people to undertake work with small groups goes beyond being articulate about what is involved: the novice will need support, and the giving of support is a skill in its own right. And since it is likely that the worker-in-charge will need to shoulder some of the more difficult cases—or at least help his colleagues with them—it is important that he should reach a reasonable level of sophistication in this area of skill and knowledge.

As we developed courses at a more advanced level, we foresaw the possibility of evolving courses designed to assist, in particular, the worker in the institutional setting. We had found that our early courses were overloaded with material, and the planning of more advanced training gave us the opportunity of transferring sections of the material —particularly that which most concerned institutional work—from the first stage to advanced training.[1] Time is an important factor in a number of ways. The initial course had been planned for about twenty-six two hour sessions based on regular field work, often supported by supplementary residential week-ends. This was found to be the kind of load that could be supported in a single year's fairly intensive part-time training. Those courses planned completely as residential week-ends were rather more economical in the use of time since the warming up period served a whole week-end rather than a single session, and it was found that a similar amount of work could be accomplished by a course of five or six week-ends, suitably spaced in order to enable the field work to be done. An intervening tutorial meeting was found almost essential to courses conducted by residential week-ends. Courses of a similar volume have been conducted as a series of one-day meetings.

We gradually realized that the first year's training could profitably be followed by a period of consolidation, after which some of the students

[1] For an outline plan for advanced in-service training, see Appendix I (b).

would be ready to follow an advanced course. I say advisedly 'some of the students', Most of the training agencies with whom we were associated had not been very selective in the recruitment to the first stage courses, and selection was largely self-selection through the realization of what the course entailed. The wastage on most courses was slight, and was usually accounted for by illness, and changes in domestic and personal circumstances. As we planned the advanced courses we felt that we might need to be more selective. Only rarely have students been accepted for advanced training who have not been through the initial training, as it has been found that even long standing workers have not had the opportunities for the relevant experience and theoretical insights.

Thus, advanced training might have as its objectives:

(a) a deeper insight into social therapy in group work;
(b) a more secure understanding of certain group processes to assist in analytical thinking;
(c) experiment and specific practice in influencing social processes in the larger and more complex establishments;
(d) learning to work through colleagues and lieutenants, and practice in supervision;
(e) gaining a better understanding of institutional organization and government.

In the actual programme of training the boundaries between these objectives become blurred, and some of the work may serve several purposes at once.

Understanding Individual Needs

By this stage in the training students have usually come to see more keenly the individual needs of youngsters, and in particular the important restorative and therapeutic value of the intimate contacts with their peers. It is often a little less readily that trainees come to appreciate the dynamics of their own intervention, and the importance of the kind of experience to which they encourage young people to expose themselves. There are several elements to be considered: first, the experience gained by the individuals through the group activity; second, the impact of the experience on the internal structure of the group and the relationships between its members; third, the roles that individual members may be encouraged to take up; and fourth, the level of communication between the members about their relationships, and the support that the group offers to one another when they are facing introspective discussion and emotional stress.

The work with small groups included as part of advanced training is not a repetition of the work done in the initial training, but is rather a different and deeper kind of experience. Trainees are encouraged to choose carefully the group they are to work with, and to make careful studies of the members of the group. They do this through interviews and by careful recording of day-to-day contacts, so that they may build up case studies of their backgrounds and personalities, and of their relationships with the rest of the group and with people outside the group. Insight into individual roles may be increased by more detailed studies of a small group which will be mentioned later in this chapter.

The outward symptoms discerned by the worker are often the expression of much deeper personal need, and in some cases help must be in terms of personality development, change, or adjustment. Sometimes it is the attitudes that young people share with their peers that makes life difficult for them, but with many it is a matter of deeper limitations of social inadequacy, or feelings of inferiority, or of a stereotyped response to people and situations. In the face of this we have felt it necessary to take students through a theory of personality.

At this level of training we encourage students to read more deeply. But we find that their reading sometimes leaves them with a confused and rather disembodied jumble of theoretical material, that only really begins to fall into place when they become involved in something practical, as, for instance, personality testing. As always, we begin with ourselves. We introduced personality testing to our trainees first very tentatively and rather apologetically, but seeing the very considerable benefit that accrued from the experience, we made it a normal part of advanced training. Like so many of the other practical approaches we have adopted, personality testing seems to serve both as an aid to intellectual assimilation, and as a stimulus to introspection.[1]

At first we concentrated too much on the mechanics of processing and explanation. We have now seen possibilities of extending the trainees' understanding of what the tests are intended to measure, and the relevance of their own profiles to what they understand about themselves. For instance, if the trainees within a tutorial group are invited to rate one another in each personality factor, they find themselves having to come to grips with what that factor is intended to express and

[1] Further particulars about the personality tests used and some supporting literature are given in Appendix 4.

a lively discussion ensues, in which differences of understanding can be aired. For full value to be derived from the exercise in terms of introspection and growth, it is important that the experience should not come before the tutorial groups have reached the point when introspective discussion, the examination of personal qualities and differences, and the discussion of the relationships within the group is customary and supportive.

Daral's group were coping with an apparent contradiction in the case of Margery who was shown as being both assertive and shy. She confessed that this really summed up for her, in a new way, one of her main struggles in life; it was true, she said, that she was shy and reserved, but she wished also for her share of prominence and this ambition had cost her fairly dearly. She was quite deeply moved whilst telling us this.

Diagnostic Practice

An essential part of the experience is a recognition of the limitation of the personality tests and of the dangers attendant upon their use, which they have in common with any other diagnostic tools. Personality tests have to be used judicially as only one of the diagnostic tools available to us. For instance, personality and sociometric tests are a useful supplement to one another. In particular it is essential to guard against brash judgements being made by students insufficiently sophisticated in psychological thinking. Our own experience is that we have been able to make very few judgements on the basis of personality tests alone, and that they are no more than an additional indicator to be weighed with the other diagnostic material and in particular the worker's own experience of the youngster concerned. For instance, if we had worked on our own preconception of the kind of personality profile we would have expected of a youth worker, we would have excluded some of the obviously more successful workers.

Several teams of tutors have debated the wisdom of trainees making use of personality testing in pursuance of their group work. Usually it has been held that it is appropriate only to the more sophisticated workers in the right circumstances, and even then only under the kind of supervision provided through the tutorial groups. I think that our early fears may have been exaggerated. We have now considerable experience of the use of this kind of material by field workers under the supervision of a tutor, both through the training programme and through research in which a large number of field workers have been collaborating. We have found a need for the same kind of safeguards as are required for other kinds of diagnostic tests, as, for instance, sociometric tests. The danger is not so much inherent in the tests as in naïve interpretation and precipitate action. We have found that the personality tests add to the insight of the worker, but must be evaluated as part of the total material that he accumulates.

Helping through Group Work

The accumulation of material resulting from interviews, tests, and recorded day-to-day contacts and conversations, is sometimes very considerable, and it is obviously only possible to work at this level with a limited number of young people. In the training situation this can be justified by the knowledge, experience, and sophistication it brings. But there are important by-products. Not only does the deeper understanding of the client bring greater effectiveness, but there is also actual help and treatment inherent in the contact between the worker and the young person at this level of conversation. The benefits are so great as to suggest that these kinds of methods may well serve the group worker in his long-term approach, which can be particularly appropriate to the young people who are most in need of help. I have been very impressed by the frequency with which the uncovering of significant information about a group of young people has both seemed immediately to suggest to the worker what his next move should be, and, by involving the youngster in some significant experience, has in itself begun a process of change and development of personality.

We have felt it important to relate the personality of the individual youngster as shown by the personality testing, to the way he relates to other people, often a long-term personal style of relationship. For instance, some young people find it much easier to make relationships with those either older or younger than themselves, and there seems to be something of special significance that attaches to intimate relationships with equals. We have found that many of those so obviously in need of our help either feel themselves inadequate in making relationships or have a limited and stereotyped approach to other people. Some offer themselves again and again for immature roles, and seem quite incapable of breaking out of a situation that brings them pain. For instance, a tape-recording of a discussion within a group of youngsters in school about some scapegoating going on in their midst, showed quite clearly that it was more a matter of the scapegoat bringing trouble on himself than his persecutors looking for a victim: 'Fred's alone at home and hasn't any friends at school. He wants to attract attention, so he calls people names and that,' with which the scapegoat himself concurred. Another group worker reported:

Sheila's aggressive nature appeared to make her unpopular with the rest of the group; and my impression was confirmed by the sociometric test. . . . On the evening when teams were needed, the group formed themselves into a single team, and because they had one member too many Sheila was promptly offered to another team.

It is difficult at one and the same time to evaluate what a group is doing and to influence its course towards the next helpful step. Everything that goes on in the group may be on several levels at once: the events may be seen as overt action, but may cover considerable expression of emotion, both as feelings about other people and as feelings about self. Similarly any group activity will have various implications: first, as a direct experience for each member of the group; second, in its influence on the structure and cohesiveness of the group; third, in its impact on the relationships within the group and the roles taken up by individuals; and fourth, as a basis for personal and therapeutic discussion. All the time the worker will need to be considering his strategy, and to be sensitive to his own intervention.[1]

A discussion of friendship led straight, as we had hoped, into a study of loneliness. Several members of the group confessed to their having been very lonely at some stage since they had been at that school, and one of the girls was very moved as she told us about her own experience. The headmaster, who was with us at the time, wondered at so many of these youngsters having been lonely in what is a fairly easy going school of over three hundred children.

The discussion moved to an expression of concern for other people, and on a subsequent occasion it was possible to arrange for them to initiate discussion with other groups in the school. As a form, they had lacked cohesion, showed very little care and sympathy for one another, and had a poor regard for themselves as a group. One of our objectives was to help them to increase their own self-esteem, and there is little doubt that the initiative they were taking raised their status in their own eyes. According to their own statements, they changed from a 'shower' to a form who took themselves seriously.

As trainees have become more skilled and assured in their group work we have found it possible to encourage them to increase their own experience and flexibility by applying their skills to different fields. We gained our first experience of informal group work in schools in this

[1] Button, *Some Experiments in Informal Group Work.*

way, and a number of trainees have undertaken group work informally with young people outside their own organization.

In helping individual young people, the group worker will to some extent be involved in counselling. There is a difference between the two functions. The counsellor is, in the main, concerned to help the individual to resolve existing problems and operates largely through crisis situations. The group worker is more often concerned with the personal development and social education of the youngster by encouraging him to expose himself to new experience, often of a stirring nature, but at the same time he must be ready as counsellor to help the youngster resolve the stresses of his new position. To this extent counselling may become an important part of the group worker's function, and following the principle of helping the trainee to cope with one element of his work at a time, we have encouraged trainees to seek situations in which their role would be largely group counselling, in circumstances where they will not also have to cope with the long-term experiences of the group concerned. It has been the concentration on the role of the counsellor that has highlighted for some trainees their special function as a group worker.

We have thought it necessary from time to time to justify so much attention being paid to informal group work with small groups on advanced courses, directed in the main to the role of the institutional group worker. We are continually challenged by the suggestion that the institutional group worker, who may be responsible for a membership of sixty, a hundred, or even several hundreds, is clearly not going to be able to relate to his members in so formative a way. To this we have responded with a suggestion that work with a small group need not occupy the bulk of a worker's time (as so many of the trainees have demonstrated) and that there is surely some intensive group work to which the worker-in-charge may contribute better than any other member of staff. At the very minimum his lieutenants—the indigenous leaders emerging from the membership—deserve his attention as a working group, and some of the more intractable problems may need his personal attention. In any case, if he is hoping to guide assistant staff or helpers into sensitive group work he must know what he is doing. I will return to this later in the chapter.

The Dynamics of Group Situations

In the initial training we tried to help trainees towards an understanding of some of the forces of group control that would affect them in their work, and in doing this we were at pains to base the study on their own inquiry and experience. There was some attempt also to apply what they had learnt to real life situations, particularly to the work they were attempting with small groups. The institutional worker is often attempting to cope with most complex group situations and requires an especially clear understanding of the principles involved, if they are to become his working instruments for analysis and influence. For this reason—as well as the mere passage of time—a revision of the concepts of group dynamics is required.

We have attempted to intermesh this stage of training into a deliberate strategy of working with groups. For instance, when returning to a study of social controls, and in particular, group norms, a complex of group controls was eased through step-by-step consultation with the youngsters.

The fact that the boys and girls sat in separate blocks and avoided working together in the small study groups may have had its roots in the influence of the school staff, but in the present situation they knew that they were quite free to choose. It was obviously part of the norms of the group to operate in single sex groups. When we first formed small working groups we discussed with them the choice of working partners—people we felt most at ease with, or groups that would include some whom we did not know so well, and should the groups include both boys and girls. After some private discussion amongst themselves they decided by general acclaim to work in small groups with people they knew well, and there were no mixed groups.

Later in the programme we raised the matter with them again and this time they decided to change their groups to include people they did not know so well, but it was noticeable that there were still no mixed groups. Two sessions later, when we were discussing topics about which the opinion of both boys and girls would be helpful, we raised the matter with them again, and this time, after further private discussion, they decided that they would like to try mixed groups. It was not long after this that several of them began to say that they thought the usual segregation of the sexes was limiting and wrong.

We have highlighted the importance of consultation on advanced courses, since it is basic to the skill of the group worker. Not only have we suggested to trainees that they should attempt some change they desire by the use of consultation; we have also required them to examine the *routine* of consultation in their institution, and the part they personally play in influencing the institution by consultation aimed both up and down the hierarchy. Many youth workers find this a most disturbing experience, and teachers no less.

Reports from students faced by the need to make change show that open discussion, the switching of roles through discussion, or role playing may be used spontaneously as the occasion demands.

At the conclusion of all the previous meetings the youngsters had rushed off without any thought for straightening up the room, and we had been left to do this ourselves, not that it had occurred to us to see it as anything other than what was to be expected. But we suddenly began to ask ourselves what kind of social training this was on our part.

At the beginning of the next meeting we raised the matter with them, and engaged them in a discussion about what they would do if they were in our shoes, responsible for helping them in their training. Although at the time the discussion seemed inconclusive, the room became almost miraculously shipshape at the end of the meeting, without our having to mention the matter.

Communication

One of the outstanding discoveries made by many trainees during the initial training is the intimacy of communication possible between them and young people, which had shown their previous contacts to have been somewhat superficial. This is one of the most challenging aspects of training at the early stages, and some trainees have only just acclimatized themselves to this new kind of relationship by the end of the course. For some it needs considerable personal adjustment. Some teachers become quite disturbed by the 'danger' of becoming involved with their pupils. Of a full-time worker:

Donald made a long statement about his own development during the course. It seems that not only has he a much better understanding of what he is attempting to do, but also his own confidence has grown. He now realizes, he says, that previously he so arranged his routine that he would avoid any really close contacts with youngsters. The course has enabled him, indeed almost required him to break through this anxiety and to relate more easily to young people in his centre. He is now engaged in encouraging his assistant staff in the same direction, and is faced with similar fears in them as he experienced himself.

We have found it fairly easy to cause students to examine the quality of their personal contact with young people; but we have been far slower to find ways of helping them to see the importance of the kind of communication taking place between the young people in their groups. One of the values of close friendship is to provide an opportunity for the sharing of intimate confidences, as a safety-valve to pressures, almost as an ever-present therapeutic outlet. Many marriages have this quality. Whether a small group can offer this kind of outlet will depend upon the customary level of conversation, which may be limited by normative controls to superficial and repetitive exchanges. A student reported:

I began to wonder whether it was May's severe home difficulties that caused the group to keep her at a distance. Did they sense danger in her predicament ? My suspicion on this score was increased as I gradually discovered that each of the girls had some kind of difficulty at home—not so severe as May's, but bad enough. Not once did any of them lead the conversation into confidences about conditions at home, and it was as if there was a conspiracy of silence on an issue likely to touch a tender spot in each of them. Thus they seemed to have outlawed one of the topics of conversation that might have given most of them considerable relief and support.

Often it seems that youngsters feel too insecure to handle an emotionally charged topic of conversation, and the role of the group worker is in helping to create a controlled situation in which deeper conversation may take place.

Thus, a deliberate study of the kinds and patterns of communication existing, not only between the group worker and the young people, but also between the members of the small group of young people, has been an essential part of advanced training. The experience of the trainees of the way that the level of conversation has been deepened in their own tutorial groups is an important example of the opportunities open to the group worker, and we shall return to this topic in Chapter 10.

The Institutional Worker as a Group Builder

The function of interaction in the growth of relationships has received considerable attention in the initial training, but for the institutional worker the study of interaction has particular significance. Most youngsters enter the larger institution in small knots of friends or acquaintances, and they may not extend their relationships beyond the small group with whom they are already familiar. In fact there is an inertia working against making new contacts that belies the fond hope of, for instance, many youth workers, that by bringing a number of young people together under one roof they will, by virtue of this alone, offer them opportunities for extending their relationships. Small groups may literally turn inward with their backs to the world, and the occasion for interaction may need to be structured into the situation before many of them can be encouraged to break out of their existing stereotypes.

Some youngsters arrive in the organization without other contacts, and our inquiries have shown that many of these are amongst the least

able to make the running in establishing new contacts. And what about
that uncommitted associate group, with whom youth workers sometimes
find it so difficult to make any real contact, how are these young people
to be engaged in inevitable interaction both with the youth worker and
with other members of the institution?

They gradually revealed their own self-doubts and the poor regard they
had for themselves as a group. Little interaction between the members
of the form had been demanded by the system of teaching current in the
school, and the sub-group loyalties and other divisive factors were much
stronger than the forces that might have drawn the whole unit together.

For a number of reasons the institutional group worker may have a
legitimate wish to increase the cohesiveness of certain groups that he is
working with. When there are tasks to perform, the solidarity of the
group will be important, and, for many young people, part of the satisfaction of their membership lies in their sense of belonging to a cohesive group and the support that this brings. The worker who hopes
to influence individuals and small groups through the overall climate
of the place is clearly interested in their commitment to the group as a
whole, for otherwise the general norms may have little effect on the
constituent sub-groups. Some youth workers choose to forego the
advantages that are inherent in cohesive situations, either through their
own policy or that of their agency, when it is felt that they can best
serve young people by making no demands on their commitment or
loyalty. I have found that workers who begin with these preconceptions
are sometimes placed under a severe strain by this form of training, as
they come to see the opportunities for helping young people that they are
denying themselves.

The study of group goals, which began in the initial training, needs
to be revived and taken further. To the institutional worker this can be
both important and baffling, since his situation may be so complex
and even disjointed that the idea of goals held by the group as a whole
may at first have little meaning. This is often particularly true of workers
responsible for general open youth clubs. By its very nature, the open
club has as its purpose the welfare of the members, which usually
expresses the agency's goals rather than those of the youngsters.

When I am faced by a group of institutional workers who have lost
their way in a discussion of group goals I tend to take them right back
to our earlier discussions about basic human needs, and to ask them
whether these might not form the basis for coherent goals that would be
widely accepted by their members. How far, for instance, does the

organization have the offering of companionship and support to its members as one of its consciously held objectives? This is quite different from members using the centre as a place where they can meet their friends. And how far does the corporate membership seek to nurture the individual member's sense of significance and self-esteem, or his adventure and curiosity? And how far also do the members see themselves as a social agency, seeking opportunities for extending this kind of service to people outside the organization, who are possibly less able to fend for themselves?

It is well worth asking any group of workers whether they have consulted their own members about this. It is most noticeable that young people, when setting up some organization of their own, frequently state their objectives quite clearly, and it is just possible that the institutional group worker may himself be an impediment by suspending a fairly natural inclination to state aims and objects.

Theoretical Concepts into On-going Work

It is important that the revision and development of this conceptual material should be fed into the daily work of the group worker, and this needs careful planning. The inquiries designed to produce the raw material for discussion, and the *ad hoc* exercises and experiments through which tentative conclusions are put into practice are not enough, because the *ad hoc* exercises may never be repeated. The trainee must be encouraged to find ways of building the new insights and skills into the routine of the establishment. Our own research has brought to our notice many instances of missed opportunities in both school and youth work. We have met numerous cases of social inadequacy and ineptitude in young people who have been virtually unnoticed during ten years in school, or in any transitory membership of youth clubs.

Earlier in this chapter I referred to the difficulty faced by the institutional group worker in seeing any role for himself in terms of work with small groups; indeed we have been challenged quite strongly about whether there is any place at all for intensive group work in the larger institution. Certainly our own experiments have brought to our attention the forces inherent in many institutions that make informal group work particularly difficult. Against this I can hear persistent protests from other colleagues who, for instance, complain about the number of times that they see youth work being equated with 'club minding', and I still have ringing in my ears the protest of a youth officer who said that she would scream the next time she was told by a club leader that his inactivity was in aid of the members' 'being free to make relation-ships'.

The conflict the institutional group worker may experience about how best he should use his time, about whether to concentrate on the points of greatest need or spread his influence over the institution as a whole, is carried over into how assistant staff should spend their time:

> Fred complained that Janet, as a result of the advanced course, had ceased to be a 'leader' and had become a group worker. Apparently she is spending a lot of her time with a small group, including some fairly seriously disturbed boys, who have been thrown out of one club after another in the district and would probably have fallen foul of this club also except for the time that she spends with them.

And later in the same course: 'Fred once again raised the difficulty that may arise in a big centre if a large proportion of the staff are doing informal group work. This, he says, reduces the staff available for general oversight.'

The routine of the larger institution may provoke difficulties in other ways. The sheer need to get things organized may pressurize the worker into breaking off conversation with an individual youngster or small group at a crucial moment. Even more important, the normative pattern of the place may not be conducive to sub-groups operating as separate entities:

> For the whole of every club evening the girls I was interested in just sat and looked. There was nothing very much to see that they had not seen a hundred times before, but they seemed to be rooted to their chairs, just in case something did happen and they missed it. I was nearly in despair until one of the girls dropped a quite unintentional hint that their inactivity belonged to the club situation and that they would be pleased to try other things when the club was not open. Having received the message I arranged some meetings with them on other than club evenings and was amazed by their keenness and ingenuity.

Quite often our colleagues undertaking informal group work have found that their first breakthrough occurred when they encouraged their small group to meet outside the club setting. Often the self-identification that resulted from doing so continued when the group returned to the club. Suitable accommodation is an ever present problem: 'Janet provoked a few hilarious moments when she described how she was closeted with this group of boys in a large store cupboard, as the only accommodation available in this magnificent, newly built, open planned centre.'

I had always assumed that one of the dangers of working in small groups within the institutional setting was that of dividing the whole into a series of cliques, and it was partly with this in mind that I suggested that an advanced course should include some consideration of how we might weld a series of sub-groups into a cohesive whole. The first time we did this the members of the course went along with it quite merrily, but when I spoke out about my fears one member said:

Well if that is what you're worrying about you can forget it as far as my club is concerned. We have four people doing informal group work now, and I have never known our club to be so cohesive. Every group we touch seems to come nearer to the centre of the club, to be much more concerned with what is going on and more responsible.

Many other workers have reported similarly. As for Fred's anxiety about being deprived of staff for general oversight, is it possible that more responsibility could be assumed by the members themselves as they gain confidence through largely autonomous small group activity?

It is at about this point that so many group workers face a severe challenge. They see needs and opportunities that they previously just did not know existed, and at the same time realize that their own personal scope for informal work with small groups is severely limited by the need to keep the whole establishment going. It is easy to say that they must involve other members of staff in the exercise, but some have very few other staff available. The more I see of this work the more I am impressed by the enlarging effect that the mere interest of an adult may have on a small group of youngsters, and I question very strongly whether we have really tapped the reservoir of goodwill that must exist in any community, if only we can introduce kindly people to an undertaking that is within their competence and the time that they have available. Judging by what some of the raw recruits to initial training have been able to achieve, it is surely not too difficult for trained workers to engage kindly and balanced men and women in a limited job of personal service to a small group of youngsters. There is much to commend the introduction of some attempt to recruit and supervise some voluntary helpers as part of the advanced training of workers in charge of larger establishments.

A similar problem has been faced with teachers in training. Their experience of the very considerable personal help that they are able to offer to individual youngsters through informal work with small groups, may induce considerable dissatisfaction in them about their relationships with pupils in their normal teaching. The problem here is three-fold: how can they adapt their teaching methods to meet their new discoveries; how can they offer a pastoral service to the young people who most need it; and how can the functions they have come to value be structured into the programme and pattern of relationships of the school? All this can be very baffling to a teacher working in a formal secondary school. Some of the routine in schools in which heuristic methods have been introduced offers in the teaching great opportunities for individual growth through group participation, but generally, we have much to learn about the development of creative group relationships in school, and of a regular opportunity for group tutorials.

Involving Other Members of Staff

A facility in guiding the work of helpers and assistant staff appears far from general. We have included training in supervision as part of advanced courses, and I have been impressed by the enthusiasm for this exercise on the part of the trainees. Some see it as taking a colleague along with them in their studies rather than as encouraging a colleague to become involved in activating a small group of youngsters. When they come to face other workers some of their courage and determination seems to falter:

Bob has not made much progress with involving one of his colleagues in informal group work. He says that he is diffident about approaching a colleague as he was at first in making direct approaches to young people— and he suspects with as little cause for fear now as then.

Some find that it does not move forward as smoothly as they would like:

The first reaction of my assistant, Danny, was one of reluctance because of the time involved, although he realized that it would be interesting and useful in his own training. Finally he agreed to do some informal group work with my support, and said that he would give some thought to a choice of group before we next met. He chose a most suitable and interesting group, who were new to the club, did not mix or accept the club's norms, and, in particular, were suspected of dishonesty. After some discussion about how he should proceed, he approached the suspected leader of the group with a friendship study form and asked him whether he would be prepared to help with an inquiry. There was an immediate rebuff, and Danny retired with his self confidence and spirits in need of repair.

We were both involved for some time in other matters and when we returned to our design the group were sitting around a table following the final moves in a game of draughts. All that could be seen of them was their rounded backs. When the game had finished Danny approached them once again and I left the room. I did not see him again until closing time, as he emerged from conversation with the last two—all smiles. . . .

The relationship between us seems to have changed as a result of this project; we are now much closer colleagues and less of the leader and assistant. Danny has successfully shouldered a number of other responsibilities, and I have to confess there have been moments when I have found myself resenting the way he replaced me as leader.

Danny's need for support adds point to May's protest that:

We are concentrating too much on the function of the worker, on what we expect him to do with the youngsters; and we are not giving enough attention to the kind of support that he needs personally during what is sure to be a very challenging experience. After all we have needed considerable support ourselves from time to time whilst on this course.

It is easy to overlook how much time and attention is given to the support of the trainees during a course of training, since it is largely incidental to whatever else is going on and does not have to be specially arranged. When trainees come to supervise members of staff in a similar venture, it is less likely that there will be any routine that fits the need for regular and consistent support, and the pressure of work will endanger its happening at all.

Some trainees, as, for instance, those who are responsible for small clubs, have no helpers or other members of staff whom they can engage in this work, and some ingenuity has to be used if they are not to be left out of this part of the training. Some will have lieutenants emerging out of the ranks of the members whom they can lead to more responsible work. Most trainees overcome this difficulty: 'Prue is quite alone in her club, but she has decided to dig out her husband in order to give both him and her this new experience. She knows just the small group of boys whom he will be able to help.' Teachers are sometimes in difficulty here, though most find some opportunity for engaging somebody else in the work. Some do it through supervising the efforts of indigenous leaders, but a number have been successful in engaging the interest of colleagues in informal work with a small group.

The contrived small group most commonly found in youth work is probably the interest or specialist activity group, ranging from drama and dress-making to weight training and youth-hostelling. Many of these are served by a specialist activity leader who has the privilege of working with a fairly small group. The potentials of this situation in terms of personal service to young people are rarely appreciated and even more rarely grasped. Many factors seem to get in the way—tradition, terms of appointment, the expectancy, and sometimes the quality of the people concerned—but above all, the slowness of the institutional group worker himself to become aware of what is possible and to be articulate about it.

We have introduced into advanced training courses an attempt to engage the interest of a specialist activity leader in his scope for informal group work. This is usually found to be a tough assignment, and the difficulty does not rest only in the trainee's own insecurity:

> Dick reported that the needlework specialist had made tremendous progress in her communication with youngsters, especially through the same kind of enquiries as he had been using as part of the training course. He was rather shaken when, after the first round, she assumed that she had completed what was required of her and said, 'Please don't ask me to do it again. I find I become involved with the youngsters.'

It may be asking rather a lot to achieve this double-take, of training the activity leader through the training for the institutional group worker; courses designed specifically for specialist activity leaders are also needed. We have made a start with this, using many of the same devices, but designed in such a way as to illuminate the activity leader's potential role. It is very encouraging to see that the achievement of good standards in the activity and the use of the group for personal and emotional experience do not clash as so many trainees seem to fear. In fact some workers seemed to have enhanced the quality of the activity considerably as a result of the growth of the more personal element of their work.

Supervision

Like so many other parts of this training, in which students find themselves coping step by step with a new operation before any name is put to it, the trainees have both experienced being supervised themselves and have begun supporting the work of others before supervision is discussed directly as a topic. First, trainees take colleagues along with them in their studies; second, they engage a colleague in informal group work, extending this, in suitable cases, to specialist activity leaders; and third, they are engaged in direct study of the kind of support their colleagues require in attempting this work. They come to see all this largely in terms of the relationships between them and their colleagues, and some find themselves trammelled by previous preconceptions about authority relationships:

When Susan was describing her attempt to involve a colleague in informal group work, she said, about the relationship she wished to grow between them, that she would not like him to regard her as a tutor. At this the tutorial group stopped their discussion to ask her how she saw the tutor. She searched into herself quite hard and finally thought that she felt it an authority relationship, and after a certain pause, punctuated by the encouragement of her colleagues, she confessed to a certain feeling of awe and dependence in her relationship with the tutor.

As we have argued the nature of supervision, we have come to regard it as a rather more active role than is sometimes suggested, but the reader will see that this is no more than in character with the fairly direct approach that goes right through this training. We do not feel that our place as supervisors is merely as respondents to the initiative of the supervisee, any more than listening is a passive occupation, for only through conversation and inquiry can we truly listen. Too directive an approach on the part of the supervisor may sabotage the initiative of the supervisee, but insufficient stimulus may result in the supervisee never having certain experiences, or facing quite crucial issues, partly because he does not even know that they are there to seek, and partly because his own timidity will prevent his volunteering the necessary initiative. We have learnt from our experience with this kind of training that timidity may be overcome through acclimatization to new experience, and we know too that, without our fairly active encouragement, a number of our most promising trainees would have been very slow to venture.

There is a danger in supervision being seen as something special and apart, and dependent upon the existence of a person who is thought to have some special skill in this respect. When one views the enormous need for support in the myriad group work situations throughout the country, it is difficult to see how anything really significant is going to get off the ground unless supervision is in some way structured into the organization itself and into the relationships of the people who make up that organization. Above all, supervision and support needs to be *structured* into the situation so that it does not depend upon being arranged specially on *ad hoc* occasions. It is difficult to escape the conclusion that its viability and continuance will probably depend most of all upon the structure for consultation that exists, as a form of mutual support and self-help. Naturally the quality of the interchange that takes place will depend upon the sophistication, maturity, and courage of the people concerned, but, with all the will in the world, consultation at the level we are inferring by linking it with supervision, is not likely to survive without periodical injections from, say, a training agency.[1]

Administration and Government

In considering how an establishment may be controlled and organized, we have begun with the needs of the individual members, followed by the contribution that might be made to individual need, through the organization. Then must follow the question: How might the institution be brought into a state in which it might be of service to its members in the ways indicated ? What is the nature of authority as it is exercised in the establishment, and what kind of experience would we like young people to have in relation to authority ? It is an interesting fact that some of the most important experience open to the members is bound up with the control and organization of the institution, especially through shared decision, responsibility, and consultation.

As each of these courses has proceeded, particularly the advanced courses, the possible forms of government for the institution have begun to suggest themselves. For instance, the trainees come to understand the meaning of personal or small group autonomy, of authority and shared responsibility, and the interplay between the form of leadership and the state of the organization. Trainees will want to know about committees and their effective functioning, but one would hope that they would not be pressed into a stereotype of a committee-based administration.

Government by committee may be the most effective way in a particular situation, but it might be healthier if the trainee is enabled to entertain this as one of the way of achieving stated objectives: there may be better ways of gaining the commitment of the members, of encouraging autonomy and shared responsibility in a particular institution at a particular time. Committee systems can have their weaknesses, especially in the division that often exists between the committee members and the rank and file of the organization. In some circumstances a better system of communication and joint responsibility may be achieved by supplementing or replacing a single committee by a combination of sectional organizations, a central co-ordinating body, working parties to cope with particular problems or events, *ad hoc* consultation, and meetings of the general body—as befits the immediate and changing needs of the organization. A system of government needs some stability and tradition, but flexibility also is a great prize.

[1] D. E. Pettes, *Supervision in Social Work*; M. Tash, *Supervision in Youth Work*.

9
Review of Method

Overall planning; interlocking studies and field work. Direct approach and emotional involvement. Relationships in the training group. Open sessions and Socratic discussion. Training in social investigation. How directive? Assessment and feedback; written work. Length of courses and numbers. Consolidation

In my treatment of the material so far I have described events as they took place and have looked briefly at some of the principles underlying what we have been attempting. It may be profitable at this stage to take a broader view of the methods being adopted. I should like also to highlight several important issues and some recurring features of our experience. The ultimate effectiveness of the worker depends upon his knowledge, his skill, and probably most of all on his personal qualities and attitudes. I shall consider how the training is addressed to each of these objectives. We need, in particular to recognize that there may be a considerable gap between knowing how to do a job and having the determination, courage, and resource to put the know-how into practice.

Overall Planning
For anyone working with groups of people, a framework of concepts is very important. But how are we to introduce theoretical material so that its relevance is clear, so that it is assimilated intellectually, and even more, so that it is absorbed into the trainee's thought and practice rather than being taken into an intellectual conserve? By causing the trainee to provide, through his own recent experience, a good deal of the evidence upon which the conceptual thinking is based, we hope to ensure, not only its relevance to him, but also that the material will be assimilated and will bite into his methods of work. It is also hoped that, through the trainee's discovery, discussion, and introspection in the company and with the support of his peers, he will be given an opportunity to develop his own sensitivity, sophistication, and maturity. In order to ensure the transference of theoretical concepts into practice, the trainee is encouraged to undertake a number of exercises, experiments, and longer projects that give him the opportunity for, indeed necessitate the use of the recently won ideas, insights, and skills.

The continuous traffic from field studies and experience, through tutorial discussion, to the formulation of principles and concepts, which are then fed back into field work is illustrated by Figure 7. The interviews undertaken by the trainees at point 1 serve a number of purposes, but their particular value at this stage is to produce a fresh and lively understanding of the backgrounds, feelings, and needs of the young people. They will also illuminate the nature of the contact and communication between the worker and his clients. The discussions with young people about their personal needs at point 2 will add an extra dimension to the experience gained through the interviews.

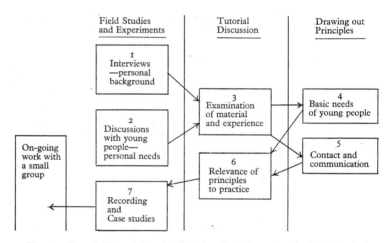

Fig. 7   Overall Plan of Interlocking Studies, Discussion, and Field Work

The interposition of the tutorial discussion at point 3 between the field work and the drawing out of principles is to give the trainees an opportunity to explore to a greater depth the significance of the material they have gathered, and to draw also from the experience of their colleagues. As the trainees emerge from the tutorial discussions their state of mind will be fertile rather than mature, and a good deal of additional discussion and study may be required when drawing out the principles at points 4 and 5.

Once the principles have been established it is vital that they should immediately be fed into the trainee's working equipment. The first step towards this will be to commit them to tutorial discussion at point 6 so that each trainee may examine their relevance to his own position.

In the case depicted, the principles could be applied in the field at point 7, through recording and through deeper case studies of individual young people. The ensuing field work, supplemented by additional studies and exercises, will in turn constitute the raw material for the next step in evolving principles.

The process is still not complete. It is vital that the principles being practised on an *ad hoc* basis should be fed into some on-going work with a small group. As indicated by Figure 7 work with a small group will be developed step by step as the trainee comes to each new point of understanding. The skills learnt at points 1 and 2 and the principles at points 4 and 5 may thus become part of the trainee's normal methods of work.

We have distinguished an interesting pattern in the way many students assimilate the material:

Ken emerged from the tutorial session flushed with the discovery that his earlier doubts about the capacity of some of his students to grasp the theoretical principles were not justified. There seemed to be a delayed action, he said. When a principle was first dealt with in open session and the tutorial discussions that followed, the members of his group protested that they fully understood what they were handling, but he was far from convinced. It seems that when they went back and tried to apply the principle they realized that they had not grasped what it was about after all, and it was not until they came to discuss their own confusion that the significance really clicked.

Ken was reiterating what several other people have noticed, and it gives us cause for thought. This is what we are saying: in spite of the fact that a principle has been based on their own sharp and recent experience, drawn out with their active participation through discussion, and reconsidered in terms of its application in the field—even then their grasp of what is involved is confused; and it is not until they come to discuss their own failure to apply the principle in practice that they begin to see its true significance. And only a few years ago I would have tried to convey such concepts through lectures and hoped blissfully that students had possession of what I had told them.

The kind of training that we are inviting trainees to share with us is informal; bystanders sometimes mistakenly see it as casual. I must emphasize, if emphasis is still needed by this time, that training in this form has to be planned very carefully. The planning should not put us into a straitjacket. In fact, there may be a good deal of room for spontaneity within a broad framework, and the security afforded by our planning may increase our room for manoeuvre. Before I embark on a course I work out the total programme as a feasibility exercise, which is important if we are to avoid taking trainees along a line that leaves them in the air because we have not enough time to bring it to some point of conclusion and usefulness.

When the programme of study has been planned, the relevant field work has to be settled and the sequence of events must be appropriate. When initiating the field work, the methods and adequacy of briefing are important. We usually devote one of the last sessions of each meeting to the briefing of the trainees for the next assignment of field work, and follow that up in writing. Even then we find that, if the assignment is for a period of several weeks, an intermediate meeting of the tutorial groups is worthwhile, indeed, almost essential. I have included in Appendix 2 the kind of notes that might be sent to trainees as briefs describing the field work, but it is unlikely that these could always be used as they stand since the group may decide to put their own special slant to any piece of field work.

Clearly, this is not a form of training for the tutor who wants to begin his preparation for a training meeting a few days or hours before it is due.

Feeding in Material

I must be careful not to give the impression that the students can be left to produce all the raw material for discussion: if the tutors have some information or a report of some experience relevant to the discussion they should be on the look-out for opportunities to feed it in. However, one is always having to judge how much can be profitably fed in at any particular point. The readiness of the student to assimilate new material seems to be influenced by whether he is stressed by a searching for solutions and by an attempt to fit new insights into a coherent body of thought.

Sometimes, when I have begun to be self-conscious about allowing students to continue a struggle for a possible resolution of a problem which I think I could short-circuit by producing an answer, students have revealed to me by a chance remark that they are enjoying the search and they would not thank me for depriving them of the satisfaction of finding their own way. Many a time I have been about to volunteer something that one of the students produced in the next minute. The process means that the teacher will be stressed as well as the students through the need to hold back and to judge the capacity of the students to make the next jump. He will be searching for material that will bridge the present discussion with the next principle to be explored, and will be noting offerings by the students that would only side-track the discussion at this point but will be valuable in the discussion likely to follow. He may need to break the tension at times by a turn of phrase that may exploit the humour of the situation, or by allowing the discussion to move away from a difficult area for a few minutes whilst everybody regains his breath.

Some trainers seem to wish to avoid technical language when dealing with in-service courses for the practitioner, but technical language, when properly used, offers economy in communication. In these courses we have tried to avoid using any technical term until it has been fully explored, unless it is a term used in common parlance in such a way as not to be misleading. We do not attempt to define the term until the knowledge, experience, and feeling upon which it is based has been examined. It is much more a matter of fitting a term to an area of understanding than of defining the term. In spite of these efforts we sometimes have angry outbursts about barren time spent upon defining words. I suspect that much of the heat has been caused by the student having, as a result of the discussion, to examine his own position and often change his ground.

Trainees first of all use technical terms somewhat tentatively but after a time begin to use them with conviction and in a context that would indicate that they have some understanding of the processes that the terms are describing. It is possible to get some feedback from past trainees who remain in touch with us, and from those who return for subsequent courses. There is little doubt that most have been introduced to a new language which represents also a new way of looking at their work. It is convincing to see the way that some youth workers, for instance, take their assistant staff into a quite new level of discussion and work, and some teachers consciously change, step by step, the normative controls operating in their class-rooms.

Field Work

Most teachers, when presenting theoretical material in lecture or other form, break it down into sequential parts so that one thing can be dealt with at a time; but both the education and social services have been slow to apply the same principle to the field work element of training. To some extent this has been accomplished on these courses through specific field studies and *ad hoc* exercises and experiments.

At first we tended, when leading trainees into the next assignment of field work, to deal with a group *en bloc*, tacitly assuming that they all had similar opportunities available to them. We now realize that this is a very insensitive way of briefing and include, as part of the briefing in tutorial groups, an opportunity for the individual trainee to relate the suggestions being put to him to his unique position. It is usually found that by adapting the exercise to any unusual situation or even offering an alternative approach, the trainee may be helped to the same basic experience. We have found this particularly necessary, for instance, when a worker is not in daily contact with young people, as, for instance, an administrator or advisory officer. Many of the principles being discussed have so universal an application that they can as readily be studied in the trainee's office or home as in the class-room.

All this is relatively easy when planning *ad hoc* exercises intended to illuminate specific principles; the incorporation of skills and concepts into on-going work, or the analysis of on-going work into its elements is much more difficult. This is easier to foresee in work with small groups, which can be built up afresh by a trainee who will see the work through, than in institutional work, where the worker inherits an on-going and complex organization at the outset.

In a study of institutional work much can be done by focusing in turn on single points of emphasis, such as, for instance, the pattern of interaction, sub-group structures, communication between the sub-groups, the normative controls (for instance, about how active the members should be), and the pattern of consultation, leadership, and initiative. This can be approached on the workshop principle. By workshop treatment I mean that a group of trainees will all be concentrating on a particular problem or aspect of their work, preferably after having undertaken some field study. The workshop, as part of training, is somewhat different from supervision. Supervision is more concerned with the resolution of the worker's own position in the scheme of things, whereas the workshop is usually about a study of particular skills or phenomena. Assignments that might be called workshop practice run right through this training. We have found that the workshop and supervision run closely together, since after the trainee has undertaken an investigation that disturbs his preconceptions he may need help in resolving his new position.

Direct Approach

The whole of this training is characterized by a fairly direct approach by the trainee to young people, which seems to be well received by the young people but can be very disturbing to the trainee; and for this we have been criticized for a number of reasons. The students themselves are anxious about the prospect:

The meeting was progressing very nicely until we reached the suggestion that we might gather some interesting information by each interviewing several youngsters. There was some sharp hostility, in particular from several teachers.

There is invariably a great difference in tone when the trainees return flushed by the success of their interviews with young people. Hostility on this score that survives until later in the courses seems to have come from people who either joined the courses late or, for some reason such as illness, have been half in and half out of the course, or from those who have failed to do their homework.

Joan, who had only just arrived in the district, was invited as an observer since she was likely to be involved in the training. She seemed ill at ease with what she saw and as the week-end proceeded voiced her opposition to the direct way in which we were involving the trainee and approaching young people.

Perhaps the most serious challenge we have to face is the charge that we are using young people for our own training:

We were led by Ann into a discussion about whether we were entitled to use young people as 'guinea pigs'. She agreed that young people seemed pleased enough to meet us and to have intimate conversations with us, but were we entitled to leave them after we had kindled their interest through conversations? In this she was joined by several other members of the group, although Frank made the distinction between interviews, when we made it clear what we were about, and the more binding commitment involved in informal group work.

I can offer very little in reply to these suggestions, except to urge upon colleagues that the young people who respond to our approaches should know our purpose and identity, and be assured that we will respect their confidences. Many trainees have found that the approach most readily accepted by young people is an appeal for their help, but if we are to receive their help it should be given willingly and knowingly. The following account is indicative of what takes place:

We conducted the enquiry by sitting in a small circle and taking one question at a time, discussing its meaning and leaving each member to make his or her own reply. They were fairly able youngsters and this approach seemed to work exceptionally well. There was no doubt about their interest, but I began to become anxious about the length of time it was taking us, particularly when normal closing time passed and the care-taker began jingling his keys within earshot. I had visions of irate parents descending upon me about having been closeted for so long with their youngsters. I was particularly relieved to overhear one youngster say, when we were sorting ourselves out in the darkness just outside the front door, 'This is the most interesting thing that has ever happened to me.'

Many trainees go far beyond gaining the acceptance of youngsters as respondents: they rope them in as collaborators, and often there is little difference between the work they do with a group helping in an inquiry, and their informal group work. To turn the statement round the other way—trainees often use the studies as instruments for their work with a small group.

Becoming Emotionally Involved

The fairly direct approach to young people is paralleled by the way that trainees become emotionally involved in what they are doing. They (and this includes hardened practitioners) often experience very considerable anxiety when they first undertake interviews at an intimate level, but they gradually acclimatize themselves to this kind of approach. Each new exercise seems to be tackled with growing confidence, although the level of anxiety usually jumps again as soon as they are invited to involve their colleagues in similar experiences.

We sometimes face a school of thought that would have us wait until experience comes to the trainee naturally at his own pace. To this I can only reply that for a number of years I tried to help students through supervision based on the experiences that a student found for himself or that came to him through the normal progression of his work, and found myself dissatisfied with the progress made through this approach. Many of them just did not have certain vital experiences because they did not reach out for them, and did not even know that the experiences were there to be sought. We face an inevitable choice between waiting for things to happen or causing them to happen.

Many trainers follow the practice of sending their trainees into the field in order to practise what they call 'youth leadership' or 'teaching'. Their trainees find themselves plunged immediately into most complex situations, of which they are sometimes required to take total control. The confused sense of inadequacy of someone placed in this kind of situation can cause considerable strain. We attempt to meet this diffi-culty by planning a series of graded steps, both in the level of challenge and in the range of function. We should like trainees to be free to tackle each step without other responsibilities pressing in on them from all sides. It would be nice to be able to argue that the steps have been worked out to suit the pace of individual trainees, but although we attempt to temper the work to suit the individual, we are still conducting the training as courses for a number of people travelling together:

Douglas seemed impatient to weigh in with a statement about the pressure he had experienced in his tutorial group about the insufficient consideration we had given individual students in their emotional difficulties. For instance, Mary may not be as secure as her outward appearance suggests, and some recent conversations we had asked her to conduct with young people had faced her with insights about herself that she did not like, and had disturbed her quite considerably.

However, it is possible to build certain safeguards into the system of training. It is important that relationships should be sufficiently on a colleague basis, particularly at the level of the tutorial group, to make easy exchange possible, so that plans can be amended as the work proceeds. The tutorial group may also afford considerable emotional support, and the tutor and leader of the course should both be available if additional and personal support is required.

One of the members of Harry's group was obviously very disturbed and talked in a way that seemed to link certain difficulties in her private life with the way she was working with young people. Harry wisely allowed the conversation to move away from the topic at a point when a confession of some domestic difficulty seemed imminent. At the close of the session I made myself available and she seemed glad of the opportunity of discussing some fairly serious difficulties in her married life, which were obviously influencing the way she was working with young people.

I do not wish to side-step criticism about the speed at which we expose trainees to new experiences and to the likelihood of their becoming emotionally involved in what they are doing, for the whole ethos of this training is based on an acknowledgement that stress may be a prerequisite to personal growth and development. This was not the premiss from which we began, but something that we have had to face as a result of experience.

Bill questioned whether it was the purpose of group work to make the client more comfortable. His own experience of 'knocking on doors in election canvassing' had made him more resilient, he said, to hostility and uncertainty! He suggested that one of the purposes of group work, or of the training of group workers and particularly of tutors, was to help the clients to become resilient to criticism and hostility. Was stress not an essential ingredient of a training situation? he asked. Were we to support people in the fantasies in their self-image or to help them face reality? The more secure person was surely not the one who was supported by an unreal self-image, but rather the person who saw himself as he really was and had learnt to live with it.

The basic safeguard resides in the exposure being by one step at a time in reasonably controlled conditions. We have noticed repeatedly that the scope for the tutorial group to operate in a supportive and therapeutic way is limited unless the members have been stirred by their experiences, but this will be considered in more detail in the following chapters.

Relationships in the Training Situation

One of the points of greatest stress has been the relationships within the training situation itself. I was at first surprised at the intensity of feeling, particularly of anxiety and hostility, that we met at the commencement of courses. It seems to arise in part out of the student's uncertainty about his role, and more particularly out of his relationships with people he sees as authority figures. Much of it probably arises from a disappointment of expectancy; he comes expecting to follow a clear and fairly strong lead and finds the situation fluid and uncertain, with more need for personal initiative than he expected. I have met this frequently, even amongst university graduates following post-graduate courses, and it would seem that most people's experience as a student has been in a didactic and authoritarian setting. The strangeness works itself out as trainees become acclimatized to the new situation; and these kinds of stresses are almost completely absent at the beginning of an advanced course with trainees who have been through previous training along these lines.

I wondered at first whether it was my personal approach that provoked this reaction, but I have been interested to notice that collaborators who have led courses have experienced the same pressures. It is interesting to note also that the reaction is sometimes most violent from trainees who are normally occupied in an hierarchical framework; those who are directive in their own walk of life very often expect to be able to express a dependence on others whom they see as being in authority.

Students do sometimes seem disturbed when they find that they may not depend upon the director of a course as they expected, they may attempt to compensate for this by attributing to him a great ability to watch their every move, and even to speak of him as 'big brother'. Or they may pin their faith on 'the method' and vest it with a certain mystique. The quest for an authority figure never quite leaves some trainees, and a colleague who sat through a course as an observer suggested that even the students' willingness to take initiative in the discussion was really a subtle way of expressing their dependence and of pleasing me. And a return to a position of dependence can come quite rapidly:

The commencement of the next session was described by Ted as a 'lecturette', and he suggested that it had been a valuable exercise in clearing the air. Something of a sigh of relief came through the recording of a number of students, and several of the tutors noted the obvious comfort that the students drew from my exposition.

Ted described the audience as 'receptive'; I noted that they quickly took on a dead pan 'audience' appearance. When treating material through small group discussions the attention of the whole company is so sharply focused, so responsive to each contribution, that the transition to the normal lecture situation is most marked: within minutes glazed eyes reveal incomplete attention, there are glances towards other points of focus, with fewer and fewer signs that the material is being actively absorbed into the students' system of thought.

On several occasions I have seen groups of students, who did much of their work through lively interchange, completely silenced by one of their colleagues who gave a didactic exposition with an authority that the rest of the group were assumed not to have. Until they were jolted out of their lethargic dependence they failed to make any headway into the real short-comings of what they had been told. The black-board sometimes seems to play a significant part in this, as if the black-board writer will see us through all our uncertainties.

The authority of the teacher's role is obviously difficult to balance. In our situation it is usually quite unreal to deny that the director of a course has insights and has had experience not shared by the members of the course, and when he questions and challenges he may easily fill a rather god-like role. When leading a course I feel it appropriate to challenge students' statements, which is all right if they feel at liberty to challenge mine, but that is more difficult to achieve. There is a danger that their challenge may be held back and come finally in the form of a revolt instead of as a dialogue in the course of a joint investigation. Now I consciously consider how the degree of distance and reverence might be reduced.

At one stage of the open session Frances suggested that I was using my authority unfairly by putting people who were raising points for me at a disadvantage. There was almost a gasp from the assembled company that a tutor should be 'having a go at Sir', but it was immediately followed by a wave of other points of criticism from various parts of the room. I wondered why we had been so slow to see a possible role for the tutors in helping to reduce the reverence expressed in open sessions.

A colleague regularly works with a fellow teacher in the class-room, whose job it is to challenge his statements and provoke the students into taking their own position.

The decision about how far we should try to alleviate the uneasiness of the trainees is a continual dilemma. Some of the anxiety experienced by them comes from a lack of clarity about where the course is leading, but this is also mixed up with their fears about the dependability of the leader. Should we allay their fears and convince them that everything has been carefully planned? This carries the danger of presenting them with a *fait accompli* and confirming them in their dependence, whereas we want them to feel and act with as much initiative as possible as partners in their own training. As the courses have proceeded we have tended to try rather more to explain what we were trying to do, possibly by using a sketch similar to Figure 7 on p. 110. It has seemed to allay some fears, although subsequent conversation has revealed that the full significance of what was explained was not understood.

The Open Session

Some of the strongest expressions of tension and hostility seem to come in the open sessions, and this is particularly true of feelings about authority. This has been the general experience of our collaborators. It is possible that the director of a course, when leading an open session, becomes the centre of hostility partly because he is the odd man out. Much less hostility is experienced within the tutorial group, probably because there are personal commitments both to the people and to what is being discussed.

The expression of feeling in open session is not something that I would be anxious to avoid: it is likely that the tension needs some outlet and since it is often a protest about the whole experience it is appropriate that it should be expressed at a corporate session. It can also be very constructive, first, in that any criticism must be faced and answered, and second, because a dialogue of this kind can sometimes serve as the first step towards better collaboration.

The open sessions have been conducted in the main through Socratic group discussions, and since so many of our colleagues have introduced similar methods into their day-to-day teaching and other work, it might be profitable to discuss in a little more detail the methods we are using. The way that this may proceed was indicated on p. 36. A question is posed for a few minutes' discussion in small groups, preparatory to a general discussion amongst the whole company. After a period of open discussion, the main flow of conversation is summarized and crystallized by the leader of the session, and this will very often lead straight into the next question. The topic raised by the question should be limited enough to enable the groups to make some progress with it in only a few minutes, and one of the skills of this manner of procedure is to visualize a programme of questions which will take the discussion along in a sequential way. The discussion in small groups is not intended to talk out the topic, but rather to spark off the members in readiness for the open discussion to follow. Thus the small group discussions and the corporate discussions blend into a continuing conversation.

The effect is impressive. If a large group is asked to discuss a topic it may have difficulty in getting going, but if we throw the same topic out to small groups for a few minutes, not only are the groups rapidly at work, but the conversation continues freely when they return to the corporate discussion. In introducing the method to the students, it is sometimes worthwhile approaching it in this way, so that they can see the difference for themselves.

I have often wondered why breaking into small groups should make so much difference. There seem to be several factors involved. Individual people seem to become committed to what they have said in the small group and wish the whole company to hear. The preliminary discussion gives them an opportunity to rehearse their statement, which may be important in the case of the more timid or less articulate. They also seem to derive a sense of support from the two or three people who have received and responded to their ideas. And when they contribute to the open discussion it is not usually merely to repeat what they have said to their colleagues in their small group, for they tend to be drawn into the dialogue and develop their ideas further.

However, it would be possible to be misled by the overall effect of the small group discussion, for a close study of the interaction within small groups, even of three members, may reveal considerable unevenness in individual contribution, and thus, of the personal experience arising from them. It may be profitable to engage the members of a course in a consideration of how everybody may be encouraged to gain the maximum benefit from the discussions. The more timid may be encouraged by their colleagues both to play their full part in the discussion in small groups and to contribute to the open dialogue, and it may also be necessary to bring to the attention of the more vociferous the effect of their behaviour on other people.

I have come to accept that the first question may have to be repeated or may even be included to break the ice.

I explained how we might tackle the day's work. As the meeting was to be a dialogue between youth workers on the one hand and teachers and headmasters on the other, I would not stand in their way as a lecturer but rather would invite them to begin this dialogue. They quite readily sorted themselves out into small groups representing different interests, and I threw out the first question. As I quickly moved round much of the discussion was completely unrelated to the question I had suggested, and I realized that there were some hoary old hobby horses to be ridden, which they might as well get out of their system.

We have tried various sizes in the small working groups. It seems that two is rarely enough to sustain discussion, that three is ideal if each of them is able and willing to contribute, but otherwise four people may be needed to produce the stimulus required. Five is already too large, since one or two people seem almost inevitably to be left out. To function successfully, a group of five people may need a chairman, whereas it is preferable for the groups to work as informally as possible. It is often worth sub-dividing even ten or a dozen people if there is some ground to be covered rapidly, or if there is a knotty point holding up progress. In the open part of the discussion there is no great difficulty in working with forty or even fifty people.

The whole process is fairly free and easy, but the onlooker should not be too persuaded by the informality of the situation. The programme of work needs to be carefully planned, and whoever is leading the discussion will find it necessary to hold the thing together so that there is a certain rigour. This mode of procedure has a discipline of its own. It is necessary to maintain good order as in any other form of teaching, and it is advisable when first experimenting, to keep the numbers down to, say, thirty. A generally accepted mode of conduct must be built up and a supportive climate that will encourage the more timid students to risk their contribution. Some groups have to learn a concern for one another and a willingness to listen to the others' contributions. This may be a point of particular emphasis in classes of children who vie competitively for the teacher's attention.

As the groups are encouraged to make use of all the space available and to face one another comfortably, the room soon gets into a state of disarray without any sense of front or back. I add to this feeling quite deliberately by operating from different parts of the room from time to time, crossing to the display board if and when this is necessary. When I started working in this way I left the groups to their own devices because I was afraid that my presence would inhibit their discussion, but I soon found it more profitable to move round to the groups, allowing myself to be drawn into the conversations, though being careful not to do the groups' work for them. I find that visiting the groups enables me to check the briefing, to assess the progress, and to time the return to the whole group discussion more sensitively. If the brief is proving unclear or unmanageable this can be acknowledged, and the brief amended. It also gives me an opportunity, possibly by a judicious question, to help some of the small groups along, or to challenge flabby thinking. It also helps to shorten the distance between myself and the individual students, and gives me the opportunity of spotting valid statements that might contribute to the open discussion to follow. Sometimes, quite important statements that are made in the small group discussions are not volunteered during the subsequent open discussion and it is helpful to be able to winkle them out.

There is little doubt that learning in this way has a skill of its own. Students seem at first to become very tired, almost as if there is a physical hurt attached to the movement of their minds. They often suggest that they are finding it necessary to think in a new kind of way. I suspect that some of the tiredness arises from the stress attached to an unfamiliar situation and different relationships, as well as from the actual intensity of work.

It is sometimes suggested by students on the courses, and even more often by bystanders, that the whole process lacks integrity:

During the discussion about consultation Jock suggested fairly forcibly that I knew very well what I wanted people to believe before I started, and that this form of teaching was just a cunning way of persuading people to accept my views—and no worse for that he added. Several other people joined him in this and although there seemed little point in protesting, I did mention how much I owed to the way that former students had broken new ground for me. I think that the discussion may have had the effect of making them more watchful, and it so happened that a few minutes later someone raised a point that was quite new to me and I was able to acknowledge the fact.

It is very important that students should not leave a course accepting Jock's suggestion, for they may approach their own students in this way if they are using these techniques themselves (Jock was already using them when this exchange took place). It might be profitable therefore to see that this discussion crops up fairly early, so that the students may be watchful from then onwards. The discussion on consultation is a very suitable time, since the willingness to be changed is one of the marks of whether consultation has taken place, and a true dialogue has a similar quality.

I have never disguised the fact that I am using Socratic group discussions as a method of teaching—not as a means of arriving at a consensus of opinion. The person leading the open discussion is inevitably in a very formative position. Although he may draw as many contributions from the company as possible, in the end, if he wishes the discussion to be crystallized, he will have to be selective. Some contributions may be merely received (though there is always a danger of an unintended but implied comment in doing so—'He didn't think much of what I said') whilst other contributors may be asked if they could develop their ideas. Sometimes there may be a contribution that will better fit a later discussion and the contributor may be asked to bring it to our attention again then. It is difficult with large groups not to remain central to the discussion, with everyone tending to address their contributions 'through the chair'; only when a group has become accustomed to this kind of situation will they conduct a dialogue across the room.

The fact that the discussion is based on a pre-planned programme may be causing the reader some uneasiness, as it sometimes does visitors and even some students. It is much more a matter of anticipation than prejudging. There are a number of issues the teacher wishes the group to consider and previous experience will suggest that certain conclusions are likely. It is thus possible to foresee a sequence of discussion. It is true that an agenda could limit the freedom of both the teacher and the student, and it is most important that the leader of the discussion should not play the ball so that it is bound to return to his chest. The security of an agenda may in fact make it much easier for him to be flexible.

It is frequently argued that in order successfully to teach in this way the teacher has to be especially secure in his subject, in order to cope with all the valid points likely to be raised by the students. It may be much more a question of being secure as a person, and in particular not to be bound up with the need for unchallenged authority. It is quite possible to be frankly sharing with trainees a new area of study, and I have often done this when covering ground that was new to me.

There is a fine line between challenging and being deprecatory:

I was a little troubled during this session by several people talking about being 'shot down', meaning apparently, that I would demolish their arguments or them personally. Several tutors took up similar themes in their recordings. Do I shoot them down? We may be trying to move along too fast, and the speed may reduce the grace of the exchanges.

And how far should the leader of the discussion engage with individual students during the open session?

In Cedric's group there is a rather aggressive young man who tends to hold up the work in his group, and in open session plays the role of professional objector. We were discussing, in open session, the proposition that the frequency of interaction might bring attachment, even if that attachment were one of hostility. Almost as if he had been sparked off by this, our objector interjected a somewhat condemnatory comment on our discussions. I responded quite spontaneously with, 'My word, you must have a lot of hostile attachments to you.' In some strange way this seemed to initiate a much more constructive dialogue between us.

We use the small groups for other purposes than Socratic discussion. Indeed, once students are accustomed to small working parties these can be used for clarification, producing briefs, for consultation and decision, or for assessment and feedback. In the school class-room the same small groups can turn readily from Socratic group discussion to problem solving and decision taking, and can serve as a means of establishing goals and influencing normative controls.

Sarah mentioned that she is using small group discussions during meetings of her council of youth. Whenever they become stuck on a knotty problem they break into small groups for a few minutes' discussion. She says it 'works like a charm'.

We have also found that for some purposes it is a most fruitful exercise to use small working parties merely to clarify questions or identify problems rather than seek conclusions.

The session on informal group work was conducted in small groups all working in the same room. It was agreed that we should not try to resolve any of the problems, merely giving enough time to identify them clearly. We did not attempt an exchange of views in open session. The agenda focused on some individual difficulties experienced by young people to which we might have to address ourselves through group work. The discussion was very lively. It rather hurt me to chop it off mid-stream when moving to the next question, but it raised no resentment amongst the trainees.

I have had the opportunity of watching several colleagues working in this way and have had reports from others, and this mode of procedure seems generally to draw the kind of response described above. It is an approach suited to topics that will receive detailed treatment later, but which the trainee is sure to meet in the meantime. It is also built upon the premiss that to clarify a problem is the first step, and sometimes a very significant step towards solving it.

Social Investigation

One area of possible dependence that has given us some concern is the way we present trainees with ready-made forms of inquiry. We accept as inevitable that it would be quite impossible for each group of students to evolve ways of uncovering the material required for the discussion; indeed quite often they do not know what is there to be uncovered until they have done it. Our anxiety is that they should also become self-reliant, capable of inquiring into something in their work situation that is puzzling them or causing them anxiety. In the earlier courses we included an inquiry to be formulated and conducted by the tutorial groups as training in social investigation, but we found it so time consuming that we discontinued it as part of the initial phase of training.

It is possible to offer some opportunities for self-help. For instance, trainees may evolve some of their own briefs, as, for instance, in preparation for club visits and observation, a form of inquiry about the background of young people, and they may progressively evolve a brief for recording. At times it is possible to invite them to compare what they would like to accomplish with a standard form of inquiry so that they can either accept or amend it. But all this is not the same as identifying a problem and having some personal responsibility for evolving ways of uncovering the relevant information.

We have felt it sufficiently important to retain some training in social investigation as part of the more advanced courses. Usually a tutorial group work as a whole on a project chosen by them, and may work through smaller groups from within their number in planning and carrying through the investigation. It seems usually to prove a most enjoyable undertaking; the important element of autonomy seems to add something to the personal satisfaction involved. My recording of this part of several courses reminds me of the agonies of effort that I have witnessed particularly as groups try to identify and delimit their problems.

One of the main dangers is that students wish to take far too big a grasp or attempt to tackle something that needs more sophistication than they can bring to it. Some may want to undertake a statistical study, almost of the market research kind, which cannot possibly have validity on account of the sample they can manage, and they can get lost in half-baked statistics. They are encouraged to do this by the aura surrounding that kind of study in the popular press. It can be helpful to suggest certain terms of reference which direct attention to the kind of inquiry that is likely to be both feasible and profitable, bearing in mind that one of the objectives of the exercise is to give the trainees an experience of the kind of social investigation that might be helpful to them as a tool in their work. It might be better for the study to be exploratory rather than statistical; and for this it will probably need to be detailed, even microscopic.

It can be a mistake in this kind of inquiry to concentrate too closely on getting answers to a series of questions: we are really examining a problem, and the form of inquiry may merely be serving as a tool to help us penetrate the problem. We should not, as it were, leave ourselves behind when we are working at the inquiry, but should be on the look-out for any signs that take us into the heart of our problem. Spontaneous conversation that arises during the interviews may offer leads that are as important as the material produced by the direct answers to the questions. Training and experience in interviewing will already have been part of the course, but may be consolidated as a preparation for the inquiry.

Here are some notes about what was included in a session introducing a project of this kind.[1]

1. (a) If we can come to know our situation clearly, we may be able to do something about it.

   (b) The skill of social investigation is something of a blank spot in those who work with young people—which locks up so much material in a closed book.

   (c) But social investigation is also a vehicle for such work:
       (i) in making contact with young people
       (ii) in activating young people.

[1] P. H. Mann, *Methods of Sociological Enquiry*; G. Kalton, *Introduction to Statistical Ideas for Social Scientists*.

2.   Planning

   (a) The idea—make it:
      (i) small enough
      (ii) deep enough
      (iii) clear enough.
   (b) Write your problem in a few sentences.
   (c) Prepare and carry through a pilot survey.
   (d) Examine the material you have collected on the pilot inquiry and make sure that it can be collated (which should also help you make sure that the material you are collecting will be usable).
   (e) Revision—prepare main survey.
   (f) Main survey.
   (g) Treatment (which should have been foreseen during the revision and preparation of the main inquiry).

3.   The questions

   (a) The loaded question—do not suggest your answers.
   (b) Type of questions:
      (i) open ended questions
      (ii) alternative or multiple choice questions
      (iii) inventory—a whole range of possibilities from which to choose.

4.   The approach

   (a) It is usually much better to interview.
   (b) Successful interviewing requires thought, sensitivity, and practice.

How Directive?

There is considerable debate within training circles about how directive we can afford to be. 'Directive' is not to be confused with my previous use of the term 'direct approach', which is more concerned with how sharply we make our entry and contact when working with people. How directive we should be in training concerns how much we should allow or invite trainees to depend on our instruction and guidance. There is a natural anxiety lest trainees become dependent upon the direction of the trainer, because most of the trainees will need to exercise considerable initiative in their professional role, and some will be working in relative isolation. Training should have as its ultimate objective the self-reliance as well as the skill of the trainee. Sometimes a distinction is drawn between directive and non-directive methods of training, but this is a somewhat blunt distinction. It is quite inevitable that we should be directive to a certain degree (even by requiring the trainee to face our non-directive approach), and it may be more sensitive to ask to what degree should we be directive and in what particular aspects of the training experience.

I have had experience of courses of training in which trainees were left very much to their own devices, and met in small groups merely within a given framework. What happened from there depended upon their initiative, their collaboration, and conflict. This kind of situation may provide a trainee with a startling experience of a particular kind, but if there is a body of information or concepts to be studied, it is unlikely that a group so structured will be able effectively to do so. They may not even know what there is to be examined or where the material is to be found. If there is a body of sequential material to be considered it is difficult to avoid the conclusion that some direction will be required.

We recognize that the kind of training that is the subject of this book is fairly directive. It is difficult for a trainee who has committed himself to a course of this kind to avoid quite a lot of experiences that we know very well he might avoid if left to his own devices. The element of direction is, therefore, in making it almost inevitable that the trainee will have certain experiences and consider a range of relevant material, but he has to live through the experience himself and draw his own conclusions as part of a working team. In all this he will face the challenge of a tutor, but he will also be supported by him and by his colleagues working as a tutorial group. Self-reliance is bred not only by trainees being required to find their own way; it may also be built up from the confidence of having lived through a number of challenging situations.

Although we may try to avoid the trainee's dependence upon us by asking questions or posing problems, we must recognize that there is even a danger of his becoming dependent upon our questioning and probing. We can only acknowledge this fact and try all the time gradually to withdraw from the centre of the questioning, so that the members of the tutorial groups may learn to question one another. The group worker faces the same problem in operating in the field: is he never to allow a group of youngsters to express any dependence upon him?

May he not be justified in using his own relationship with them judicially, acting as a stimulant, even as prime mover if this is the only way of initiating the relevant experience for his clients ?

On most courses there have been moments of considerable doubt and turbulence when trainees have begun working with small groups of young people and have faced the level of dependence upon them that some of the young people have wished to express. There is always a danger that, when trainees become self-conscious in their work, they will become alarmed by commitments implied in relationships that they would formerly have entered into cheerfully and unquestioningly. Their fears of invoking the dependence of young people are valid; but they have difficulty at the initial stage in visualizing the developmental phase of the work, and the period of the worker's withdrawal and growing self-reliance of the youngster. We may try to allay their fears by describing the later phases of work but we should not be too surprised if it does not mean very much to them. Sometimes, the best we can do is to remind them that the initiation of a piece of work has, as its prime objective, the client's self-determination and the worker's withdrawal.

In this context, it is interesting that we have noticed a recurring tendency at the end of the courses for a certain hostility and rebellion to be shown to those directing the course, and it has occurred to us that this might be a symbolic cutting of the umbilical cord. I have been through my recording of a number of courses, and although the reasons have been different from one course to another, it is a curious coincidence that criticism, hostility, and rebellion should erupt so often near the end of a course which has been proceeding industriously and happily. The reasons for these strong feelings are undoubtedly complex. Some of them have been expressed in a way that would suggest that some of the people concerned are acting out their own catharsis whilst the situation is still open for them to do so.

Written Work

I was at first stopped short by questions about what written work we demanded of the students on these courses, because if by written work is meant essay type material on a particular topic, that can be assessed and marked, then in the case of the in-service courses the answer is 'none'. And yet the trainee's written reports and aide-mémoires are integral to the whole programme. He notes his observations, conversations, and field studies; he records any experimental work he does and is encouraged to develop the systematic recording of his daily work.

He may also prepare some longer reports as a stock-taking of certain parts of his field work. Much of the written work is in note form since the skills of recording include being selective and brief. Elaborate recording by practitioners is always in danger of being dropped as soon as the pressure of work increases.

In particular, trainees are encouraged to write up an account of their informal group work, and they quite often tell us that they did not really begin to see themselves at work until they attempted this. Many report step by step in the same kind of way as they attempted to tackle the work: why they chose that particular group, how they made contact with them, what served as a focus for the group including the worker, what they learnt about individual people and how far the experience involved in being a member of the group was suited to individual need.

Most important of all, the written statements serve as a basis for discussion. In some courses, where formal assessment takes place, the written work may be collected as part of the material of interest to an assessment panel.

Assessment and Feedback

Several of the training agencies that undertake a formal assessment arrange for the trainees to be interviewed by panels, which include some educationists and social workers not connected with the training. Where this is well done it might even be described as an extension of the experience of the trainee, for it is based on a continuation of the dialogue with him. I am always a little doubtful about what is being assessed. It would be difficult to claim, in most cases, that this is an assessment of the trainee as a worker. At best it is an assessment of the effort, application, and progress of the trainee during the course, and this must be relative to where he stood before he began the training.

Equally important is the opportunity for the trainer to take stock of what has been achieved by the course. The practice of asking trainees what they have gained from the course is probably not a very reliable way of becoming informed, especially since the opinions one hears are sometimes so much at variance with one another. Feedback needs to be more intimately bound up with the whole process, and one of the outstanding features of this form of training is the continuing dialogue by which the trainer is able to assess the effectiveness of the course as it proceeds. For this reason alone it is important that the distance between the trainer and trainee should be shortened, so that the trainee may make spontaneous comment and criticism.

Length of Course and Numbers Involved

There are three major elements to be considered when planning the amount of time to be given to the course: first, the time needed for field studies, and the way these need to be spaced (for instance, we have learnt to take care that the periods of field work are not prejudiced by the normal seasonal holidays); second, the actual time to be spent together as members of the training group; and third, the pace appropriate to the assimilation of experience and change rather than information. The base plan included as Appendix 1 (a) indicates the time that may be needed to accomplish the kind of programme laid out there.

If there is little time available it would be better to attempt less work than to cover it less thoroughly, but there comes a point when less time means a falling effectiveness. The advantages of the longer course include being able to build one topic upon another, to reiterate earlier lessons as they apply to new and related topics, and to help the trainee, with the support of a tutorial group, to accept change. I cannot see much of value being accomplished on in-service training of less than five or six months' work. The real measure is the field work that can be accomplished: the actual meetings of the training group may be seen largely as supporting and capitalizing upon the trainee's field work. It is not just a matter of scurrying through a programme of conceptual learning; we must remain long enough with the trainee to help him to apply the learning to his practical work and to acclimatize himself to new positions.

In calculating numbers it is advisable to see the basic unit as the tutorial group. This can be too small as well as too large. Five tends to be too few unless the people concerned each have quite a lot to offer, and illness can cause a thin meeting and discussion; seven appears to be a better number and most agencies have settled for between seven and nine, in so far as they are free to choose. Above this number, the intimacy of the group begins to suffer and there is real difficulty in processing the mass of material brought in by the members of the groups.

If the course is to consist of a number of tutorial groups who will meet for corporate sessions—as, for instance, open sessions with Socratic discussion—an upper limit will be set by the feasibility of maintaining a real dialogue. About thirty might be enough whilst trying one's hand, and each teacher will gauge his upper limit as his experience grows.

Consolidation

Fred had recently visited a number of the people who had been on last year's training course, and he was disappointed with the work of several of them. They had done some most promising work whilst they were in training, but a break seemed to occur as soon as the pressure of training was relaxed.

This and a number of other experiences like it have faced us with the question of whether, in the end, our own training was to have as little effect as we had seen with other methods. Whilst the course was actually in session trainees were bound to meet a number of young people at an intimate level, and, as we have found, were immediately caught by an urgency of addressing themselves to the youngsters' needs. Was it that, when the routine of intimate conversation that was demanded by the training was removed, the sheer pressures of daily work pushed aside this level of personal contact as something that would be tackled tomorrow but never quite today. Clearly, it was necessary for the kind of work represented by the training to be absorbed into the daily work of the trainees as a matter of course.

Perhaps we were moving too fast and time should be spent during the training to ensure that this application was made. There is a difference between applying the training to the trainee's practical work—which is the essence of the whole course—and absorbing it into a routine. The latter is difficult to do piecemeal, because earlier experiences are related to later parts of the training, and in any case the true significance of some of the earlier experiences does not become really apparent to the trainee until some of the later work has been attempted. It has seemed to us that a course should be completed so far as it was to be taken, and then a renewed round of work study should begin to ensure its application and consolidation. It is essential that the practices should enter the day to day work as part of a *routine*. As for means of accomplishing this, we saw that it was wasteful to put all our resources into the initial training without reserving some to see that there was a consolidation of effort. It would be more economical to allocate, say, twenty-five per cent of the tutorial resources to consolidation even if this meant reducing the volume of initial training a little.

Thus we set about visualizing a programme of consolidation through which individual skills and insights learnt through training would be built into the routine of daily work. The consolidation would be approached on the basis of a regular workshop, and a possible plan of action is outlined in Appendix 1 (c). At a series of approximately monthly meetings (too frequent meetings leave too little time for serious action in the intervening period) a plan for the next period's application is worked out by the group, who, at their following meeting, report progress and plan for the next step.

10
The Tutors

The central role of the tutor. Processing the students' field studies. The tutor's leadership. Personal change and development. T-groups. Therapy in group work: the emotional undertone. Agendas for discussion. Recognizing signals. Questioning. The tutor's personal style. The team of tutors

It will hardly be necessary at this stage to emphasize the central position of the tutorial group in this form of training. It is through the tutorial group that the individual trainees are offered support in their field work, are helped to see the true significance of what they have uncovered, and when any general principles have been elicited from the material that they have produced, to study the application of those principles to the practical work in the field. In courses based on residential periods, where a number of tutorial groups are coming together, the formulation of general principles may take place in open corporate sessions; but in many smaller in-service courses, run mainly as weekly meetings, this part of the work also is the business of the tutorial group.

Although the quality of the members will influence the standard of work that can be achieved in the tutorial group, the effectiveness of the group as a whole will be influenced even more by the skill, sensitivity, and personal resource of the tutor. He in turn will need support, which he will normally find in the team of tutors, which serves not only to foster the personal effectiveness of the individual tutor, but also as a working party to plan and see through the whole course.

There has been some uncertainty in training circles about how strong a leadership a tutor should offer. He has been encouraged by some trainers merely to observe and make summaries, a mode of procedure often introduced in order to prevent the members of the tutorial group from becoming dependent upon him. It is true that there is always a danger of the tutor occupying, indeed relishing a central position, but the tutor who remains outside the discussion may sometimes seem threatening and can produce a strained atmosphere that may hold up the work instead of facilitating it. The subtle balance that must be maintained by the tutor is only gradually learnt by most of them. His objective is to establish a colleague role. This does not imply necessarily an equal role, and certainly not the rather godlike presence of the non-participant. We have found that most tutors come to achieve the balance by maintaining their part of the dialogue largely by questions, as they carefully avoid offering a resolution to the problem.

I felt that Sam was trying to jump his tutorial group to a point of definition before they were really ready for it, by almost telling them the conclusions that they should come to. I wondered whether he was wanting to demonstrate his own technical understanding, but I doubt it. He is probably a little over anxious that they should come to viable conclusions.

Processing the Material

One of the persistent problems of the tutorial groups is how to cope with the very large amount of material brought in by the members. There is rarely time to give detailed attention to all of it and some students may feel a little deflated by their offerings not being considered. The group will need to develop its own modes of dealing with this problem, which may change from session to session. There is not much point in dealing superficially with all the material presented, and the groups usually decide to choose certain pieces of work for detailed examination. Whatever happens, it is important that individual members should not feel that their work is being neglected; the less able students need their share of attention and it is important that the group should not choose always the 'best examples'. The feeling of personal neglect usually diminishes rapidly as the group become involved in the decisions about the mode of procedure.

Some groups evolve a rough rota, but others compromise by running quickly through a general report from each member of the group to see what is available and then selecting certain reports for special attention. Sometimes they will process one piece of work as a whole group, and having established the kind of approach and rigour appropriate to the exercise, will break up into smaller groups so that each member's work may receive attention, possibly returning to the total group in order to report any salient items. The tutor will need to consider, when encouraging the group to work in this way, whether the material being handled during the session is likely to give rise to introspection and personal change, in which case he may wish to encourage the group to work as a whole so that he can be formative in what takes place.

The tutor has to consider all the time how active he should be. Whilst he will wish to stimulate questioning at a rigorous level and may avoid providing the answers, he may find that trainees come to depend even on his questioning. It is not very difficult to side-step this as long as the tutor is clear about what is happening and what he wants to achieve.

I found Larry very leading in his questions—almost dictatorial—and seriously limiting the range of response open to the group. I managed to focus the attention of the group on the nature of the exchange, and chatted with him about it after the close of the session. I showed him a sketch I had drawn of ten minutes of the exchanges. He decided that he would recede into the background next time, and when I visited the group there was certainly a much freer interchange taking place, without each contribution being channelled through him. But during the last session his questioning was again dominating the situation.

The theoretical component of the course is not something that can be ladled out in chunks; it matures bit by bit as experience brings new enlightenment. To this end, the tutor must be secure with the concepts used in the training. It is true that in developing these courses I have been acting as a visiting specialist, but my function has been rather different from that of the usual information giver. Our joint purpose has been to make sure that the necessary expertise will be vested in the local tutors by the end of the course. The tutors concerned with a course can do much to help one another as a team. They will be looking forward to the material to be dealt with in the near future, and a certain specialization amongst them can sometimes enable each to stimulate the discussion within their own special field of interest.

The Tutor's Leadership

Since the training is very much concerned also with the attitudes and the personal development of the trainees, the way in which the course is conducted, and the state of mind that this induces in the trainees is as important as the content. There are a number of general qualities in the trainee that are usually seen as important, such as self-reliance, resilience, flexibility, and openness to new ideas.

In coping with tutorial discussions that bring stress, the tutor will need a high level of resilience, and tolerance to uncertainty, criticism, and hostility. In some cases a tutor may have a great deal to bear.

I responded to an appeal from June to join her group for the next session. She has had a very tough passage particularly with three of her group: John whose previous approach to his work has been so challenged by the course that at first he condemned each new move as unethical, impracticable or just not suited to his circumstances; Brinley, who seemed to want to avoid anything that might involve him in change and new thoughts; and Roger whose whole bearing was formidable.

They had combined, each for very different reasons, in opposition to June and the rest of the group, and had made life pretty unpleasant for her. I have only recently realized how much more support she needed in the early stages of the training than we offered her.

Our tutorial teams have always had considerable discussion about how challenging the tutor should be.

John was anxious about Harry who seemed excessively rigid, and John thought that we were making little impression with him. We asked him how rigorous and demanding he was with the members of his group, and he considered this as if he were thinking about it for the first time. He thought that perhaps he had not been as forceful as he should have been.

In this respect the tutor's approach seems often to be determined more by his personality than policy, and even his policy may be an expression of his personality.

We were discussing whether we should lead people to see their own short-comings through the exchanges in the tutorial group, and several of the team feared that this might be cruel and harmful. Cyril thought that the habit of keeping private thoughts to ourselves was one of the happier elements of our civilization; Paddy said that he could see the logic of not sweeping things under the carpet but found himself constitutionally unfitted to face people with anything unpleasant.

There is little doubt that the whole tone and level of discussion between the members of the tutorial group is set largely by the leadership that the tutor offers to the group.

As Susan was about to deliver her account of her experiment in establishing communication, she prefaced it by saying, 'Well, you may think that this . . .', at which point the whole group, led by Laurie, the tutor, cut her off by a volley of encouragement. I suspected that she was about to confess a sense of inadequacy, and I asked Laurie and his colleagues why they had not waited to hear what she had to say. This led to a renewed outburst of similar assertions, and when I repeated the question rather more pointedly, protests were added to the assertions.

Although I earned a certain hostility by my persistence, the group did finally address themselves to my question and decided that whilst they wished to reassure Susan, they may also have been expressing their own discomfort at hearing her confession of inadequacy. Finally, with some amusement, they turned to Susan and said, 'What were you going to say anyway Susan?'

As I left the group I wondered whether we avoid hearing other people's statements merely to save them pain or also possibly to avoid hearing our own sense of inadequacy echoed by somebody else. I was interested to notice that the level of intimacy in that tutorial group deepened quite rapidly after the exchange that I have reported, and they took a pride in the supportive nature of their group. My recording much later in the same course also reminds me, about the same person: 'Susan felt that a change in her own personality began on the day that she and the group faced her feelings of inadequacy.'

All of this is closely bound up with the subtle question of what kind of relationship the tutor is seeking with his group as a whole.

Almost out of context Reg said that he felt that he should be 'one of them'—meaning his tutorial group, but Cyril was very doubtful whether we could ever be 'one of them'. He suggested that we were set apart, however little, by our role, and whether we liked it or not the group vested a certain authority in us. After all, here we were meeting as a team of tutors before anybody else had arrived.

Sandy seemed to wonder what we were all talking about. He doesn't feel there is any deference shown to him—he merely tells his group that he and they are all equals!

A similar balance is involved when a director or leader of a course is working with a team of tutors.

Personal Change and Development

There was an air of great uneasiness as we asked ourselves whether our work as tutors went beyond helping trainees to understand; were we also concerned with the personal qualities of the trainees? As was quite rightly pointed out, we were really asking ourselves whether we were concerned with changing people. At this point the discussion faltered, and I had the feeling that several of us would prefer not to take it beyond this point. Geoff sat us all up sharply by stating roundly that it was quite inevitable that we should be changing people, and if we weren't prepared to face this he wondered why we were in the business.

In the debate that followed several people described how they had been changed by the work they had undertaken as part of the course. As we left the room at the end of the session Paddy said that he felt that there had been 'a moment of truth'.

This kind of exchange has been repeated many times in my experience, and seems almost inevitable as groups of tutors face the complexity of their role. In the early discussions about possible development and change in the trainee, the tutors tend to assume that the only two alternatives are either to cause change or to leave things as they are. Gradually they come to see first, that some change may be inevitable as a result of the training; and second, that their role may be one of offering opportunities for change rather than directly causing it. The initiative and personal autonomy will remain with the trainee.

Boris revealed that when he first took up a post as a full-time youth worker he was quite unable to conduct a conversation with the youngsters about anything intimate. He could now see that he set up all kinds of barriers so that it would not be necessary. He had found some of the contacts that he was required to make as part of the training quite frightening. He felt that he had broken through a bit as a result of the initial course, and he had asked to come on the advanced course quite deliberately in order to increase his skill and confidence in making close contacts.

He was remarkably inarticulate about his feelings when struggling to convey all this to us. He was able to say that he had always retreated from deeper relationships, but was unable to express the feelings that led to his retreat from intimacy. Responding to the obvious concern and sympathy of the rest of the tutorial group, he went on to tell us that the changes that had begun in his professional life had extended into his private life as well—'My wife says she doesn't mind how it has happened; if it is going to make me easier to live with then it is all right by her.' He was very moved whilst telling us all this.

Janet told me later that, following this confession, Boris seemed to have become more articulate even during the same weekend. She felt that he had gained strength and confidence from the obvious and warm support of the rest of the group.

The reader may wonder that someone who finds intimate (as distinct from functional) relationships difficult should enter work of this kind, but the number of cases that have come to our notice as a result of these courses has led us to suspect that it is not as uncommon as might be expected.

Attitude Change

The attitudes that influence the approach to our work are partly inherent in our personality but are as often caught from the milieux in which we move. We have already noted that attitudes, for a variety of reasons, may be persistent and resistant to change. Here is an identifiable problem. A frontal attack—for instance, at its most obvious: 'This is the way that you should teach (or do youth work), not like that'—is setting one opinion against the other and may merely build up its own resistance. Neither does the mere statement of evidence seem to be enough to ensure a challenge to existing attitudes. We even seem to be able to accept an intellectual position without its necessarily changing our behaviour: to absorb it, as it were, into an intellectual conserve.

It seems that in order to challenge a prevailing attitude we may need to reach areas of thought and concern more primary than the attitude itself, and to argue our way through from this point forward. For instance, in discussing teaching or youth work, if we begin with the more primary question: 'Whom do we want to serve and what help do they need of us ?' and if we conduct our inquiry by real life discovery rather than by the canvassing of opinions, we may bring existing standpoints into a state of flux and enable the trainees to move to new positions. And as long as the objectivity of actually looking at real situations is maintained throughout the study, there is a chance that previous attitudes about how we should do our job will all go into the melting pot. But even then we should not be too optimistic about making any impact on the way that the worker actually approaches his job. We shall need to encourage him actually to apply his new ideas step by step as we proceed.

A simple and frequently recurring example of fixed attitudes we meet during this training is the blockage presented by entrenched attitudes against a direct approach to young people, which is often regarded as either impossible, unacceptable, ineffective, or unethical. If we allowed this to remain a subject of opinion we should often have made little progress by the end of the course. By giving trainees a legitimate reason for making a direct approach to young people, we may enable them both to gather the information that they are seeking and to discover what effect their approach has on young people and on their work with them.

Many of our attitudes, although quite deeply embedded in our outlook, are drawn from the working milieu and are often accessible to the trainer. But the business of helping a trainee in deeper attitudes and in his own relationships, both of which are bound up with his total personality, is quite another matter. It is sometimes possible for the tutorial group to initiate introspection that may reach deeper attitudes and predispositions.

At the first meeting of the tutorial team some five weeks ago, Cedric seemed to have been ill at ease, and he revealed during today's session that the disturbance that had begun at the first meeting had remained with him during the intervening period. His anxiety seemed to centre on the dependence—authority relationship between him and me. He indicated that he was beginning to get it into focus. He had experienced parallel uneasiness in his relationships with members of his tutorial group.

Whether the tutorial group will contribute to the resolution of this kind of problem will depend upon the willingness and ability of the tutor to lead the discussion into areas of personal intimacy. We may have to accept that there are springs of behaviour that are not readily accessible to rational examination and modification. These deeper elements of personality are the target of social and psychotherapy. To some degree the tutorial group may have, as part of its function, an element of social therapy.

There is a growing literature on group therapy. Group therapy began as group psycho-therapy for the treatment of the mentally sick,[1] but more recently similar techniques have been used for the personal development and the social and emotional education of normal people.[2] Much of this has gone under the general label of 'T-groups'. Ottaway describes it as 'the ordinary man's therapy'.[3]

As most teams of tutors deepen their understanding of their role, therapy and personality development become the subject of lively discussion. The very mention of therapy may at first raise considerable alarm amongst a group of tutors. It seems to conjure up a picture of surgical incision rather than the opening of doors to the individual, who retains his autonomy of action. During this discussion there is sure to be some mention of the T-group, which will be very hazily understood by any members of the team who have not had personal experience of a T-group, and it may be helpful if I attempt to identify the main features of the T-group situation.

T-groups

A small group of people meet, without any formal task, in the company of a 'tutor', 'consultant', or 'conductor', who, whilst offering some interpretations of what is taking place, does not directly help the group along any line of discussion. It is obvious from the terms in which different experimenters describe their experience that the form of leadership differs somewhat one from another. It varies from the conductor who engages in fairly free conversation with the group, to the 'consultant' who does not allow himself to be consulted, and does not respond directly to any remarks or questions addressed to him. I have come across cases of consultants who go so far as to be patronizing and deprecating in their comments, and whose conduct is seen by the group members as being rude and offensive. Most of those conducting

---

[1] W. R. Bion, *Experiences in Groups*; S. H. Foulkes and E. J. Anthony, *Group Psychotherapy*; C. R. Rogers, *Client Centred Therapy*.
[2] E. Richardson, *Group Study for Teachers*.
[3] A. K. C. Ottaway, *Learning through Group Experience*.

T-groups seem to have in common that they will not direct the group or even suggest any lines of discussion.

The form of leadership offered by the tutor is a very interesting one. As soon as he is recognized and identified as a member of the establishment, he seems to be imbued in the minds of the members of the group with a certain authority, as a person to whom they may reasonably expect to express their dependence. His inactivity as a leader is very unsettling. The group might fairly rapidly bypass him if it were not for his occasional interjections which re-establish his position. Not everyone who leads this kind of group would analyse it in these terms, nor for that matter would agree with my analysis, but I am being guided by my own experience in varying the form of leadership. I would describe it as, to some degree, a 'spoiling' leadership—the leader offers no direction or encouragement, but he maintains his position sufficiently to prevent the group throwing up its own structure of leadership which might usurp his position. In a subtle way, it is a very authoritarian form of leadership.

The group does throw up leadership, which may be quite transitory, but the tutor does not make any indigenous leadership legitimate by delegating what the group sees as his authority. The reader may recognize in this description certain elements of the leadership practised by some youth workers, or by tutors and organizers of some training courses, and of phases of leadership in many other walks of life, including even family life.

The early discussion that arises in a T-group tends to be sporadic, may not follow a logical line, and there may be long silences. Some find it a most disturbing experience. They wish to express their dependence upon a leader who does not respond as expected, and their discomfort is increased by the rapid change that may take place in role and status. Most of us like to know where we stand. Many at first become anxious and hostile, and there has been a recognizably recurring pattern of feeling and events in the groups of which I have been a member and have led.

In normal life we tend to deal with one another through the medium of a task that is outside both of us, even if that task is merely making a cup of tea or discussing the weather. In such circumstances it is appropriate that emotion should be harnessed to the task in hand, and any free expression of inappropriate emotion is likely to be discouraged. Some would insist that the T-group has as its task the consideration of the feelings of the members and their relationships with one another in the 'here and now', but this is not a task outside themselves for which they must get themselves organized. As a result of this it is unnecessary—inappropriate might be a better expression—for the group to become structured into a set of roles and a hierarchy, and the situation in which the members find themselves may be extremely fluid and changeable. Many find this extremely uncomfortable. Most groups spend much of their earlier meetings casting around for 'something to do'.

If we are deprived of a task we are left facing one another as inner people, and in the course of time the T-group may come to be seen as a situation in which the expression of personal feeling is appropriate. In these circumstances spontaneous expression of feeling may well up, and the group may become strongly supportive of a member in difficulties. Although personal behaviour and feeling may be explored by rational discussion, the real therapy seems so often to follow an adventitious and spontaneous *expression* of feeling, although *talking about* the feelings that have been expressed may help the individual concerned to come to grips with what is happening within him.

I have embarked on this aside since the T-group etches more sharply certain events and features that may be encountered in training sessions, particularly in the tutorial group, and even in normal group work. It may also illuminate the therapeutic element of group work. It is even possible that a tutor or group worker may produce a T-group situation unintentionally.

Celia, a training supervisor, reported that several members of Roger's tutorial group seemed to be anxious and hostile, and as far as she could tell this was associated with the way he did his job as a tutor. He was reserved, almost taciturn; she had difficulty in talking easily with him herself and seemed to find him a little threatening. In answer to our questions she confirmed that she had attended some of his tutorial meetings and found him very quiet. We went on to distinguish between not doing the work for the tutorial group by answering their questions, and not responding at all.

In a discussion of a trainee's informal work, similar features may be distinguishable:

Janet was working with eight fairly disturbed boys who had formed themselves into a discussion group. She had initiated the earlier discussions on topics like sex, gambling, and drugs by saying a few words at the beginning of the session, but she modified this a little when they came to discuss what it was like to be young, by suggesting to them they were the people who knew all about the topic and she would be interested to learn from them.

The following week they approached their evening together without any topic having been suggested and she decided to take no action herself and to see what would happen. She is quite a gentle and reserved young woman, and when she withdrew herself there must have been very little stimulus emanating from her. There was an hiatus and a good deal of giggling that she thought covered some anxiety. Then several youngsters each tried to initiate discussion, but the topics were not taken up. I suspected that she had inadvertently created a T-group situation, and when she said that she did not know where to go from there I was not surprised.

When a worker leads a group into a situation in which a task is appropriate—as, for instance, following a programme of study—but behaves as if he were the tutor of a T-group, then the lines really become crossed and great frustration can arise.

I visited the group in which Malcolm and Roger were sharing the tutoring. They were due to be discussing the progress of the trainees in informal group work, but I could find absolutely no relevance to the topic nor any coherence in the desultory discussion that was taking place. The tutors remained silent—almost glum—and the trainees were floundering.

I learned afterwards that Roger thought he had taken on too much of the leadership and should leave the field clear for Malcolm. But they had not agreed and out of sheer perversity, it would seem, had left the session to one another. I found it interesting that this group, usually so voluble and not particularly dependent upon the tutors—should have been so hamstrung in a discussion to which each had so much to contribute. It was clear that they were all very frustrated by the situation which seemed a cross between a T-group and a working session, with all the conflicts that this mixture can bring.

Therapy in Group Work

I used to imagine that something like a T-group situation would be necessary for any therapy to take place, but more recent experience has caused me to question this. In fact I doubt whether the T-group is the most effective approach to 'the ordinary man's therapy', for the leader of the T-group must forego, as a result of his relatively inactive form of leadership, many opportunities to lead into relevant emotional expression. Concurrent experience has enabled me to compare the T-group approach with the kind of tutorial work I am describing in this book, and some of the intimate discussions that we have experienced during in-service courses have developed more rapidly than I have experienced in any parallel T-group. The T-group is sometimes used for 'sensitivity training'—helping the participants to increase their sensitivity to other people. For this also I would prefer to use the more even and equal dialogue of the tutorial group, especially if members are exposing themselves to significant experience as part of the training.

I had assumed that the absence of an outside task is a prerequisite to therapy, but I have now come to see that we can distinguish between tasks that either lead into or remain outside the intimate self. The majority of the field work undertaken in connection with these courses in some way involves the trainee personally, and many of the studies lead straight into introspection. For instance, we have been told repeatedly by trainees who have undertaken friendship studies that they have found themselves looking at their own pattern of friendships and the way that they relate to other people. When studying the personal qualities and needs of young people they find that they take a cool look at themselves, and this kind of experience is deepened when they study their own personality profile following a personality test. The intimate contacts with young people, both through the studies and through group work, often evoke an emotional response in them, and the discussions with colleagues represent a series of experiences that can form a springboard for the expression of emotional feeling.

Therapeutic expression seems most of all to take place when the person concerned has been emotionally stirred. The T-group is inherently disturbing, and this may be the basis of much of its therapeutic effect. In training through discovery and experience the trainees become deeply involved with the hopes, joys, cares, fears, and unhappiness of the people whom they meet so intimately, and this helps to set off the intimate exchanges of the tutorial groups. Contact with young people may affect us in several ways; it may, for instance, stir our compassion, or it may reawaken quiescent emotional conflict within us.

In Douglas's group the last two sessions have given rise to a good deal of intimate exchanges. May has become deeply involved, perhaps over involved, with a group of youngsters each of whom seems to have quite serious personal problems. Douglas told me that during the morning's session May had unloaded a lot of her anxieties and seemed a little lighter, but when I joined the group later there was obviously much more to come. She said that the youngsters had reminded her of her own troubles when she was seventeen and she wanted very much to help them if she could. It looked as if the experience may have revived some stresses in her as much as reminded her of them, for she was very stirred.

The mood of a tutorial group—indeed any group—may be contagious, and the emotional difficulties in one person may raise sympathy in some but also trigger off quite strong feelings in others. At other times members of the group may be encouraged by the intimacy of the occasion to speak about things that are troubling them.

The atmosphere was tense but sympathetic and supportive. Brian addressed a linking question to Andy who responded by talking quite out of context, about his disablement and what he obviously considered a disfigurement, and the difficulty it gave him in meeting other people. He stumbled through his statement and I had the impression that he had never before stated this clearly even to himself. The response of the group was very sensitive and supportive.

The examples above reveal a confessional element, and it would appear that people often find a good deal of relief—almost cleansing—in a kind of public confession in tutorial discussion. For instance, many colleagues have repeatedly returned to the tutorial group in order to work through the change that has been going on in them during the intervening period. On one course a headmaster felt bound to make quite considerable changes in his professional approach—which seemed fairly basic to his personality—as a result of his experience as a tutor and as a member of a team of tutors. In particular he was exercised about the kind of authority relationship he should establish. He seemed to be inviting the group to attack his position and he would often conclude a discussion with a confession that revealed a slight change of position. He was soon using the group also to discuss the very disturbing response that his colleagues at school were showing to his change in behaviour.
Sometimes the matter is urgent and yet painful, with the result that the person concerned procrastinates until he has to hurry it in at the last minute.

We were just about to conclude the meeting when Tom stopped us short by raising 'a very important matter in this context', which really had nothing to do with what we were talking about. He wanted to tell us about his group of boys. He was obviously deeply moved by his contact with them and in particular by the death of one of them. It did not seem so much the death of the boy that had moved him as the tender and responsible reaction that his death had evoked amongst the other boys.

The reader may well ask why we place so much weight on the discussion of personal qualities and problems, as if the command of language had intrinsic value. This may well be the case. Being articulate is, of course, not just a matter of having a flow of language at our command, for it is equally important that the person concerned should be able to identify the feelings that he is wishing to describe. The function of being articulate is to enable a person to explore feeling as well as to express it. In the context of introspective and confessional discussion, the ability to sort out areas of confusion and diffuse feeling is the prerequisite to expressing it, but both draw upon the same ability to be articulate.

Being Sensitive to the Emotional Undertone

There is a conflict inherent in trying to cope with a programme of learning and the trainee's emotional development. First, there is competition for time, and the pressure of the business may very easily squeeze out the discussion of personal concerns, which may well be time consuming. Second, the task is comparatively safe; the expression of personal feeling and the exploration of the trainee's emotional position may be much more challenging, and in particular more frightening to the tutor. I have seen tutors scampering along, anxious to keep everybody busy, as if there was a danger of something just below the surface that might erupt. It is for this reason, I suspect, that some training agencies tend to do most of their in-service training through open-ended discussion in small groups, and thus avoid the competition of a programme of work.

We have regarded the programme of work as essential, indeed, a major part of the course, but we may reasonably be asked whether we are being realistic in combining these two competitive elements as part of the same operation, actually taking place concurrently. If, before all this started, I had been able to distinguish clearly that these two competitive elements existed, I may have wanted to provide for them separately; as it was, we just got on with the programme and discovered by accident that many of the situations we would have to cope with were emotionally charged, and gradually learned how to provide for both elements at once.

Some kinds of operation especially seem to generate an intensity of feeling, and this is something that we have learnt to provide for in our planning. It is necessary to consider how deeply the trainees will have become involved by any particular stage of the training, to consider those areas of experience most likely to have stirred them emotionally and to allocate time in the programme for wide ranging discussions when these matters are considered. Several different parts of the experience are overlapping in terms of the trainees' feelings, and the programme must therefore be viewed as a whole, with blocks of time, although devoted possibly to difficult exercises, being seen as opportunities for the discussion of personal feeling. But all this will come to nothing unless the tutor is sensitive to the emotional undertone of what is being said:

His statement was somewhat muddled and irrational, and I was probably not alone in suspecting that the anxieties that he was expressing were not really those that were troubling him. Later in the evening he confessed to me, in a somewhat roundabout way, that some changes affecting his job were making him feel insecure, and it became apparent that his statements during the session included a covert attack on a colleague who was with us.

It is most important that the tutor should not only have the sensitivity to detect when what is being said carries an emotional charge and may be implying quite a different covert message from the overt statement, but he should also develop an ability to switch the conversation fluently from the business to personal expression. But before he can do this with any effect it must be accepted by the group as a norm, and the situation must be sufficiently supportive to assure the person concerned that it is safe to venture into more intimate realms. The relationships between the members of the group may be a legitimate part of this personal exploration, and in some cases may be one of the only ways of enabling a trainee to face himself as others see him. Some tutors, when they recognize this, seem to want to make a special occasion of looking at the relationships within the group in a manner that I have from time to time described as an 'emotional jam session': 'Ann is anxious to be what she calls "insightful", but may be working rather obviously. Apparently she likes to leave time at the end of a session so that "we can all look at ourselves and the way we are relating".'

I fear this approach a little. There is a lot of difference between coping with anxieties as they arise, and digging around indiscriminately. This kind of approach is in danger of feeding the complicated personality one sometimes finds in training, who has difficulty in accepting any homely explanation for anything. I prefer to deal with matters that may arise (or be caused to arise) naturally, spontaneously, and in context, but for this I grant that the tutor must develop considerable sensitivity:

Reg said that he was very chuffed when he recognized covert hostility being expressed to him by two members of his group, which illustrated what we had been talking about at our last meeting. We asked him what he had done about it and he replied that he had rather neatly changed the subject. He seemed a little nonplussed when we asked him why he had done that.

Agenda

The suggestion that we may be able to prepare for a discussion of personal and intimate matters which are likely to arise spontaneously may appear a contradiction in terms, but we have gone so far as to consider whether it is possible to prepare an agenda with this in mind. The purpose is not merely to provide for an intellectual examination of emotional positions—this is relatively easy—but rather that individual members may find it appropriate to express anxieties that may cost them something to reveal. There may be a general and a specific element in this. In general, an open and supportive atmosphere will be necessary; but more specifically, the discussion may need to move into areas of concern to particular individuals. This may happen accidentally, but if the tutor can foresee the areas of concern he may be able to guide the discussion more deliberately.

Through an agenda we may provide not only for a logical order of progression, but also for a deepening of discussion. For instance, I find that it takes some time for a team of tutors to get back into tune after an elapse of time between meetings, and a progress report of the work that has been done during the intervening period is a useful way of coming together again. The discussion is likely to be factual—a straightforward report and memory recall. This can lead naturally to an exchange about the progress of individual trainees, and that in turn to a discussion of any personal difficulties and the demands that individual people make of us. By this time we are touching upon our own ability to help students, and it would be surprising if a discussion of this kind were not to give opportunities to focus on feelings of inadequacy, in ourselves as well as related to specific demands made upon us.

It is quite unnecessary to conduct a meeting on a one-two-three agenda as we might with a business meeting. We may have to initiate the first item, but beyond this point it should be possible to maintain a free flowing open-ended conversation, but at the same time, by building upon what is said by our colleagues, to steer the emphasis from one area of concern and expression to another. We shall hope that the discussion may proceed in a relaxed way, but there may be moments when we shall be content for it to hang fire if we suspect that there is more to be said, which may be slow to come because it is emotionally charged.

Within this general agenda there is the possibility of something a little more specific. When facing a meeting of a tutorial team I often consider both my own problems, and the position and progress of each member of the team, and from this prepare a series of specific questions to myself which may help me guide the discussion. For instance, I may be personally concerned with how to reduce the deference paid to me as the director of the course; one of my colleagues may be persistently conducting his group sessions in a didactic manner; another seems anxious to cover up any gaps through which embarrassment may enter; a third, though efficient, finds it difficult to flow and unbend, and so on. How can openings be offered to each of us for the discussion of these matters? It is uncanny how the flow of discussion will offer the tutor opportunities to focus on one thing after another without his having to wrench the conversation round to a new topic. It is not that the tutor tells anyone what he suspects—he may in any case be quite wrong—but rather that the group may create spaces in front of individual people which will give them an opportunity to explore matters of personal concern if they are ready to do so. At these times there may be a pause almost as if everyone is waiting for a colleague to use it.

We touched lightly on our own anxiety when faced by our tutorial groups, and there was a pause which I did nothing to fill. A movement by Paul drew attention to him and we all waited for him to speak. He looked embarrassed and said 'What are you looking at me for boys?' There were some desultory exchanges in which Paul's agitation gradually grew and several members of the group asked pointed though sympathetic questions about how he was getting on with several fairly formidable members of his group. His answers were non-committal, though I had good reason to suspect that a certain lack of cohesion in his group arose from his own timidity. Immediately after the meeting he drew me into his room and revealed that he was feeling very uneasy with his group.

Following this occasion Paul began to discuss his difficulties freely with his colleagues in the tutorial team and his assurance and skill as a tutor grew rapidly.

By focusing attention especially on the agenda affecting the discussion of personal matters I do not want to reduce the importance of tutors having a clear agenda to guide the discussion of more factual material, for I have noticed that tutors sometimes neglect their homework even at this level. In this respect also the prior preparation of an agenda need not lead to a formally regulated discussion, but if anything, to increased flexibility and spontaneity on the part of the tutor. The tutor must have a very good idea of the directions in which the discussion might go and seize upon the leads offered by his colleagues, but he must also be prepared to allow the direction to change if the immediate events and needs of the trainees suggest it.

Signals

What is going on in the minds of the members of a group can sometimes be read from what they say, but the tutor must be able to recognize a whole range of signals. Signals will arrive in a variety of ways, and the watchful tutor will soon be able to recognize the characteristic signals put out by each member of his group. It is often the hesitant contribution, the one that a member has not properly framed or has difficulty in expressing that is the helpful contribution both to the individual and the group, and the signal that this is rumbling in the background may be very faint. Many signals come through the eyes; looking up or down, brightening or narrowing;[1] through bodily movements—the head, arms, fingers, or the whole posture; or through an air of agitation or merely drawing breath. Positioning is extremely important.

When tutoring Barbara tended to engage, in direct eye contact, the person who was speaking. I think it was her form of encouragement, but it had the effect of riveting the speaker to her, which both excluded the other members of the group from the conversation and limited her own ability to see the many signals being made by them. We discussed as a group what was happening, and considered also the square layout of the seating. Barbara moved back a little so that she could see the people on either side of her, and attempted both to deflect the speaker so as not to engage him personally, and to watch the reactions of the whole group. Within a few minutes the pattern of discussion had changed markedly.

We must be careful that sensitivity to the other people in the group and concern for them should not be seen as the responsibility of the tutor alone:

This was the last official session that the group would be together, and I was surprised that Jennifer had said nothing for about half an hour. I drew the attention of the group to this, and when they turned to her she said 'Well, yes, I did want to say something really, but the longer I left it the more difficult it was to get in.' The group were a little shocked at their own insensitivity.

The degree to which everybody has participated is, of course, a rather simple way of viewing the success of a discussion, although it does seem that it may be necessary to express an idea with our own

---

[1] M. Argyle, *The Psychology of Interpersonal Behaviour.*

mouths before we are really in possession of it. But we shall want to avoid, if possible, dragging people into the discussion unnaturally. In this form of training there is very little difficulty in getting a discussion going: there is so much to be said and reported that the real problem is to find time to enable everything to be dealt with, and to stimulate some depth in the examination of ideas and material. The tutor will also be wanting to ease himself out of a too central position. In doing all this he may use, whether knowingly or not, a number of well worn practices.

When a statement is directed to him he may *bounce it back* to the person who made it—either by a word or two, by gesture, or even by making no response—in the hope that the person who originated the statement will be prepared to develop it. It is interesting to notice how often, when we are asked a question, the questioner is really only waiting to answer it himself. Bouncing back a statement is quite different from *mirroring it*, by which I mean that in some way we hold it up for the clearer view of the person who made the statement. Sometimes it is only necessary to repeat the statement or even a single word, or to ask him whether he really heard what he said, but on other occasions we may need to engage in a short conversation and clarification. We may otherwise encourage—or *draw on*—a member of the group to continue talking on similar lines, and our action to achieve this may vary from a nod of encouragement, eye contact, or gesture, to developing the theme in conversation. In general I find a tendency for tutors to use rather too many words: it is really quite remarkable how economical we may be in influencing the course of conversation.

Frequently the tutor is wanting to see the conversation widened to include other members of the group, in which case he may *deflect* something that is addressed to him to another specific person, or to any other member of the group. Once again, this might be achieved without words, as, for instance, by an inquiring look to members of the group. Clear headedness and some skill is required when *linking* one contribution with another. The tutor may often wish to link a present statement with one made sometime ago, and much will depend upon his ability to store relevant contributions. We are all the time being offered gems by members of the group which, though not particularly valuable at the moment, will clearly be of great value at a later stage. To profit by *storing* contributions, the tutor's preparation and agenda must be good, and he must have the ability to tuck items into a pigeon-hole awaiting later use.

This may need conscious practice, and if the tutor's memory is in danger of letting him down (for he is likely to have several other things to bear in mind at the same time) noting a single word may serve as an aide-mémoire. It also requires a lot of restraint on the part of the tutor to let pass an important point that is not of prime relevance to the present discussion, and an ability to store items will reduce the temptation to lead a butterfly discussion. Storing an idea may help the tutor when he knows that soon he will be wanting to initiate a *change of direction*, and only rarely should it be necessary to initiate a new line of discussion away from the flow of what has gone before. And all the time we shall be challenging any loose statements, or better still, *creating spaces* for other members of the group to challenge them.

I am fascinated by the economy with which some tutors perform their role, with interjections of only a single word or a short sentence, a gesture of encouragement, the initiation of humour, and here and there a pregnant silence. It is an interesting exercise for the tutor to count and to note the number of words in his own contributions. I have noticed that when a tutor has been saying just a little too much, he has had the effect of cooling the temperature: the exchanges bubble up, the tutor's incursion is a little too wordy, and the thing has gone off the boil and has to warm up again. And one of the tutor's main objectives should be to share the leadership with the other members of the group.

Many tutors have difficulty in living with silences, and tend to rush in, in order to avoid any discomfort. The tutor should be able to tolerate silence, and learn to allow a silence to continue for just as long as it is constructive. A tutor may induce a silence by indefinite leadership, and may even use silence with special effect: as for instance, when he feels that a group is reluctant to shoulder certain responsibilities, or when members of the group might profit by being thrown on their own musing for a few moments, possibly about the next moves. As the members of a group continue to work together their silences may become easy and relaxed. The quality of silences is a matter of great interest in itself:

Janet's tutoring was kindly and sensitive—she really has made tremendous strides since we began. On one occasion there was a long silence, which she finally interrupted with a question to Paul. We decided that we would ask one another what had been going on in each one of us during the silence, and Ben revealed that when Janet broke in he was about to make a statement about some difficulties he was facing. All of us had been actively pursuing our thoughts and had not been embarrassed. It was a very important experience to all of us to realize just how much a silence might have within it, and how it might be used creatively.

Questioning

The reader will have noticed the prominent part played in this form of training by questions and programmes of questioning, and we have found ourselves examining some of the principles of questioning. A question induces a state of stress, however mild, in the respondent. For instance, the simple question, 'What was the first thing you did this morning?' may send the respondent searching within himself, and it is quite remarkable how natural it is to respond to a question with some kind of effort. Thus the respondent may become involved, or may be moved from merely being involved to a real partnership. By comparison with didactic teaching, working through a programme of questions tends to put the student in a relatively stronger position, according to the amount of autonomy implied by the questions.

It is possible for a question to be wide, to be an entry into a whole area of thought and discussion; but it is equally possible for the question to be so close as to leave almost no room for manoeuvre. An extreme example of close questioning may sometimes be seen when a teacher is questioning a class in order to revise what has recently been taught. It is possible so to phrase a question as to leave only one right reply, and that could be a single word.

In discussing this we have come to ask what level of autonomy our questioning leaves the respondent:

The previous meeting of the tutorial team had obviously made Ken conscious of his didactic approach to his group, and he seems to have replaced this by close questioning. It seems as if he is so keen to put over his own views that, as he has foregone the more direct way of doing this, he is attempting to do it, as it were, by proxy through the inescapable answers to his close questioning.

If one of our purposes is to nurture the self-reliance of the trainee it is important that we should leave with him considerable responsibility for the direction in which the conversation goes. It may be helpful to see the exchange in Socratic terms, in which the reply from the trainee may serve as the basis for the next phase of discussion. Some quite deliberate thought and study may be required of the tutor if he is to learn to combine flexibility with a consistent line of inquiry. In this context, it is often helpful to consult the trainees about how the agenda for the ensuing discussion should be arranged.

Styles of Tutoring

It is interesting to notice the differences in the overall styles of the tutors. Some are anxious that everything should be explained clearly to the trainee, and others may hurry them on, not realizing how long it may take some trainees to assimilate the material. Some short circuit the discussion by providing the answers because they seem to be stimulated by the knowledge burning in them, but others seem unable to live with the uncertainty of whether the trainee has grasped the point:

I thought that Sam was asking his group questions that just could not be answered from the evidence they had in front of them, and I wondered why he was hurrying them so. I suggested to him afterwards that there may be times when we just could not come to conclusions and would have to tolerate some doubt.

Some enjoy the intellectual exercise, and may even be enjoying a sense of importance in displaying their own knowledge, whilst others are friendly and chatty, and try to keep the atmosphere buoyant and happy. A few play it with a straight bat, and the exchanges fall back into the group without much of the tutor sticking to them:

Frances' style of tutoring is staccato, and she gives the appearance of being reserved, which is not noticeable in normal conversation. She has had some experience of rather inactive leadership of open-ended group discussions, and I wonder whether this has led her to a rather standoffish style.

Some approach their tutorial group quite naturally as if it were a working party of colleagues, but most tutors have a period of uneasiness before settling down to their particular form of leadership.

The Tutorial Team

I began this chapter by mentioning the importance of the tutors' functioning as a team and I should like to return to this in the context of the relationship between the tutors and the person who is leading the whole course, or the director as he is so often called. Their relative and overlapping functions need thought and discussion.

For instance, I am always anxious to clear with a group of tutors what my own function should be, as the leader of a course, when visiting the tutorial groups. The reader will have gathered, particularly from the extracts from my recording, that I have usually paid regular visits to the tutorial groups at work. When doing so I have seen my role as a fairly active one, which I gather is largely the case with our collaborators who are themselves directing courses. I engage in conversation with the group, more by way of questioning and stimulation than as an informant, but this needs careful handling and a good understanding between the members of the tutorial team. I am personally anxious not to weaken the position of the tutors, but this again depends upon the kind of colleague relationship that we have developed at all levels.

I feel fairly confident that I made a contribution to the understanding and insight of the students in both the groups I visited. Both the tutors gladly sat back and seemed to enjoy my intervention, for in both cases it sparked off a lively exchange. But I have felt unsure of the legitimacy of my intervening in this way and must raise this with my colleagues at our next meeting of tutors in the hope that they can help me sort it out.

In some ways the position of the leader of a course visiting tutorial groups may be a privileged and useful one, for he may be free to challenge more sharply—particularly the attitudes, behaviour, and manner of thinking of the trainees—than the tutor feels free to do. He is not a permanent fixture in the group and as long as he is accessible, in the sense of being freely rebutted and challenged, he can even afford to occasion some heat in discussion. I have discussed this matter with several groups of tutors, and in each case it was felt that the intrusion of the director of the course in this way, although disturbing, could be most helpful, particularly in helping the tutors to see the emotional undertone of what was going on. It may be significant that most of my own intrusions into the tutorial discussions have been about attitudes, emotional positions, and relationships, and less about the factual content of the discussion.

Just as we have accepted it as legitimate that the team leader should participate in tutorial discussion, so we have also learnt to profit by the tutors' invading what at first we saw as the director's domain. The tutors take care of much of the corporate briefing and lead some of the open sessions. When the director is leading Socratic discussions in open sessions the tutors are about, helping on the discussion and conferring with the director about the progress being made. But possibly their most creative role in open sessions is to fan the probing and the challenge emanating from the general body of the trainees, and to reduce reverence accorded to the 'director'. So much depends upon the evenness of relationships, the ease of exchange, and accessibility of both tutors and the leader of the course.

11
The Training and Support of the Tutor

In-service training. Programme of training for tutors. The team of tutors. Tutors' anxieties. Support and social therapy through the tutorial group. Resilience to hostility. Training each new generation of tutors

We were slow to appreciate how much preparation and support was needed by the tutors responsible for this kind of training. On the early courses our objectives were limited to safely seeing through the immediate course of training for a group of students, and any tutor training was quite incidental and accidental. But having convinced ourselves of the effectiveness of the approaches we were adopting, we foresaw the possibility of long-term and continuous schemes which could be carried through by local people. Thus we began to ask ourselves how we might train tutors who could continue the work without the presence of an outside specialist.

In our first attempt to do this I joined nine experienced youth workers, all drawn from the same district. We spent a week together in a residential centre where we evolved a number of field studies and experiments, and tried them out for ourselves. We had an exhilarating, if somewhat challenging and exhausting week's work, and left assuring one another that if the training did only half for the trainees what it had done for us, they would have a significant (a word chosen as neutral amongst disturbing, stimulating, daunting, interesting, informative) experience.

We did not call this specifically tutor training; we had merely worked out a course and considered how to run it. We imagined that, added to the tutors' past experience and future reading, our week together would fit them to carry through their own local training course. To their great credit they did see through an exciting course—as I could judge when I met their trainees during and at the end of the course—but we learnt, as they went along, how woefully inadequate their preparation had been. In the first place their purchase of the theoretical material was insecure. They did not appreciate what they did not know until they tried to take other people along with them, and we had not foreseen the need for them to revise the theoretical material. Some pretty odd by-ways were traversed by all I could hear. Second, although the tutors had had the experience of conducting a number of exercises, and of making the discoveries for themselves, they were not really articulate enough to give the trainees the help they needed.

Above all we had not foreseen, and much less prepared the tutors for the personal stresses and individual difficulties that they met. We were faced with something of a crisis in our thinking: was it really possible to prepare tutors for this part of the work before they were actually meeting their problems? Would discussion about the emotional support required by the trainees mean very much until they were coping with real situations? And what about their own emotional difficulties arising from the challenges they met in their contact with trainees—we could hardly build up in advance a reserve of personal support.

In-service Training

Out of all this we realized that if we attempted the preparation of the tutors before they started work, we lacked the basic material for their training—the experience of actually tutoring, of handling the theoretical material, of guiding the approach to field studies and exercises by the trainees, and of nurturing support in the tutorial group. And we had no opportunity to address ourselves to the tutor's own emotional problems. There seemed nothing for it but to conduct the future preparation of tutors as in-service training.

The opportunity to try this was presented by a consortium of local education authorities who wished to experiment with this kind of training. They gathered a course of about forty potential tutors. We set to work quite confidently and only gradually realized the complexity of the task we had undertaken. The trainee tutors had to make themselves familiar with the content of the training, which was new to them; and even more important, they had to acclimatize themselves to this mode of learning. As is often the case with experienced practitioners, most of them found this very challenging. 'In-service' also meant that they were, at the same time, learning how to take a group of trainees through the programme.

The combination of these two elements proved extremely exacting, and we realized that in future it would be wiser to separate them and conduct tutor training in two steps: the first devoted to taking the potential tutors through the training themselves, and the second angled more specifically to working with a tutorial group. We have also met the persistent problem of trainees—for instance, youth officers—who would seem an obvious source of potential tutors but who are not in regular face-to-face contact with young people.

Bronwen made a strong plea that all students, whether they were advisory officers or not, should be encouraged, indeed almost required to do the field work. She did concede that the recording might be done as it were proxy by supervising the recording of a friendly practitioner. But as for the other exercises, it was generally agreed that all students should make opportunities to meet, interview and converse with youngsters.

For the *ad hoc* field studies and some of the exercises, it has usually proved possible for an advisory officer, for instance, to attach himself to a centre where both staff and young people have welcomed his interest. The problem here is only one of time and ultimately of priorities. As for the recording, it has been argued by many of our colleagues that the trainee should record his own work, whatever that may be. The informal group work has sometimes presented more difficulty although many advisory officers have gained their first direct experience by encouraging a face-to-face worker to experiment and standing by him as a consultant. It is possible for us to underrate the value of the vicarious experience that a tutor gains through his trainees. Whilst it may be true that some personal experience gives greater insight and security to the tutor, his direct experimenting is in any case likely to be limited, and in time he may learn more through the efforts of his trainees than his own.

Some of the difficulties experienced when introducing this kind of training are caused by the way that the approach departs from the accepted tradition of teaching. In those areas where training has been proceeding along these lines for several years, the training of tutors has been found to be very much easier. Even those who have not had personal experience of the training seem to catch a receptiveness from the prevailing climate.

Programme of Training for Tutors

The reader will find in Appendix 1 (d) an example of the kind of training programme that has been found feasible for tutor training. It assumes that the trainee has already worked through the theoretical material of the course and has had experience of the relevant field studies and exercises, and of informal group work. There is quite a lot of common ground between their new role as tutor and the experience that they will have gained in contact with young people through informal group work. For this reason a number of tutorial teams responsible for tutor training have insisted on an extension of this element of the experience of trainee tutors.

The pragmatic approach of using the trainee's recent experience as the raw material for training causes the discussions to be relevant, fresh, and lively, but it has its disadvantages. Events that arise spontaneously during the trainee tutor's contact with his group may be fortuitous, and may thus have certain limitations as a basis for a sequential and systematic discussion of method and experience. The personal contacts out of which this material will arise are not as susceptible to pre-arrangement as are, for instance, the *ad hoc* field studies and exercises structured through the course. This it has in common with informal group work. The reader will remember that we have managed, in the case of informal group work, to distinguish a recurring flow in the type of event and emotion that occurs at various stages, and to some extent to provide for this by focusing on a series of points of emphasis. Could this also be done as the work with a tutorial group progresses?

We have attempted to do this by focusing, step by step, on a series of questions that seemed to have come into prominence at the various stages of progress of the tutorial group. Here are some of the questions appropriate to the early stages of tutor training:

(a) What do you know about each member of your tutorial group? What methods do you use to get to know them as quickly as possible? Have the methods that we have used in our work with young people anything to offer here?

(b) Does your own recording help you in this respect? Do you work to a brief when you are recording?

(c) What preparation do you encourage in your trainees before they undertake each piece of field work? For instance, how do you help them in their skill of interviewing?

(d) How do you ensure that the reports brought back by the trainees receive critical scrutiny? Do you find it necessary to lead the probing, and how far are you able to encourage the trainees to initiate the questioning amongst themselves?

(e) How do you overcome the difficulty of processing the very large volume of material that they bring to the group meetings?

(f) Do you find that they face stresses as a result of their early field work; do you wish to offer them support, and if so what methods do you use?

We have found it necessary to use a series of questions more than once for each group of trainees. The questions may be asked tentatively as the trainees approach the problems concerned, in order to focus on the possibility of their existence, but we may well find it necessary to return to the same questions several times. It is not possible to hurry a discussion beyond the perception of the trainee, and each time the same question is discussed it may be in a rather more sophisticated form.

Later questions may include:

(a) Can you give a short description of each member of your tutorial group? What are the features of his personality?

(b) In what ways do you feel that each of the trainees may need help in his personal development?

(c) In approaching these needs how far are you able to make use of:
    (i) the kind of new experience in which the trainee is being involved;
    (ii) the internal relationships within the group;
    (iii) intimate and confessional discussion within the group?

(d) By what means are you building a supportive atmosphere in the tutorial group; what is meant by a supportive atmosphere? How well does each member of the group know the others, and have you considered how you may encourage knowledge and trust to grow?

(e) Are you able to overcome possible competition between the business and the intimate elements of the discussion—do you find it possible to plan for this?

(f) What kind of agenda do you work to in order to reach the personal elements in the discussion?

(g) How far does your recording help you in all this?

The Team of Tutors

It is within the team of tutors responsible for a course that the most significant experience is gained and the sharpest training takes place, particularly in the case of a team of tutors' conducting a course of training for potential tutors. This is, of course, as it should be, for the members of the tutorial team are often responsible for the training schemes for their own areas. Since there may be a dilution of skill as it is passed from one level to another, it is particularly important that those who hold the overall responsibility should be keenly aware of, and articulate about the processes through which they are working.

One of the senses in which a group of tutors must be a team is in their general responsibility for planning a course together, but some of the first meetings with new groups of tutors have been amongst the most tricky I have experienced. The incident I reported on p. 9, which was one of great tension, arose from my suggestion that we might consider together what we were hoping to achieve in the skills and development of the trainees. The question seemed to me a perfectly reasonable way of beginning our preparation, but several members of the team had obviously expected me to give clear direction. Another team spent some of the time at their final assessment meeting talking about 'that dreadful first meeting'.

The feelings engendered at some of the early meetings have been so strong that I began to think that my leadership must be at fault, or that the reaction was personal to me; but since then a number of colleagues have found that they have met a very similar situation as they began working with their own teams of tutors. Although this would suggest that the reaction is not associated with a personal approach, there is little doubt that it is the response to the form of leadership that we are all tending to use on these occasions. I have already mentioned that a leader may provoke anxiety and hostility when he does not fulfil the expectancy of the members of the group, and many people seem to be seriously disturbed by a working party instead of a directive approach. This is made very clear by the difference between the reaction of one person and another; somebody who is normally held within an authoritarian framework, or who tends by personality to operate in an authoritarian manner often finds the adjustment to this new kind of situation most unsettling, whereas it is very noticeable that others, who have been accustomed to a situation based on consultation seem to have little adjustment to make.

It is possible for the leader of the team of tutors to ease the early tensions by focusing on organizational matters first, but he will need to consider the primary objectives of the discussion. For instance, members of the team will quite happily consider the kinds of people likely to be recruited to the course, their geographical distribution, and how they might be brought together for tutorial meetings. But it can reasonably be argued that this is the kind of consideration that should follow a declaration of purpose rather than precede it. Basically, the training is concerned with attitudes, relationships, and personal competence, and the relationships established within the training situation are one of the most formative and urgent matters for concern. The effectiveness of the team of tutors will be quite strongly influenced by their relationships to one another as intimate persons rather than as functionaries. And we inevitably face, at the first meeting, the question that will recur throughout the experience: how far do we wish to shield people from emotionally charged situations?

The Anxieties Carried by the Tutors

Although the early meetings sometimes carry a special emotional charge, there is very often a new settling down to be accomplished at each of the periodical meetings of a team. The teams I have worked with have usually begun their meetings with a loose and discursive progress report about the work done, the tutorial meetings held, the misunderstandings about the brief for the field work, and other matters of fact and straightforward memory recall; all of which helps everyone to get his bearings and to renew contact with his colleagues. But before very long, we have moved into a discussion about the progress and difficulties of individual students, which has led, if only covertly, to the tutors' own feelings of personal inadequacy.

Sometimes it has seemed from the discussion of a team of tutors at their preparatory meeting, that the whole course was going wrong. This is how it appeared to me when I reported the pilot course:

I had noticed that at both the first and second weekends the 'review of progress' took a long time and led to the expression of a lot of anxiety. At the preparatory meeting before the first weekend there were so many doubts expressed about the exercises undertaken and the validity of our methods that I began to wonder whether we had made a complete mistake in our approach. But suddenly I sensed a change in mood and a desire to move to the next item on the agenda. The whole group settled down to earnest work, and the rest of the meeting, and indeed the whole weekend was carried through with considerable assurance. When the students arrived and we saw what they had accomplished, it was difficult to see what grounds there were for tutors' pessimism. Something similar happened at the second weekend but it was not until the third that I realized that this might be an essential ingredient of our work together, a cleansing session when anxieties were publicly confessed.

This possibility was emphasized by the following event. On Friday evening Alan was prevented from being with us when the normal confession of anxieties took place, and when he arrived on Saturday morning the meeting of tutors was already under way and there was a calm air of business. As we concluded our meeting at the approach of lunch time, we were a little startled by a sudden and violent outburst by Alan, who protested that he had no idea what this was about, or where he was going, and the whole thing was getting out of hand. The group was already standing, but paused, somewhat nonplussed, until one of our number said, with slight amusement, gently, and with great consideration: 'Well, of course, Alan, we all went through that last night.'

The anxieties carried by the tutors are very considerable. The authority relationships on the course trouble many of them, and some tutors find it quite difficult to settle into what is for them a new role. To that may be added quite reasonable anxiety about their ability to handle the theoretical material and to guide the field studies of their trainees. Above all they are anxious about their own adequacy to meet the face-to-face challenge of the members of their group, and to help individual trainees who are in personal difficulty. The confidences passed to them may be quite a load to carry:

One of Rhiannon's trainees had blurted out to her, during a private conversation, some very intimate information about a liaison he was having with a woman member of his staff. Since both the trainee and the woman were married the situation was fairly dramatic. Although Rhiannon felt that the affair was not having a direct effect upon the trainee's work with young people, she wondered what her responsibilities were to the management committee of the centre. Knowing all the people concerned she was conscious of the very complex issues involved.

It is very interesting to watch a tutorial team at work over a period of time, and to notice the change in their level of anxiety and in their attitude to what the training is all about. In the early meetings the main focus of their anxiety is about the programme and their ability to see it through, but as time passes they become much more relaxed about this side of the task and concentrate on the intangibles, on the more personal progress of the members of their groups and the relationships between them, on the relationships within the team of tutors and on their own feelings. It becomes very obvious that their early anxiety about seeing through the programme is deeply intermeshed with their own standing in their groups, with their being open to challenge, and their anxiety to be well thought of. In the latter part of the course their purchase of the new material to be handled is no better than with the earlier material but they become much less anxious about their own competence and find it much easier to live with their own inadequacies and uncertainties.

In the early stages of discussion, so anxious are the tutors to get square with the factual side of the work, that I have to exert some effort to persuade them to leave time for more personal discussion. In the later meetings, however, it often becomes necessary to remind the team that we ought to leave time to consider the theoretical material we shall have to handle with the trainees, but they are usually in no hurry to get down to this side of the business. This experience has caused me to think a good deal about those many hours I have spent in committees, where what was being said represented as much an emotional as a rational position of the contributors. If only some of our committees could be conducted like our tutorial groups, so that there could be a cleansing of personal anxiety and a growth of understanding and support for one another, how much more expeditiously and rationally the business might be conducted.

Personal Development and Support

The major anxiety and skill of the tutor in this kind of training is probably that of coping with intimate exchanges in the tutorial situation. At the early stages there may be a lack of awareness of, or apprehension about what is under the surface; later, as it becomes impossible to ignore the underlying emotional positions, anxiety grows and there may be protests about the danger or ethics of what we are engaged in.

There was almost a complete rejection of the possibility of personal adjustment and therapy arising through the work of the tutorial groups. Ron, in particular, seemed anxious, and the whole idea of anybody's personality being influenced rather frightened him. He was at pains to point out that he was not a very confident person and feared our knocking down his present position without replacing it with anything else.

The two words 'probing' and 'therapy' invariably seem to become a focus for anxiety. Gradually tutors begin to see that it is not so much a question of 'curing' anything in the members of their groups, as of giving them an opportunity of revealing themselves to themselves, of talking about themselves with other people whose support they can feel, and of hearing from other people about problems similar to their own. The interpretation of therapy as a direct 'interference' is very general amongst groups of tutors at a certain stage of their progress.

Only gradually do most tutors come to appreciate that social therapy, so far as we are able to lead in that direction through tutorial work, is largely a matter of opening doors to the individual trainee, and of leaving with him the choice of whether he wishes to make use of the opportunities before him. It is vital that we should all appreciate the importance of the trainee being the architect of his own development, and of making sure that the responsibility for conducting his own life and affairs is left firmly with him. Colleagues have expressed the kind of fears that would suggest that the tutor may be squeezing confessions out of the members of his tutorial group. In fact, the individual is unlikely to move into intimate conversation, let alone confession, until he senses that the situation is sufficiently supportive for him not to be hurt by his disclosures, and the nurturing of that supportive atmosphere is one of the skills of tutoring.

There are tremendous stresses under the surface in this team of tutors, which I suspect is complicated by their knowing and having dealings with one another outside the immediate situation. A competitive element seems to be present and I must try to build a more generous and supportive atmosphere so that individual tutors may use the meetings to air some of their difficulties and anxieties. I was rather shaken to learn, quite by accident, that Harry has been distressed to the point of losing sleep as a result of the hostility expressed to him by some of the members of his group. He clearly did not consider the tutorial team sufficiently supportive to air his anxieties to us.

Supportive Situations

The early discussion, within the team of tutors, about the support that can be given by tutorial groups usually scarcely gets off the ground; I find that this is not something that most people can visualize until they have experienced it, either through being a member of a group, or even more, after having tutored a group that has become supportive. 'Support', as the term is being used here, usually involves intimate exchanges, whereas most groups seem to want to keep things 'safe' by concentrating on the factual and the business-like. Indeed, support may be a misnomer for the earlier intimate exchanges, judging by the way that most people exert themselves to avoid them. The next stage is often what I would describe as 'cosy'—the group is intimate but comfortable, and someone (so often the tutor himself) is ready to smooth ruffled feelings or start diversionary action if things get at all uncomfortable. Strangely enough, what I have already referred to as 'introspective jam sessions' may also remain at the cosy level when the group concerned takes care that the exchanges do not bite below what is pleasant to hear.

A supportive atmosphere does not mean the avoidance of embarrassment and pain; on the contrary the sympathy and help that a group can bring to a member who is talking through his own trouble can be extremely warm and supportive. Indeed, some groups reach their most supportive moments when they are pointing out to one of their members his own short-comings, during which they are accepting and identifying with him even though they might be quite incisive in their criticism. And they will go on bearing with him even when he takes it badly. This is difficult to convey to trainee tutors without their having had the opportunity of relevant experience.

A question that tutors are often asking themselves is how far they should allow and encourage their tutorial group to mount a personal attack on one of their number:

It seems that Paddy has in his group one member who sometimes makes it quite difficult for the group to get on with its job; Paddy knows him of old and says that the man upsets every group he goes into. He says further that if he were not such a coward he would bring to the attention of this man the kind of reaction that his behaviour caused in other people, but Paddy does not seem to have realized that the man's peers might be able to help him in this respect more than he can as the tutor of the group.

What are we to do about the person who seems to think that the hostile reactions he meets arise always from the perversity of the other chap; or the youngster who has no real friends because his approach to life keeps potential friends at a distance? Are we so sure that the kind thing is to join the conspiracy of silence? The group worker regularly faces this problem, especially when working with inept or anti-social youngsters, and it is surprising how much help a group of peers can give one another through their frank speaking, as long as this takes place in a controlled atmosphere.

Handling Hostility

We also spent a good deal of time on how to handle hostility. Cleo seemed to be suggesting that we should not bring it into the open if it were possible to avoid doing so, but the rest seemed to feel that it would be better to clear any hostility as it arose, especially if it was getting in the way of the work.

The whole question certainly seems to receive a good deal of attention at the meeting of most tutorial teams, and this is not surprising, considering how intimately the comfort of the tutor is bound up with it:

A statement by Frank initiated a long discussion about hostility. It looks as if he may be acting as a sponge to the hostility expressed to him, and may not be reacting resiliently enough. He has not seen that the person who is expressing hostility is at least engaging himself in the business in hand. We illustrated this point from several people on the present course who had first become committed to the work through their expression of hostility.

The hostility that Frank is provoking is considerable. By not examining the position with the people concerned, he is not checking how far he justifiably gives rise to hostility by his own leadership. In Frances' case, she is aware of the hostility rumbling under the surface but she seems to be allowing it to poison the atmosphere rather than encouraging its overt expression.

There are two steps in dealing with hostility. First, hostility may be cleared by its full and overt expression in a controlled atmosphere; and second, the person expressing the hostility may be helped to explore the real feeling lying behind it. It may come as a surprise to him to discover that the feelings are his own, and do not attach to the object of his hostility.

New Generation of Tutors

As we have pursued these courses we have been impressed by the willingness of the practitioners in the field to engage in a completely new look at their work. But generation after generation of practising workers will need opportunities for adequate training, and a continuing operation of this kind will need a lot of resources. Above all, considerable efforts will be required in order to maintain a flow of trained tutors. There is a natural wastage of trained people, and the geographical distribution of would-be students for in-service training means that tutors must be available over a wide area, even if their services may not be used continuously. Seen on a broad scale this is a mammoth task, and its accomplishments will make quite imperative that a local cadre of tutors should include in their responsibilities the maintenance of their own numbers.

Much of the tutor training we have undertaken so far has been the training of a local nucleus of tutors, who will take in hand the training of additional tutors as the work gets under way. We have therefore seen a number of schemes for the training of additional tutors in operation. Spurred by their sense of urgency, some teams have conducted crash courses for the training of additional tutors. A number of these courses have suffered from all the difficulties we experienced in other courses of training for tutors, but with some added by the haste of the programme and the relative inexperience of the nucleus of people who have been involving others in the training. The fact that such schemes have survived and prospered can only be as a result of the enthusiasm of those who have seen them through. The strategy of the operations has not always been well thought out, and some teams have moved forward before they had sufficient experience to ensure their own security when faced by daunting odds. One is only conscious of the need that fired their sense of urgency.

Many of the training teams found it difficult to take along with them the many people in their areas who felt entitled to comment on what was taking place, and this is a dimension of the task that is sometimes inadequately provided for. Something new may be seen as threatening, and if we are not party to it we may be tempted to denigrate it. We faced, very early on in our experience, the need to win the collaboration of anyone responsible for or central to the establishments in which field work might take place. But the problem is wider than that. There are many other people looking in on what is taking place, some of them in very formative positions, whose support is important, and whose opposition might be quite disastrous. It is an essential part of the job of the training agency to win the interest and sympathy of these people.

In areas where the training has existed longer the situation has been much easier. Potential tutors can be drawn from those who have had experience of being students themselves, and may have some understanding of the therapeutic element of group work. Potential tutors can also serve their apprenticeship as co-tutors or assistant tutors and this practice is being followed quite widely.

There is always a danger of the momentum of training slowing down and of the courses becoming ordinary and uninspiring, and something more than just support will be required if the training is to prosper in the long term. Tutorial teams will need regular workshop sessions when they may deepen their penetration in one area of perception after another, and if the whole principle of training by discovery is to mean anything, their own work should be taking them on to new fields of understanding, and to special developments through which they may contribute to their colleagues in other areas.

That, after all, is the way this form of training was developed in the first place: it arose from our own research and experiment and we fell upon much of it almost by accident. The same kind of contribution is open to anyone who has the wit to see the relevance and the potential of anything interesting that he turns up.

12
Wider Horizons

Evaluation; personal progress and change. Training for the recreative centre. Introducing the activity specialist. The potential of discovery methods. Feedback. People influencing their environment

Evaluation

We have not been able to make any scientific tests of the effectiveness of the approach to training that I have been describing; in any case the techniques of objective evaluation of training are very much in their infancy. Since we began personality testing we have had several examples of marked changes in the personality profiles of trainees that would suggest more than coincidence, but since we have still been at the stage of evaluating the tests in terms of training rather than the other way round, it is not possible to work, with any confidence, from this evidence. We have had, therefore, to rely in the main on our own subjective judgements, which have been embodied in recording of events as they occurred. I have quoted from this recording, and the reader may be able to judge for himself how balanced it has been.

Each group of tutors with whom I have worked seemed to have distinguished significant changes in some of the trainees. The most obvious area of progress has been in knowledge and understanding, and the kind of conversation at the end of the course has been so different from that at the beginning.

When Harry began the course he seemed something of a duffer, not allowing himself to understand rather than not being able to do so. In the last session he was at times leading the theoretical discussion with great assurance and in a way that showed that he was describing and analysing real events in his work.

But it is equally possible to be recording:

David is still in considerable difficulties. He has great difficulty in grasping the principles we are dealing with and even more in putting them into practice. His responses are desperately slow, and a straightforward question from Liz about how he would approach a colleague about a certain piece of work caused him to seize up. His tutorial group have exerted themselves in an attempt to help him, but there has been very little improvement in his performance. All this seems especially surprising in view of the fact that he is a trained full-time worker. He is inclined to explain his difficulties in terms of outside restraints, either of circumstances or other people, but I doubt the justification for this. It looks as if he is in the wrong job.

Much of the help that has been brought to trainees has been in their attitudes and approach to their work, and there is little doubt that causing trainees to make their own discoveries has often had a very powerful impact in this respect.

Although Stan cannot resist the logic of the discussions taking place, he is very anxious not to be hurried and is reserving his position all the time. On a number of occasions he has led a rearguard action by a small group, and on others has claimed to be questioning as 'devil's advocate'. On one occasion he suggested that the course was not altogether reasonable because it was requiring him, as a teacher, to train himself all over again. In spite of all this he stands out in this group by the way that he has applied the theoretical material to his teaching, and to the organization of the pastoral work in the school.

And sometimes the impact can go far beyond the people actually engaged on the course:

We were surprised a little by Margery's account of the work done by the two colleagues she had already involved in some informal group work in school. Not content with this, the three of them are about to involve another four members of staff in some study of groups within their classes, plus some pastoral-cum-tutorial work with them. She is a very modest person and it is quite extraordinary that she should dare so much.

Involving trainees in making their own discoveries, backed by lively and sensitive tutorial discussion, has proved a most potent way of causing them to question their own attitudes and approach. Most tutors have reported significant changes in the position of at least some of the members of their tutorial groups. Many trainees have described themselves as in a state of flux at some points in the discussion, and most of them, as they crystallize their new position, do seem to allow the evidence and their experience to have sway.

It is the trainee's development in personality that is most difficult to judge, but in some trainees it is the most impressive change that has taken place.

Sue was full of the experience that she had had as a result of the course and wished to tell me what had happened to her. She talked about her high level of dependence when she began the course—which was obvious enough at the time—and named several important events that had first revealed this to her, and others later that had helped her to cope with it. She also felt that she had become much more articulate about what was taking place between her and other people, and, she thought, more sensitive to other people's position. She felt that she had done quite well for a 'mere housewife running a club part-time'. In fact she is a potential tutor, and I must make sure that Fred has spotted it.

Statements about individual cases, although revealing in themselves, do not indicate the amount of change taking place in the body of trainees as a whole. Some trainees are very experienced and mature before they begin, and they mainly add knowledge and skill to an already settled personal outlook. At the other extreme a few trainees change quite dramatically in their daring and social skill; and others occupy positions between these two extremes. It is probably the potential for personal growth presented by this training that has most impressed the people central to it, especially since it was only as personal development began to take place that we realized the potency of the training in this respect. The potential for change seems to be inherent in the actual experience that the trainee finds himself involved in, though much may be added by the skill of the tutor and the support of the tutorial group.

It is quite unreal in most cases to attempt to separate the development of personality from the understanding of the material, and both facets feed into the trainee's or, as in this case, the tutor's general ability:

I was really impressed by Janet's tutoring; both her questioning and her own contributions were brief, crisp, and clear, and nicely timed. She has developed out of all recognition. She seems to have left her previous rather prim, inflexible style—it was only two months ago that she said that she was 'working on it'—and when she took an open session this week-end she conducted it with spontaneity and assurance.

The final test of the personal progress of the trainee is, of course, in his performance. Not only have I had the opportunity to follow individual trainees back to the practical situation, I have also been kept informed by those around them; and it is possible also to glean a good deal from the trainees' frank discussion of their problems. To judge from the trainees' own testimony, they are very soon seeing things that previously they did not know were there to be seen; they are daring to venture in directions that they previously imagined were closed to them; and they are offering positive though sensitive help to young people whereas many had previously merely hoped that they might be seen as available. The same may be true of tutors:

When we first met he was anxious, intellectually out of his depth, and seemed even not to be the intellectual equal of some of the people he was tutoring. He was diffident, and confused beyond his lack of understanding; he seemed to have a very considerable sense of hierarchy and showed strain when concerned with people in authority. During this week-end he was confident, clear, and guiding the discussion in a most competent manner. He avers that his relationships with his colleagues, and particularly with superiors in his daily work, have improved greatly. It looks as if he may have gained from the course more than most of his trainees.

As for the attendance and persistence of the students, although these in-service courses have made more demands than most on the trainees, both in overall time and in the challenging nature of the work, the level of attendance has on the whole been very good. We have had few people drop out because they found the work too demanding; the great majority of the casualties have been caused by personal and domestic changes, usually to the great regret of the persons concerned. I have the impression that the increased demands have increased the willingness of many people to join the course and to give their time rather than the reverse. The problem of most training agencies has not been the recruitment of trainees, but finding the tutors to cope with the numbers coming forward.

Maintaining a Balance

There has been a good deal of emphasis throughout this treatment on the personal outlook and development of the trainees. I have in part chosen quite deliberately to add this emphasis as it is the side of training that has received all too little attention. However, I should like to acknowledge the reminders we have sometimes received that group work may be addressed to a wide range of purposes, and that the personality development of the client is only one of several directions that group work may take.

Many group workers have, as their major responsibility, the organization of a recreative centre, and some of our own fraternity drew attention to the very ordinary things that the institutional group worker must see are done efficiently.

We wondered whether Fred had been under some pressure recently, for within the hour he reminded us several times, and with some heat, that a youth leader has to face such mundane matters as opening doors, collecting subs, keeping the peace, writing a few letters, and he thought that these matters were particularly important for the new recruit. Muriel joined him to add that it would be nice if he could also learn to hold the floor sufficiently to make some simple announcements.

There is also a danger, through an over concentration on the more informal personal development, of not merely neglecting but even devaluing activities and skills:

We were paying far too little attention to the very exciting things that we should be encouraging young people to do, said Peggy, somewhat forcibly. It is not enough, she said, to see this as a supplement that might be added to the course; it should be written into the scheme.

It is too easy for the worker to become so concerned with the social development of young people that he neglects the opportunity for them to pursue or extend their interests and activities. It can become fashionable to regard activity as being valuable only or mainly as a vehicle for social experience, and it is repeatedly necessary to make a case for a whole range of physical and cultural activities that have intrinsic worth to the individual.[1] In order to prepare the group worker for this side of his work, it is important that his own sights should be raised both to the range of activities and the scope within each of them. As a general organizer, he must be able to converse reasonably about a variety of pursuits, and he may even need to nurture the enthusiasm before he can justify approaching a specialist.

At the same time the specialist activity leader, or instructor as he may be called, has the privilege of working with a small group, and may have opportunities for informal work with young people not open to any other member of staff. The person in charge of the establishment should, for this reason, be able to engage the interest of the specialist in the personal growth of the young people in his group. To do this effectively he needs not only to be able to do informal group work himself, but also to be articulate about it. The organizer of the recreative centre must cope also with the formulation of a total programme, which will include corporate events as well as sectional interests, the regular and the *ad hoc*, the highlights, and other points of variety.

In introducing these elements into training we have tried to get away from the succession of talks by specialists. We have asked ourselves whether discovery methods are appropriate to this area also, and have sought ways through the mists—almost mystique—that sometimes surround discussions about 'cultural' activities. We have taken as our premiss that every man's culture is his particular means of personal expression, both through which he expresses himself to others and through which others may communicate with him. This means that a

[1] B. Davies, 'Activity in Youth Work', in *Youth Review*, no. 14, Spring 1969.

man has in his cultural armoury only those means of expression in which he is personally skilled; what is so often called 'cultural' may be no more than a store which he may visit but certainly does not possess.

Every man, every youngster, according to this thesis, shares a distinctive culture, and one of the best points of departure is to examine, with the youngsters concerned, just what means of expression they have at their disposal, and how adequate they find them. Just as we have found the youngster's personal needs a most profitable point of departure, so his cultural position offers a similarly productive study. We are much more likely to engage most youngsters in their own cultural extension if they set their own goals than if we are pushing at them our own preconceptions of culture. There is an urgent need to help young people enrich a culture which is addressed to their state of life, and we may, in so doing, reveal to them the passions of past generations who have contributed to our heritage. Here again, leading young people to their own discoveries, including the discovery of their own limitations, is a way of firing their ambition.

In attempting to inform trainees about the disciplines and potentials of a number of activities, we have tended to introduce the visiting specialist through a dialogue rather than a talk. We have found that this requires considerable preparation, with the tutorial groups first discussing the topic and preparing to raise matters on which they would appreciate guidance. Very often there has been a very considerable amount of knowledge and skill amongst the trainees, and we have at times had to recognize that the normal specialist talk would have insulted many of them. Indeed, many of our visiting specialists have been stretched and stimulated to quite new thought about the treatment of their own subject. The specialist is not left entirely at the mercy of what happens to be raised for he is at liberty to draw the trainees' attention to matters that he thinks important, but the trainees, for their part, are able to focus much of the discussion on matters about which they need help. One of the difficulties about this kind of exchange is the briefing of the specialists, for we have found that for most of them it is a new, and for some an exacting experience.

Wide Application

Experience has shown us that training through discovery and experience is relevant to a wide range of skills. Our main concentration has been on the in-service training of teachers and of youth workers as group workers, but we have addressed similar approaches to training of workers in adult education, the initial training of teachers, and to a variety of teaching. A special contribution may be made in this way to the training of any worker whose service to young people is likely to be affected by their peer or other group relationships, or who is concerned with the social skill and behaviour of the client.

The contacts we have had with industry have led us to believe that there is great scope for well designed schemes of training making use of discovery methods; indeed one may wonder how else the very considerable changes in attitudes that seem to be necessary are likely to be achieved. As far as we can ascertain, little deliberate work is being undertaken in the personality development of young people in industry, and some experiments in the tutoring of apprentices, inspired by the approach to informal group work, have shown great promise. The wide range of application of these methods has been brought home to us by some fairly slight pieces of work we have done within the hospital service, with occupational therapists and ward sisters. There seems a very sharp experience waiting for anyone whose job is concerned with serving people, particularly if the state of mind of those people is of importance to the service.

The Use of Field Work and Feedback

A much more economical use of field work is amongst the most important new experience that this programme of training has brought us. It has enabled us to pack so much more experience into the time available for field work, as well as providing much of the raw material for theoretical studies. We have been able to ensure that theoretical concepts are really applied to the practical situation, and there has been a continual feedback to alert us to the effectiveness of the tools that we have been fashioning, the concepts that we have been using, and the degree to which individual students have understood what has been discussed.

So often field work is used as a separate part of training and any relationship with theoretical studies is fortuitous. Theoretical courses may be conducted as a separate column of work, without any guarantee that the content of the course will be fed into practice, or that the experience gained in the field will be streamed back into theoretical discussions. Those responsible for social science courses face similar difficulties when they have to depend upon the accident of what happens to turn up whilst the student is with the field work agency. It is this kind of situation that we have learnt to change by more deliberate planning, and there is reason to believe that a similar approach could be applied to quite a number of professional courses.

In teacher training a number of interesting experiments have taken place in the planning of teaching practice,[1] but often the objective of these has been to try out a variety of approaches, rather than to ensure the crossing, backwards and forwards, of theory and practice. It is difficult to justify a continuing division between theoretical courses that are descriptive of the flow of human events inherent in the educational process, and its practical application to what one teaches and how it should be taught. The complaints, so often repeated by those who have recently passed through teacher training establishments, that the theoretical courses they have experienced are irrelevant to the actual teaching are probably ill founded; what the complainants may be saying is that they were not invited to test the relevance of their studies to the actual job of teaching.

Feedback is not just a matter of asking the student what he has thought of the course or what he has learnt, but should be seen as a continuous dialogue which cannot fail to inform the teacher about the student's progress and about his own effectiveness. This dialogue is unlikely to be set in motion by the student. It should not be left to chance but should be structured into the very process of teaching. Feedback should not be confused with examination and other tests of performance: these may tell us what the student has retained at the time of the test, but tell us little about the subtleties of our own approach and presentation. This is a very urgent matter in the field of teacher training, and not least over a wide area of university education, where teaching methods have been slow to change and have remained largely unexamined.

Of course, all this turns on the relationship between the teacher and taught, about which I have already had so much to say. We have found that the pupil in school will quite rapidly begin to inform his teachers if they demonstrate that they will be receptive to his views, and it has been noticeable that many teachers who have achieved this kind of relationship seem to have increased their own enjoyment of teaching.

As a Means of Change

Teaching through discovery leads to a high level of commitment to the work being undertaken, and, in the school context, seems in itself to be a

[1] W. Downes and K. E. Shaw, 'Innovation in Teaching Practice', *Trends in Education*, 12 October 1968.

major contribution to the ambition so frequently expressed of causing young people to be partners in their own education. It also may ensure that the material will be really assimilated by the student, and if it is accompanied by a critical analysis through discussion there is every likelihood of the student assuming a more critical and more creative role in life.

When dealing with matters of attitude and behaviour, learning through personal discovery has an impelling effect, especially, once again, when accompanied by an openness in discussion on the part of all concerned. This has relevance, not only to teaching and professional training, but to many aspects of life in a world going through rapid change. The application to industry is obvious and is not particularly difficult to achieve. Not least important is its application to moral issues. Day by day the controls of fear and conformity decline, and the ordinary person is presented with choices in his behaviour that are quite unprecedented. If society is to survive in this era of personal choice—one would like to be able to substitute personal responsibility—our young people in particular must be faced in a much more dynamic way with the issues involved. Didactic teaching is just not equal to this task.

I am very conscious of the dangers of the techniques we have evolved. They represent a powerful means of persuasion that may be lifted out of context by the professional persuader, whose only ambition may be that the client should believe what is most profitable or rewarding to the manipulator. My fears in this respect are not restricted to the field of commercial advertising or political campaigning; they could apply equally to the educator or the religious teacher. It seems to me that for work of this kind to have integrity the student or client should be brought to a point of responsible choice, and above all, the teacher should himself be really accessible and open to change.

Social Education in School

One of the prices that we are paying for modern technical progress and the increased mobility that has come in its wake, is a loss of the automatic therapy inherent in so many settled community groups, and some of this will have to be replaced by other social institutions. The school is the one universal agency available for social education, and our own experiments, although limited, have brought home to us the potential of the school for personal development and adjustment. Although this is seen most clearly in relation to the less tractable youngsters, our sights should not be limited by the problem areas in the school. It is just as important that the more intelligent, who have within their ranks many of the future leaders of the community, should be given real opportunities for creative social growth. It is an unfortunate fact that the education of so many of this group is amongst the most formal and personally cramping.

The focus of this book, as far as the school is concerned, has been on the potential for personality development of work designed specifically for that purpose, but it is vital that we should appreciate that there is an element of social experience inherent in every minute of school life. This might lead to creativity or conformity, to enlargement or belittling, to a sense of social worth or a feeling of failure that may be compensated by anti-social activity. We have scarcely begun to examine the part played by the school as an inevitable agency for social education. What I am suggesting here should not be confused with vague discussions about the value of example in school (those who base their practice on this philosophy may not know about normative controls and the differing frameworks of expectancies that surround, for instance, the roles of teacher and of pupil), nor with the equally confused trust in team games and school mottoes, nor with the largely irrelevant discussion about the compulsory act of corporate worship or the uncertain effect of religious education. All these factors may have their effect, and some, as for instance religious education, might have greater influence if more of those responsible for it would take young people into their confidence as colleagues, as fellow seekers.

Youth work requires urgent reappraisal from the same point of view. The efforts of the youth worker to bring young people enjoyment, relaxation, and recreation have their place, but in the course of research we have met many young people who have been in contact with a youth service that does not appear to be addressing itself to their really urgent needs. There is room for a good deal more intensive work with young people than can be accomplished in the loose, mobile, and sometimes transient membership of a large proportion of youth clubs and centres. There is a danger that we may be streaming off the energies, ambitions, anxieties, and even the angers of young people to the innocuous or irrelevant, rather than inviting them to engage themselves with us, with the surrounding community and with the urgent matters that face the modern world.

People and their Environment
An essential element of our work with individual people has been to find out as much as possible about their social background and their

personal needs, and it is possible to visualize the person in front of us as the product of the interplay between their inherent qualities and temperament and of their experience through life. The difficulties in which some youngsters find themselves are attributable directly to the social environment, and this has raised amongst us questions about how far it is possible and realistic to help them by treating them away from their wider environment. Some are much more influenced by the whims of fortune than others. Although what they now are may be very much a result of their family and neighbourhood experience, if they could be helped in their personal resilience they might cope much more effectively with adverse conditions. But we have been led to consider the wisdom and ethics of helping somebody to change without appropriate changes also being effected in their environment.

It is an interesting thought that forms of behaviour that sadden the educationalist may in themselves be viable adjustments to actual social environments. Apathy may be an apt adjustment to an oppressive situation that is beyond individual influence. For some, this could describe school. Apathy may avoid the self-destruction that, for some kinds of personality, may be inherent in rebellion; though rebellion may be an appropriate adjustment for another kind of personality. We should be tolerant in our judgement of anti-social activity, since it, too, may be a viable adjustment for some, whose mental health is kept intact by their attack on a society which brings them so much pain. Is it possible that by changing the individual we may cause him to move out of adjustment with the environment in which he must continue to live, and are we able to escape some responsibility for helping to change that environment?

Even more fundamentally, we might ask ourselves whether part of our job might not be to help the clients to become agents of change in their own environment. In this context the danger of the youth worker deflecting the natural anger of young people on to the innocuous becomes rather more urgent: by so doing he may be merely providing a sedative and thus preventing any real change in the situation. Perhaps that is what some youth workers feel that they are employed to do, rather than to draw the fire of young people on themselves and the community they may be seen as representing. May there not be far too much readiness to serve young people rather than to stimulate (almost incite) them to play an active role in the community?

For instance, for some youngsters the school is a confirmation of failure, an important statement about their lack of social worth. Their response to the school situation may be one of apathy or destructiveness and rebellion, and who is to say that these responses do not have their own validity? If the youngsters are to be changed, then clearly the school may have to change as well, and one of the possible forms of therapy in this situation may be one of creative protest. But creative protest is possible only if the lines of communication are open.

It is unlikely that the victim of the situation will be capable of initiating the dialogue—his natural reaction is much more likely to be one of mindless destructiveness—and it is therefore incumbent on the senior partners in the relationship to open up the dialogue. The group worker will often be able to make the contacts necessary for this to happen. Is it not therefore, an inevitable part of the group worker's function both to act as liaison with any inflexible forces in the environment, and to help his clients to work on their environment in a creative and responsible manner? At this point we stand at the overlapping borders of group work and community development.

Appendix 1 (a)

Training through Discovery and Experience
Outline of an Initial In-Service Course

The following programme might serve as a common core for a variety
of workers who are responsible for helping people in group situations.
For the group worker it may be advisable to bring forward the actual
work with a small group and feed most of the field studies and exercises
straight into some on-going group work. The sessions are planned as
weekly meetings, but they may be grouped for full day meetings or short
residential periods.

Session	Preparation	Tutorial
1.		Discussion: (a) What is the purpose of your work? (b) How would you describe your job? Leading to: Prepare brief for visits of observation.
2.	Visits of observation.	Discuss visits of observation. Preparation of inquiry (1): What do we want to know about our clients?
3.	Visits of observation.	Discuss visits of observation. Brief for job analysis. Preparation of inquiry (2): Proforma for interviews. Brief for observation of an episode of group behaviour.
4.	Job analysis. Observing an episode of group behaviour.	Discuss job analysis. Discuss episode of group behaviour. Inquiry—brief for interviews (Look forward to group work with a small group).

Session	Preparation	Tutorial
5.	Observing an episode of group behaviour. Inquiry—commence interviews (with an eye to finding a small group for group work).	Discuss episode of group behaviour. Inquiry—brief progress report. Brief for recording general leadership. Look forward to work with a small group.

6.	Recording general leadership.
	Inquiry—complete interviews.
		Discuss recording.
		Discuss inquiry:
		  (a) What kind of people are they?
		  (b) What do they need of us?
		Study session:
		  Setting up two-way communication.
		  Brief for discussion with young people about basic needs (preparation may need to be done carefully).
		  Look forward to group work with a small group.

7.	Recording general leadership.
	Discussion with young people: Their basic needs.
		Discuss recording.
		Study session:
		  Basic emotional needs.
		  Discussion about friendship and brief for friendship study (and have an eye to work with a small group).

8.	Recording general leadership.
	Friendship study.
		Discuss recording.
		Friendship study—progress report.
		Study session:
		  Why do we join groups?
		Brief for work with a small group:
		  (a) Identification of the group.
		  (b) Getting to know them.

Session	Preparation	Tutorial
9.	Complete friendship study.	Friendship study—prepare sociogram.
	Work with a small group— exploration and recording.	Work with a small group— progress report.
		Brief for recording—recap: basic emotional needs.
		Brief for discussion with young people about making relationships.
10.	Record work with a small group—asking ourselves 'What are the personal needs of the individual members?'	Discuss recording of progress with a small group.
	Discussion with young people about how some of their relationships were formed.	Discuss findings from friend- ship study.
		Study session:
		The function of interaction in making relationships.
		Brief for study of interaction in a certain part of the establishment.
11.	Record work with a small group, with special emphasis on the relation- ships within the group.	Discuss work with small group.
		Revise brief for recording— recap: friends, associates, and other relationships.
	Study of the pattern of interaction in a limited area of the establishment.	Study session:
		Report on study of interaction.
		Context of interaction, and the task-personal axis.
		The possibility of the worker influencing interaction.
12.	Record work with a small group, watching pattern of interaction.	Discuss group work. Discuss the context of the group's being together.
	Continued study in the establishment:	Discuss the study of interaction.
	(a) pattern of interaction;	The climate within which interaction takes place.
	(b) context of interaction;	The scope for influencing interaction: Report and brief for experiment.
	(c) consider the scope for influencing the observed pattern of interaction.	

Session	Preparation	Tutorial
13.	Record group work, giving special attention to the context around which the group has gathered. Commence experiment in influencing interaction.	Discuss group work. What is the context? What is the influence of the context on the life of the group? Experiment in interaction—interim report.
14.	Record group work with special attention to context—does the context enable the group worker to help? Continue experiment in influencing interaction.	Discuss group work. The relationship of the group worker to the group. Recapitulation—the purpose of group work. Report on experiment in interaction.
15.	Record group work, with special attention to the needs of individual people and their roles in the group. Discussion with young people: Do they feel a sense of belonging to the organization? If so, why?	Discuss group work. How should the group worker use himself? Dependence on the worker. Study session: Cohesive factors (producing identification or a sense of belonging): (a) attachment to people (interaction) (b) clear purpose (group goals).
16.	Record group work, with special attention to the relations of the group worker to the group. Consider the interaction and attachments between the sub-groups within the organization.	Discuss group work. Special attention to dependence of group on worker. Individual roles. Report on the interaction and attachment between the sub-groups. Prepare inquiry about goals appropriate to the establishment.

Session	Preparation	Tutorial
17.	Record group work, with special attention to the purposes of the group and its effect on the experience of individual members. Conduct sample inquiry into goals in the establishment.	Discuss group work, the group goals, and the experience they bring. Discuss inquiry into goals. Study session: Identification and consultation. Brief for experiment in consultation.
18.	Record group work, with special attention to the experience brought to the members—in terms of helping them with relationships. The discussion of the relationships within the group. Prepare for experiment in consultation, e.g. about club goals or any other suitable matter. Discuss with members—what influence does our group of friends have on us?	Discuss group work. Revise brief for recording—recap: the flow of interaction, climate of the group, group goals, relations of group worker to the group. Report plans for experiments in consultation. Study session: (a) Why do we conform? (b) Group norms.
19.	Record group work with special attention to the influence of the group on the behaviour of individual members (group norms). The growth of intimate discussion in the group: a supportive climate. Experiment in consultation.	Discuss group work—the influence of the group on the social responsibility of its members. The nurturing of a supportive climate. Report experiment in consultation. Brief for inquiry into norms.

Session	Preparation	Tutorial
20.	Record group work with special attention to the encouragement of social responsibility. The growth of introspective discussion. An inquiry into some part of the expectancy of members of one another (normative climate).	Discuss group work. A review of progress. Attention to individual need and growth. The possibility of social therapy. Report of inquiry. Can the worker influence the normative climate? (Some might like to try this through inquiry or consultation.) Brief for study of leadership.
21.	Record group work considering the *difference* in individual need. Record the acts of leadership by adults and young people, and the delegation of responsibility.	Discuss group work. Consider individual roles and satisfactions. Report on study of leadership. Study session: Shared responsibility. Brief for experiment in delegation.
22.	Recording work with a small group. The quality of each person's experience. The growing autonomy of the group. When will the group worker be withdrawing? Plan experiment in the delegation of leadership. Record as general leader— with special emphasis on personal behaviour as leader.	Discuss group work. How do we serve these individuals through the group? Discuss plans for experiment. Study session: Leadership continuum; authoritarian—encouraging autonomy.
23.	Record work with a small group, with special attention to the relationships of the group worker to the group. Record as general leader: How do I operate on the authoritarian-autonomy continuum?	Discuss group work. Achieving independence in the group. Discuss recording as general leader. Study session: Leadership continua: *Laissez-faire*—forceful; protective—exposing.
24.	An examination of personal style as a leader.	Discuss behaviour as leaders.

Appendix 1 (b)

Working with Groups
An Outline for Advanced In-service Training

| Preparation | Meetings |

FIRST STEP

Initiation of informal group work:
  (a) Choice of group.
  (b) Making contact.
  (c) Finding a provisional context to allow the group and group worker to act together.
  (d) Commencement of diagnostic procedures.
(a background and friendship study might be appropriate)

Informal group work:
  (a) General discussion of the group, mode of contact, provisional context(s), and commencement of diagnosis. Examination of recording.
  (b) Discussion of purpose.
  (c) The next step—with special reference to the context(s) of the group.
Resumé of theoretical background:
  (a) Basic emotional needs.
  (b) Communication.
  (c) Relationships: the function of interaction.
  (d) The study of interaction.

SECOND STEP

Informal group work:
  (a) The context(s).
  (b) Changes in the group.
  (c) Discussion of the relationships within the group.
Interaction:
  (a) A study of the pattern of interaction within a limited aspect of the institution.
  (b) An experiment in changing the pattern of interaction.
Communication—a study of the areas of communication:
  (a) Between the appointed leader and the members.
  (b) Within groups of members.

Informal group work:
  (a) Assessment of progress.
  (b) Recording.

Interaction—report and analysis.
Communication—report and analysis.

Theoretical analysis:
  (a) Norms.
  (b) Roles.
  (c) Cohesiveness.
  (d) Group goals.
  (e) Identification.
  (f) Consultation.

13A

Preparation   Meetings

THIRD STEP

Informal group work:
    (a) The use of discovery methods
       in the work with young
       people.
    (b) Introspective discussions in
       the group.
    (c) Initiate a colleague in the
       work.
Norms and roles—a study of the
norms and roles in a small group or
in some aspect of the institution.
Consultation—an experiment in
consultation.

Informal group work:
    (a) Assessment of progress.
    (b) Social therapy in group
       work.
    (c) The skills of supervision.

Norms and roles—report of study.
Attitudes and attitude change.

Consultation—report of an
experiment.

FOURTH STEP

Informal group work:
    (a) The problems of the
       worker's withdrawal.
    (b) Nurturing the leadership
       being exercised by members
       of the group.
    (c) Taking a colleague through
       step-by-step.

Norms/attitudes—an exercise in
influencing social controls.

Study of the worker's institution:
    (a) Sub-groups and sub-group
       structures.
    (b) Lines of influence.
    (c) Patterns of communication.

Informal group work:
    (a) Progress report.
    (b) Prepare for written stock-
       taking.
    (c) The support needed by the
       group worker.
    (d) The scope for small group
       work within the institution.
    (e) Helping the subject special-
       ist through insights gained.
Norms/attitudes:
    (a) Report on experiment.
    (b) Application to other
       situations.
Study of the worker's institution
    —report.

Leadership—structure within the
institution.
Restatement of purpose (leading
to job analysis).

Preparation   Meetings

FIFTH STEP

Informal group work:
   (a) Opportunities within the
       institution—consultation
       with colleagues.
   (b) Introducing informal group
       work to a subject specialist.
   (c) Prepare written stocktaking.

Job analysis of trainee's own work.

Leadership:
   (a) Pattern of responsibility in
       the institution.
   (b) Experiment in delegation.

Counselling—initiate a group
   counselling situation.

Informal group work:
   (a) Extension within the
       institution.
   (b) Guiding the subject
       specialist.
   (c) Review of programme—
       towards the development of
       a model.
Job analysis:
   (a) Trainee's own work.
   (b) Involving colleagues in
       similar analysis.
Leadership:
   (a) Analysis of field study.
   (b) Experiment in delegation.
   (c) Study of the elements of
       leadership.
Group counselling.

Supervision:
   (a) The skills of supervision.
   (b) The role of the worker res-
       ponsible for an institution.

SIXTH STEP

Informal group work:
   Initiate contact with young
   people not attached to the
   institution.

Leadership:
   (a) Study and variation of
       trainee's personal style of
       leadership.
   (b) Modifying the structure of
       responsibility in the institu-
       tion, possibly through con-
       sultation.
Supervision:
   (a) Consolidate the position.
   (b) Involve a colleague in
       supervision.

Informal group work:
   (a) Work with young people
       outside the institution.
   (b) Consider written stock-
       taking.
Leadership:
   (a) Trainee's own style.
   (b) Inducing change in the
       structure within the
       institution.

Supervision:
Report.

The institution as a corporate
   entity.

Appendix 1 (c)

Programme for Consolidation

The consolidation of the basic course of training might be accomplished through approximately monthly meetings, each of which would have its own point of emphasis. The following programme is designed for a series of nine meetings lasting a whole day—or the equivalent. The whole programme has the two elements running through it: informal group work with small groups, and institutional group work; but these assume varying weights as the programme develops, with the informal group work taking precedence at the beginning of the programme and institutional group work in the second half of the programme.

The business discussed at each meeting is intended to initiate the practical work for the ensuing period of field work. There is a considerable continuity in the material, and it is appropriate that a review of progress of the preceding period of field work should lead immediately into the new business planned for a meeting.

Programme of work to be initiated at each meeting

First Meeting
Making Personal Contact
1. Making contact and setting up communication with individual young people (with the experience gained in interviewing as a background). What is the routine of the organization in this respect?

The Institution
1. Do we record our observation? How do we encourage other members of the staff in their observation?
2. The encouragement of regular recording, moving the points of emphasis as the meetings develop.
3. Job analysis—Shall we begin job analysis by studying the role of the trainee?

Second Meeting
Informal Group Work
1. How do we discern individual needs?
2. Deepening the relationship with the particular individuals who seem most to need our interest.
3. How can we surround the youngsters whom we wish to serve with a small group, or how do we locate small groups who should be encouraged by a group worker?
4. How are we to encourage the group to act together with the worker?

The Institution
1. Discuss the scope for group work with colleagues.
2. Continue job analysis by encouraging colleagues to analyse their own jobs in collaboration with us.

Third Meeting
Informal Group Work
1. What are the personal needs of the young people concerned? What diagnostic procedures have been used?
2. A study of the relationships within the group (possibly using socio-metric studies).
3. Review the provisional context forming a focus for the group—considering the quality of the experience that the context is likely to bring to the members.
4. Engage the interest of other members of staff in informal group work.

The Institution
1. Is there proper scope for informal group work in the institution as it is at present organized? Is there a need for some adjustment in order to make intensive work possible?
2. Relate the job analysis to the stated purpose of the organization and the ambitions of the workers concerned.

Fourth Meeting
Informal Group Work
1. A review of the progress and needs of individual youngsters.
2. Fitting the context to the need.
3. The degree of autonomy in the group and the group worker's relationship with the group.
4. Methods of supporting the other members of staff in this work.

The Institution
1. Consider the overall pattern of the establishment:
   (a) the sub-group structures within the establishment;
   (b) the patterns of interaction which exist—especially the interaction between the sub-groups.

Fifth Meeting
The Institution
1. Becoming aware of the pattern of communication and consultation in the institution.
2. The spread of leadership through the staff and young people.
3. A study of normative controls, undertaken in discussion with other members of staff.

Informal Group Work
1. The degree to which other members of staff are now involved in this work and in discussion about this work.
2. How do we activate and stir the groups (with special attention to the need to involve certain youngsters in emotional experience)?
3. Do we use discovery methods and other means of exposing members of groups to experience (and what experience should we expose them to and why)?

4. Watching the internal relationships of the groups as the situation of the groups changes.
5. The support of colleagues by talking through their problems.

Sixth Meeting
The Institution
1. What is the routine for consultation?
2. Has recording become a focus for discussion amongst members of staff?
3. What jobs within the institution have to be done, who does them, and who carries responsibility?
4. What responsibilities are carried by groups of young people, and to what extent are those groups autonomous?
5. Are attempts made to influence normative controls by consultation?

Informal Group Work
1. Who are your young lieutenants, and do you work with them as your personal group work?
2. What is the relationship between the worker and the groups he is concerned with—how does the worker use himself?
3. What about specialist activities? Are the potentials for informal group work in these being exploited?

The Study Group
Is the group undertaking this programme being nurtured as a self-reliant working party?

Seventh Meeting
The Institution
1. Have you developed a *system* of recording—each person recording appropriately to his situation?
2. How do you acknowledge this recording;
   (a) by being informed by it?
   (b) by responding to it?
3. Have you developed—do you need—records about individual members?
4. Are there clear club goals (corporate group goals—not just the leader's ambitions but goals that include the leader and members together)? Consider undertaking some consultation about this.
5. How far does the programme of the group express the needs, interests, and ambitions of the members? Do we need to renew our contact with them about this?
6. What is your style of leadership? Could you ask your colleagues to help you examine this?

Informal Group Work
1. A stocktaking of the progress of the informal group work in the establishment. Is the institution orientated to this kind of thing? Are adjustments in the structure/programme/physical conditions required?
2. Consider the counselling element of informal group work.

3. How are the discussions with the specialist activity workers progressing? Do you need to introduce background and friendship studies, etc., to them?

The Study Group
Have you encouraged a self-consciousness amongst the members of this study group about their helping one another? Helping means criticism as well as support.

Eighth Meeting
The Institution
1. What is the form of government in your club?
    (a) How far does responsibility and autonomy spread down the structure and membership?
    (b) Is there a committee? What are the regular and functional links between the committee and the members? Is there any sense of 'constituency'? How do you reconcile the autonomy of the members and groups of members with the responsibility of the staff?
2. How does the club express its corporate nature through its programme?
3. How does the club express its social concern in the community?
4. Do the goals of the club include support and friendliness to all its members? How is this expressed?
5. Are individual members encouraged (by group goals and group norms) to develop themselves as individuals in their own way?
6. Have you encouraged your colleagues to study their own style of leadership?

Informal Group Work
1. Does each member of staff carry his own personal group work?
2. Have you looked for volunteers who might be encouraged to work with a small group of youngsters?
3. What about the specialist activity leaders—are they now making a contribution in this respect?
4. Are you nurturing indigenous leadership—even amongst the less able youngsters?
5. Are you encouraging the emergent young leaders to look around for opportunities for their own contribution to others in the community, e.g., with junior clubs?

The Study Group
Are there emergent leaders in the tutorial group who might convene meetings of the group to continue the supervision when this series has ended?

Ninth Meeting
Discussion of Material and Plans for the Future
1. Does the group feel a need for continuing discussions?
2. Could the group formalize its continuing existence? Is there sufficient indigenous leadership to carry on with only occasional encouragement from some outside person?

Appendix 1 (d)

An Outline Programme for the In-service
Training of Tutors

This outline is formulated on the assumption:
   (a) that the trainee tutor has himself completed a programme of study
       through discovery and experience;
   (b) that he is in-service, in that he bears some responsibility for a group
       of trainees who are working their way through a course based on
       field studies, exercises, and experiments.

The field work of the trainee tutors will therefore consist largely of
their work with groups of trainees. This element of field work is not
listed specifically; those items below that are italicized would normally
involve field work additional to the normal tutoring.

PHASE ONE
Review of Content and Presentation
   The pattern of the course.
   Brief for visits of observation.
   Brief for initial recording of general leadership.
   Brief for interviewing, and for inquiry about the personal background
      of some young people.
   Study sessions on communication and basic emotional needs.
   Informal group work—the purpose and first steps.

The Individual Trainee
   How can the tutor become informed about the previous experience and
      personal needs of each trainee? *Prepare a report.*
   Check that each trainee has adequate opportunities for field work and
      experience.

The Tutorial Group
   What is the tutor's role in leading the tutorial group into:
      (a) learning the theoretical principles;
      (b) becoming a working party;
      (c) becoming a supportive group?

The Trainee Tutor and his Personal Needs
   What will be required of the trainee tutor and what support is he likely
      to need?
   The training course as a support group.

PHASE TWO
Review of Content
   Relationships, and the use of sociometry.
   The study of interaction, leading to an *experiment in influencing
   interaction.*

Informal group work:
  (a) identifying the group;
  (b) making contact and deepening the relationship;
  (c) finding a context that will encourage the group to act together
      with the worker.

The Individual Trainee
  How should the tutor set up personal communication with each
    trainee?
  The personal needs of individual trainees—the kind of experience/roles
    that would be helpful to him.

The Tutorial Group
  How can the tutor encourage the group to accept some responsibility
    for the programme of work?
  How is the group to organize the processing of the very considerable
    volume of material brought in by the individual members?
  What support can the tutorial group offer to the individual trainee?

The Trainee Tutor
  What kind of relationship is each trainee tutor making with his groups?
  How is he recording his work?
  A personality test and processing the profile.
  The skill of questioning.

PHASE THREE
Review of Content
  Influencing interaction.
  Group norms, leading to an *experiment in influencing group norms*.
  Personal roles; hierarchies.
  Cohesiveness in groups.
  Informal group work:
    (a) discussing personal need—diagnostic procedures;
    (b) addressing the group experience to the need of the individual;
    (c) role-taking within the group.

The Individual Trainee
  *Prepare a personal description of each member of the tutorial group,
    including the part he plays in the group.*
  Report any special support that seems to be required by individual
    trainees.

The Tutorial Group
  Creating a supportive and intimate climate in the group.
  Introducing discussions about the relationships within the group.
  Coping with the competition between the business/content of the
    course, and the discussion of personal issues.
  Recognizing the emotional undertone.

The Trainee Tutor
  The tutor's personal leadership of his group:
    (a) repertoire of responses;
    (b) tolerance to silences and uncertainty;
    (c) coping with hostility;
    (d) creating space for the personal expression of the members of the group.
  Revise the brief for the tutor's recording.

PHASE FOUR
Review of Content
  Influencing group norms, attitudes.
  The commitment of individual members to the group.
  Group goals.
  Consultation, leading to an *experiment in consultation.*
  Informal group work:
    (a) review of method, especially the contribution of the context of the group activity to individual need;
    (b) change in relationships arising from the group activity;
    (c) discussion by the members of their relationships within the group as part of the group experience.

The Individual Trainee
  A Statement about the progress of individual trainees:
    (a) in understanding;
    (b) in sensitivity;
    (c) in skill;
    (d) in attitude and outlook;
    (e) in personal resource.

The Tutorial Group
  The tutor as a group worker.
  Introducing introspective study and discussion.
  Preparing an agenda to help the exploration of personal issues.

The Trainee Tutor
  The trainee tutor's personal relationships with his group of trainees.
  The support he gives, and the support he needs.

PHASE FIVE
Review of Content
  The place of consultation in work with groups.
  The elements of leadership, leading to:
    (a) *a study of styles of leadership;*
    (b) *an experiment in the delegation of responsibility.*
  Informal group work:
    (a) the worker's use of himself;
    (b) introducing introspective group discussion.

The Individual Trainee
 Review of the needs of individual trainees, their recording and their
 need for supervision.

The Tutorial Group
 The growth of intimate and confessional discussion.
 Social therapy through the tutorial group.

The Trainee Tutor
 The trainee tutor's assessment of:
  (a) his own development;
  (b) his continuing needs.
 Revise brief for recording.

PHASE SIX
Review of Content
 Examination of styles of leadership.
 Informal group work:
  (a) development and change in the individual members of the group;
  (b) the social therapy of groups;
  (c) the changing role of the group worker.
 The training programme:
  (a) review of method and content;
  (b) consolidation and advanced training.

The Individual Trainee
 The assessment of the trainee's progress; the trainee's part in his own
 assessment.
 Looking forward—support and further training.

The Tutorial Group
 Review of the function of the tutorial group.
 Socratic methods in discussion and study.

The Trainee Tutor
 The support required beyond the training course.

Appendix 2

In this appendix are included some examples of the briefs and forms of inquiry used to lead trainees to appropriate discoveries and experience.

The trainee's efforts are usually supported in any or all of the following ways:

(a) by a briefing session at a meeting of the trainees to prepare for the next assignment of field work;
(b) written guidelines to confirm or initiate each assignment;
(c) intermediate meetings of the tutorial groups (in the case of courses conducted by, say, monthly overnight residential periods).

On several of the forms, repetitive headings are omitted as indicated. Some examples of notes of guidance are included in this appendix.

Appendix 2 (a)

Conducting an Inquiry into the Personal Background of Some Young People

Would you please *interview*, say, six young people making use of the form entitled 'Personal Background'. In making your approach to young people, you will be well advised to begin by stating your identity and purpose. Assure the interviewee that the inquiry is confidential and that, should he not wish to answer any of the questions, he will not be pressed to do so.

Most young people respond readily to a request for their help in this way; indeed, you may find that some would welcome an opportunity to talk more deeply about some of the matters raised by the inquiry. By sympathetic listening you may be able to help the young person a little, and he in turn may offer us a good deal of enlightenment for our work and study.

In choosing the people whom you will approach you may look for a cross-section of the membership of your organization, or concentrate on what seems to you a natural small group. Treat the exercise as an opportunity to meet a number of people whom you would like to know better. Later we shall be looking for a small group with whom to work more intensively, and these interviews might give you an opportunity to identify such a small group.

CONFIDENTIAL

PERSONAL BACKGROUND

1. NAME................................... ADDRESS....................................
   ....
   ....

   Age: Male/Female   Married/Single/Engaged/Steady

2. School last attended ....
   School standard ....
   Any posts of responsibility ....
   Other Comments ....
   ....

3. Occupation ....
   Grade of work ....
   Training Commitments ....
   Previous jobs ....
   Any ambitions...
   ....

4. Family Background ....
   Father's occupation ....
   Mother's occupation ....

Brothers		Sisters	
Age	School/Occupation	Age	School/Occupation

Movement of family during childhood:

Any other information offered about family experience and background, e.g., stability?

Further education ....
....
....

Affiliations (clubs, societies) ....

....

....

....

Church Attendance: Yes/No   Denomination ....

Interests: Present: ....

Past: ....

Would like to follow..

....

Other information:

Appendix 2 (b)

The Observation of an Episode of Group Behaviour

The Brief

When inviting trainees to undertake an exercise of this kind it is usually helpful to send them an example of the kind of observation that they might attempt, and a few notes of guidance such as the following:

The paper enclosed is an account of a few minutes' observation of group behaviour such as may be seen all around us. Would you please try this for yourself.

Look for a fairly simple situation involving only a few people. Restrict your observation to a few minutes' behaviour, but observe in the greatest detail possible; you will be well advised to make notes very soon after the occasion. Although the enclosed description is written up in prose form, you will be presenting your own report to your tutorial group and you may be as well served by an aide-mémoire in note form.

Take this in your stride. Opportunities abound for this kind of observation, which may be accomplished in public transport, at a bus queue, in a cafe, a pub, in someone's home, or in any other place where a few people are gathered together.

The Observation of an Episode of Group Behaviour

An Example

As I walked into a rather scruffy little café in search of a cup of coffee, I noticed a young couple, seated together at a table, who were snuggled into one another. The lights in the café were low and it was a few minutes before they emerged sufficiently for me to be able to regard them separately.

They were sitting as is shown on the plan, at table A. There were another three young people sitting at a table B, and I was the only other

person in the café as I observed from table C. The girl at table A was a
petite fifteen or sixteen year old whom I shall call Tina. She had fairly
long hair tied in a bunch at the back, and was wearing a light overcoat
over a short dress. She was not wearing an engagement ring.

Her foot, from which a sandal was suspended by the toe, was hooked
under the calf of her escort. He was a long slouching young man of about
eighteen, dressed in untidy jeans, boots, a shirt open at the neck, and a
nondescript zip jacket. I shall call him Lanky. Tina, to Lanky's left,
was snuggled into Lanky's left shoulder with her right arm resting along
his thigh.

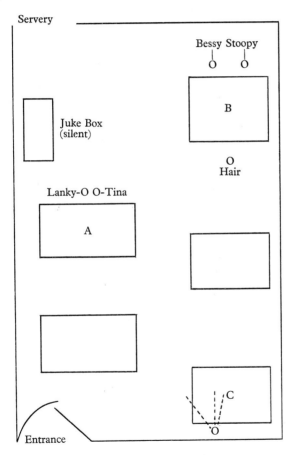

Lanky leaned back motionless, with his arms down by his sides,
making no response, as far as I could see, to Tina's using him as a cushion.
He wore a dull expression which remained unchanging. His gaze seemed

fixed unseeingly on the door of the café, and his eyes did not acknowledge the passage of people along the pavement outside.

Tina made a little snuggling movement with her head and shoulder from time to time and the movement rippled down her body. Lanky did not stir. Tina's eyebrows rose as she looked up, but Lanky's face was not within her vision.

About five minutes after my entry, Lanky extracted himself from Tina's embraces and without any apparent explanation left the café. At this, Tina turned half backwards and engaged the three young people sitting at table B in an exchange of glances and a few words. Communication began by a slight shrug from Tina that was enjoined by a hot whisper and some gesticulation from a girl at table B, all of which conveyed to me that Tina had arranged for the other three to meet her at the café. With a shrug and upturned hands Tina seemed to suggest that she was the victim of circumstances, and confirmed this impression by looking furtively at the door through which her escort had departed.

The other girl in this exchange was rather rounder than Tina, positive in all her actions, and seemed to be a focus for the attention of two male companions. I shall call her Bessy. In front of her—with back to me—sat a boy with long, rather lank hair, whom I will call Hair, and beside her, sitting sideways on his chair with his back against the wall and feet on the rail of Bessy's chair, sat Stoopy, who was, at this stage, obscured from my view by Hair. Bessy jerked herself about in her chair as if to convey that she was not pleased.

About seven or eight minutes after his departure Lanky reappeared, having changed into trim trews and a jacket, and long pointed boots. He resumed his seat beside Tina, who received him fondly by encircling his left arm with both of her own. Thirty seconds later Bessy stood abruptly and made for the door. Hair jumped up and followed closely whilst Stoopy more deliberately gained a standing position and trailed after the other two with his head so bent forward as to be hardly higher than his shoulders.

As I left the café I noticed that it was situated beside a public house where a lot of young people were taking drinks in an open courtyard.

Appendix 2 (c)

Friendship Study

This inquiry will enable us to chart the friendship patterns of the people in the group you choose—their relationships both within and outside the group. It will be necessary for you to *interview* each person. You will need to be clear about the definitions of friendship that we are using, and to make sure that the interviewee is describing his situation in these terms.

Do not attempt the inquiry with too big a group. The interviews, if done sensitively, may take some time, and it would be better to get under the skin of a small group than look superficially at a larger one. Consider carefully your choice of group, which might be an activity group, or a group who merely spend a lot of time together.

Remember that we are looking forward to working more intensively with a small group, and you may wish to use this inquiry to help you identify and make contact with the group with whom you wish to work.

FRIENDSHIP STUDY   CONFIDENTIAL

1. Name ....
   Address ....
   ....

   Age: Male/Female   Married/single/engaged/steady

2. School last attended: ....
   School standard:..

3. Work: (a) Interviewee's occupation:...
                 Grade of work: ....
            (b) Father's occupation: ....
                 Grade of work: ....

4. Have you any *close friends*?
   (Someone you like and probably meet frequently, whom you trust and rely on, and to whom you would confidently tell some of your secrets—and expect them to do the same to you.)

   (a) Name................................. m/f............. Age...........
       How long have you been friends?..
       ....
       How did you first meet him/her? ....
       ....
       What do you do together? ....
       ....
       Where does he/she live? (District/Distance) ....
       ....

   ((b) to (e)—repeat (a) four times)

5. Have you any *other friends*?
(People you like and possibly meet frequently, whose company you *seek*, and who are more than associates* or acquaintances† but are not close friends.)

    (a) Name.. m/f.............. Age........

        How long have you been friends?..

        ....

        How did you first meet?...

        ....

        What do you do together?...

        ....

        Where does he/she live? (District/Distance) ....

        ....

    ((b) to (f)—repeat (a) five times)

  * Associate: You may not go out of your way to meet this person, but if he happens to be about you would probably join up with him.
  † Acquaintance: Someone whom you would acknowledge upon meeting him, but would not normally choose as a companion for a social occasion.

Appendix 2 (d)

Brief for Visits of Observation

1. Membership
    Numbers, sex, age, socio-economic background and kind of area, geographical distribution.
    Membership commitment, including fees.

2. Premises
    Siting, accommodation, condition, use of space.

3. Equipment and facilities
    Equipment available, its distribution, its condition, its use.

4. Programme
    Group activities and how they are conducted. Their standard, and the commitment and adherence of individual members to them.
    Corporate activities and programme.
    Informal activities—not organized and without regular membership. How are they initiated and maintained?
    Informal facilities, and how used and supervised.

5. Staff
   People and designation: hierarchy.
   Allocation of duties.
   How they tackle their jobs.

6. Member-staff relationships
   . Contacts observed.
   What is said on the subject.
   Who is in control ? Is member-staff contact built into a routine ?
   Initiative observed.

7. System of government, responsibility, and consultation
   Any committee ?
     How elected and officered.
     Frequency of meetings.
     Functions.
     Staff relationships with the committee.
   Other areas of initiative and responsibility
     Other initiative taken by individual young people.
     Staff meetings and other means of consultation.
     Management committee's system of inspection and supervision.

Appendix 2 (e)

Job Analysis—Form 1

1. What is *said* to be my job.

   Designation:

   Who determines the way the job should be done ?

   Main duties:

   Statement of purpose:

   (Enter the work actually undertaken during a single session on *Form* 2).

2. *Chain of responsibility*
     (a) I am responsible to (i.e., a person who carries responsibility for
                             what I do, directs my work, etc.):

        (i) Name: Designation:

Area of responsibility; how instructions are conveyed, frequency of contact, etc.

(Repeat heading (i) as required)

(b) These are the people who are responsible to me:

(i) Name: Designation:

What he does: How I supervise his work:

(Add further names as required by repeating heading (i))

3. I am concerned with the following decisions:

(a) Kind of decision:

How the decision is taken and my part in it:

(Add further decisions by repeating heading (a))

4. The following are people who act as advisers to me:

(a) Name: Designation:

Matters for advice, frequency of contact, etc.

(Add further advisers by repeating heading (a))

5. The following are my nearest equals:

(a) Name: Designation:

What we share or how we are in contact:

(Add further names by repeating heading (a))

6. This form leaves the following aspects of my job unexamined:

Job Analysis—Form 2

Use this form for the analysis of a single session's work.
Describe briefly the work done during each interval in the appropriate
spaces.
Include names and number of people where appropriate.

Time (e.g., ¼ hour intervals)	Contact with members			Contact with staff/helpers		
	Personal support	About activities	About general organization	Personal support	About activities	About general organization

Time (e.g., ¼ hour intervals)	Administration				Outside contacts	
	Personal support	About activities	About general organization	Other	Representing the organization	Other

(These four headings are usually placed side by side as a single line across a brief size
paper.)

14

Appendix 3

Briefs and Forms for Recording

Briefs and forms for recording should be used judiciously, as trainees may sometimes be inhibited by too complex a brief. Brief and form 3 (a) is an example of a fairly simple form of recording that may serve to initiate recording, and with more sophisticated treatment might also serve the trained institutional worker. Brief and form 3 (b) is appropriate to the recording of fairly sophisticated work with a small group, and it would be inadvisable to present the brief to the novice. It would be far better to develop a brief step by step as the trainee deepens his skill and insight. The brief given here may serve as a point of reference whilst this is being done.

Appendix 3 (a)

Recording of General Leadership

The Purpose of Recording
Recording should assist the person doing it to make clear to himself what is taking place and the issues involved. It is, therefore, more than a narrative: it should include some analysis of the situation and reflections about future action. Recording should also serve as a basis of discussion with one's colleagues, and in particular with anyone who can assist the worker to gain insight into his own situations and actions.

Daily Recording
A separate report form should be used for each session's recording. Be selective in your recording. Make sure that you record important details, but do not make a burden of it.

The following suggestions may be helpful in considering the kind of things to record.

(1) Work undertaken
    A clear and critical statement of how you spent your session is required here. It should lead you to an examination of your choice of action and the effectiveness of your use of time.

(2) Contacts and discussion with helpers and members of staff
    This will give you an opportunity of seeing the way in which you helped and stimulated the work of other adults, and encouraged

them to use their time. You will also be able to keep a record of the arrangements and decisions you agreed with them.

(3) Contacts and discussion with members
As you record you will build for yourself a picture of how much responsibility you have delegated to young people and the kind of support you offered to them. You will also wish to note your dealing with disciplinary matters and the personal counselling you have done.

(4) Observation
Here you will wish to note behaviour and events you observed which did not involve you in any direct action. Seemingly trivial events may suggest a great deal.

(5) A space is included in case you wish to report additional material.

The Skill of Recording
The skill of recording is to penetrate beneath the surface of passing events and to build up a sensitivity to what is happening to individuals and groups of people. In particular we should be interested in our own behaviour as leaders, the influence we are having, and the opportunities we may be missing.

RECORDING OF GENERAL LEADERSHIP

............day   Date........... Club............................. Recording by...........

Climate of session...

1. Work undertaken

Time		Function	Persons Involved	Comment
From	To			

2. Contacts and discussions with helpers/members of staff

Persons concerned	Matter	Comment and action taken/required

3. Contacts and discussions with members

Persons concerned	Matter	Comment and action taken/required

4. Observation

Persons concerned	Matter	Reflections/ action required

5. Any other matters for recording.

Appendix 3 (b)

Recording by Group Worker

RECORDING BY GROUP WORKER

A prompt list which may suggest areas for special attention at certain stages in the development of a group

A. The Main Events

This section is intended to include, not only the activities of the group and individual members of the group, but also the part that various people took in running the group, and in maintaining its existence and cohesion.

1. The activity of the group
   (a) group activity
   (b) individual action.
2. Maintaining the group—organizing its activity and keeping the group going.
   (a) Discussion of plans
      (i) of immediate concern
      (ii) plans for the future.
   (b) Were decisions taken ?
      (i) the problem
      (ii) who initiated ?
      (iii) how did the discussion go and who took part ?
      (iv) what decisions were taken and who decided ?
   (c) What responsibility was exercised by which members of the group ?
3. Development or changes in the purposes, ambitions, and values of the group, including required or forbidden behaviour.
4. Relationships between the group and people outside (e.g., if the group is part of a larger group, to what extent is the group drawing upon or contributing to the larger group ?).
5. Environmental factors that are aiding or limiting the group.

B. Relationships, Role-taking, and the Discussion of Relationships

1. The emotional climate of the occasion (e.g., friendly, hostile, apathetic, lively, cohesive, supportive, discordant).
2. Who was present and any change in membership.
3. The pattern of interaction and communication induced by the activity.
4. Were there any developments or changes in the control of the group.
5. Relationships
   (a) The structure of attractions and rejections.
   (b) Who initiates, who follows.
   (c) Cliques and their relationships.
   (d) Any special roles, e.g., leadership, clown, scapegoat, peacemaker, etc.
6. Discussion of relationships within the group.

C. Personal Matters
1. Significant items of communication, introspection, revelation, and confession.
2. An assessment of the personal outlook, difficulties, needs, change, and growth of individual members of the group.

D. The Worker's Position
1. The attitudes of individual members to the group worker, and the group worker's approach.
2. The affairs of the group—level of dependence or autonomy.
3. Contact with other workers or outside bodies.
4. Action required of the group worker
   (a) in respect of the group activity;
   (b) in support of individual members;
   (c) in contact with other workers.

GROUP WORKER'S REPORT

Group and Function.. Report by.......................... Date...............

The Main Events	Relationships, role-taking, and discussion of relationships	Personal Matters	The Worker's Position

Appendix 4

Personality Tests

Tests used on these courses:
For young people over the age of
  16 and all adult trainees   16 P.F.

For young people up to the   High School Personality
  age of 16   Questionnaire (H.S.P.Q.)
Prepared by Professor R. B. Cattell
Published by The Institute for Personality and Ability Testing
Obtainable in Great Britain from:
  National Foundation for Educational Research in England and
    Wales,
  The Mere,
  Upton Park,
  Slough, Bucks.

Materials included
Question books and answer sheets
Scoring keys
Norm tables
Personality profiles

Instructions
Manuals and handbooks are published with the material.

Comments
The subject is scored in each of 16 factors in the 16 PF and 14 in the
H.S.P.Q. Although the factors are described briefly in terms such as
'emotional stability' or 'reserved—outgoing', it is not possible to equate
any one factor with actual behaviour. Overt behaviour is influenced by a
combination of a number of factors.

A good deal of caution is required in interpreting the tests, and in our
own use the tests have served as only part of the diagnostic indicators
we have used.

Further References
R. B. Cattell, *The Scientific Analysis of Personality*, London 1965.
R. B. Cattell, *Personality and Motivation Structure and Measurement*,
  London, 1951.
H. J. Eysenck, *The Structure of Human Personality*, London, 1970.
Carl Rogers, *Client Centred Therapy* (Especially Part III), London,
  1965.
Boris Semeonoff (ed.), *Personality Assessment*, London, 1966.

217

Selected Bibliography

Argyle, M., *The Psychology of Interpersonal Behaviour* (London, 1967).
Association Press, Leader-training Workbooks (New York, 1962).
Banton, M., *Roles* (London, 1965).
Bany, M. A., and Johnson, L. V., *Classroom Group Behaviour* (New York, 1964).
Batten, T. R., *Training for Community Development* (London, 1962).
Batten, T. R., *The Non-Directive Approach in Group and Community Work* (London, 1967).
Bion, W. R., *Experiences in Groups* (London, 1961).
Button, L., *Some Experiments in Informal Group Work* (Swansea, 1967).
Cartwright, D., and Zander, A. (eds.), *Group Dynamics* (London, 1961).
Cattell, R. B., *The Scientific Analysis of Personality* (London, 1965).
Evans, K. M., *Sociometry and Education* (London, 1962).
Foulkes, S. H., and Anthony, E. J., *Group Psychotherapy* (London, 1965).
Goetschius, G. W., and Tash, M. J., *Working with Unattached Youth* (London, 1967).
Goldman, R., *Angry Adolescents* (London, 1969).
Hargreaves, D. H., *Social Relations in a Secondary School* (London, 1967).
Hauser, R., *The Fraternal Society* (London, 1962).
Homans, G. C., *The Human Group* (London, 1959).
Jahoda, M., and Warren, N. (eds.), *Attitudes* (London, 1966).
Jennings, H., *Leadership and Isolation* (New York, 1950).
Johnson, J. A., *Group Therapy* (New York, 1963).
Kalton, G., *Introduction to Statistical Ideas for Social Scientists* (London, 1966).
Kaye, B., and Rogers, I., *Group Work in Secondary Schools* (London, 1968).
Kelly, E. C., *The Workshop Way of Learning* (New York, 1951).
Klein, J., *The Study of Groups* (London, 1967).
Konopka, G., *Group Work in the Institution* (New York, 1954).
Konopka, G., *Social Group Work* (New Jersey, 1963).
Mann, P. H., *Methods of Sociological Enquiry* (London, 1968).
Milson, F. W., *Social Group Method and Christian Education* (London, 1963).
National Association for the Study of Education, *The Dynamics of Instructional Groups* (New York, 1960).
Newcombe, T. M., *Social Psychology* (London, 1952).
Odlum, D., *Journey through Adolescence* (London, 1961).
Ottaway, A. K. C., *Learning through Group Experience* (London, 1966).
Pettes, D. E., *Supervision in Social Work* (London, 1967).
Richardson, E., *Group Study for Teachers* (London, 1967).
Saunders, R. L., Phillips, R. C., and Johnson, H. T., *A Theory of Educational Leadership* (Columbus, 1966).
Sprott, W. J. H., *Human Groups* (London, 1958).
Tash, M. J., *Supervision in Youth Work* (London, 1967).
University College of Swansea, Faculty of Education, *The Psychology of Adolescence* (1966).

Index